T0330099

Market Platforms, Industrial Clusters and Small Business Dynamics

Market Platforms, Industrial Clusters and Small Business Dynamics

Specialized Markets in China

Ding Ke

*Associate Senior Research Fellow, East Asian Studies Group,
Area Studies Center, IDE-JETRO, Japan*

INSTITUTE OF DEVELOPING ECONOMIES (IDE), JETRO

Edward Elgar
Cheltenham, UK • Northampton, MA, USA

Published by
Edward Elgar Publishing Limited
The Lypiatts
15 Lansdown Road
Cheltenham
Glos GL50 2JA
UK

Edward Elgar Publishing, Inc.
William Pratt House
9 Dewey Court
Northampton
Massachusetts 01060
USA

A catalogue record for this book
is available from the British Library

Library of Congress Control Number: 2012935332

ISBN 978 1 78100 627 6

Typeset by Servis Filmsetting Ltd, Stockport, Cheshire
Printed and bound by MPG Books Group, UK

Contents

Acknowledgments

This book is the final outcome of the research project on "A Study of China's Industrial Clusters and Specialized Markets" at the Institute of Developing Economies, Japan External Trade Organization (IDE-JETRO).

The creation of this book has been affected by various academic traditions. The author searched through the literature on Japanese small business history during graduate school. After entering IDE-JETRO, I gained many opportunities to hold discussions with colleagues engaged in area studies on developing countries. Benefiting from these experiences, I learned how to clarify the essentially different economic logic behind seemingly similar economic phenomena in different countries through the methodologies of fieldwork and historical analysis. Armed with this academic background, I was able to discover the unique development mechanism of the specialized market described in this book.

Methodologically, this book has also been affected by the two-sided market theory, an important field of the novel theory of the *platform*. Although cutting-edge studies on two-sided markets are concentrated in the high-tech sectors of developed countries, I noticed that this framework is also extremely powerful for explaining many industrial phenomena in the developing world. By using the *market platform*, and a series of related concepts (e.g. the indirect network effect, critical mass, platform governance, and platform competition), I was able to gain a profound understanding of the nature of the specialized market.

Throughout the process of studying the specialized market, I have learned while being supported and encouraged by many people. As my supervisor at Nagoya University, Professor Johzen Takeuchi guided me through the vast field of small business study, and taught me how to conduct thorough fieldwork. The work of Professor Yukio Watanabe at Keio University on the Ota District of Tokyo, which is a model case of Japanese SME clusters, helped me to recognize more clearly the completely opposed feature of China's small businesses. Professor Hubert Schmitz at Sussex University in the UK told me that the majority of buyers in National Value Chains are small buyers, which greatly deepened my understanding of emerging markets, especially their low-end segment. Professor Bernard Ganne at the National Scientific Research

Center, France, gave me an important opportunity to present my study on specialized markets at the workshop entitled "Industrial Clusters in Asia: Old and New Forms." Professor Yasuharu Tanzawa at Chuo University, Japan, and my colleagues Momoko Kawakami, Tomohiro Machikita and Toshitaka Gokan introduced me to much important theoretical literature on the platform, the two-sided market, and new economic geography.

Since complete statistical data do not exist, the only way of obtaining the whole picture of specialized markets is to go into the field, interviewing the people concerned and collecting scattered materials. I was very fortunate to join in the research projects "A Comparative Study on Urban Small Business and the Rural Industrialization in East Asia" funded by a grant from the Japan Society for the Promotion of Science (JSPS) and directed by Professor Johzen Takeuchi; the research project on "Sustainable Development in Asia and the Role of Small Business" funded by a grant from the JSPS and directed by Professor Masakatsu Tamaru; the research project on "Chinese Enterprises: In Quest of Industrial Upgrading amid Transition" funded by a grant from IDE-JETRO and directed by my colleague Ken Imai; the research project on "The Flowchart Approach to the Formation of Industrial Clusters: Focusing on the Mechanism of Endogenous R&D and Innovation" funded by a grant from IDE-JETRO and directed by Professor Akifumi Kuchiki at Nihon University, Japan; and the research project on "Industrial Clusters in China and Asia" funded by a grant from the National Institutes for the Humanities (NIHU) and directed by Professor Tomoo Marukawa at the University of Tokyo. Thanks to their invitations and kind assistance, I was able to continue to conduct fieldwork for a decade in Zhejiang Province and Jiangsu Province where specialized markets are the most developed.

During the process of the field surveys, I have been also supported by many Chinese researchers. Concerning the survey in Yiwu and other industrial clusters in Zhejiang, I gained full support from the research team led by Professor Jin Xiangrong at Zhejiang University. According to my understanding, among China's economists it is his team that attaches the most importance to field surveys. During my survey in Changshu, Mr Zhu Xinghua, former director of Changshu Township and Village Bureau, and Mr Xia Zuxing, one of the founders of Zhaochang Market, not only arranged many important interviews for me, but also related to me, without any reservations, their own experiences of the development of this market. Professor Xu Yuanming and Professor Xu Zhiming at Jiangsu Academy of Social Sciences kindly helped me to conduct the later stage of the survey in Changshu.

Lastly, I would like to dedicate this book to my family. Without their long-term warmth, care and steadfast support, this book would not have become a reality.

Ding Ke
Tokyo
October 2011

Introduction

Source: The author.

Figure I.1   International Trade City: the fifth-generation market in Yiwu

As a huge transitional economy, China has her unique development experiences. The *Specialized Market* that is the subject of this book is a typical
example of this uniqueness. Specialized markets (Zhuanye Shichang) are
generally marketplaces located in industrial clusters, specializing in the
wholesale supply of local commodities and their related goods. Their
sellers and buyers are the countless number of small and medium enterprises (SMEs). In developed countries, such marketplaces appeared on the
eve of the industrial revolution and gradually disappeared. In developing
countries, most marketplaces have tended to be part of a large informal sector. In contemporary China, however, specialized markets have

appeared in many of the modern industrial sectors, such as daily necessities, apparel, metalworking, molds, eyewear and cell phones, and were paradoxically upgraded and expanded along with the development of the industrial clusters (Ding 2010; Ding and Pan 2011).

The specialized markets on the one hand linked with the industrial clusters, and on the other hand, have extended their tentacles to distant markets. Various smaller markets with names such as Commodity City, Apparel City, Cell Phone City, and Auto Parts City are grouped together in the cities and towns in China. Most of these markets have tight links with specialized markets. Some were even established by the manager of a specialized market itself. It is now difficult for ordinary Chinese consumers to survive without these markets.

In accordance with advances in communications and logistics technology, specialized markets further began to form links with emerging overseas markets. There are a number of marketplaces opened by Chinese merchants in Dubai, Johannesburg and Sao Paulo. Merchants from developing countries also come to the marketplaces in Guangzhou or Yiwu, in China, for purchasing.

The specialized markets in the industrial clusters, the markets in China's cities and towns, and in the emerging economies, have thus joined to form a powerful *Specialized Market System*. With a seemingly primitive, but in fact brand-new form, the specialized market system is constantly circulating products from China's industrial clusters to emerging markets, and through this significantly strengthening the competitiveness of Chinese SMEs.

As a result of the emergence of the specialized market system, China has dramatically become the most *market*-oriented country in the world. During the period 1978 to 2003, the total number of marketplaces in China increased from 33,302 to 81,017. In a mere ten years from 1990 to 2000, the share of the transaction volume of consumer goods traded in marketplaces accounted for between 26.1 percent and 62.1 percent of China's "Total Retail Sales of Social Consumer Goods" (NSTGMSS 1991–2001).[1]

In spite of the importance of the specialized market in the real world, its academic significance has not as yet been sufficiently clarified. Based on Western experiences, most Chinese scholars treat the specialized market as merely a primitive institution appropriate for the initial and middle stages of industrialization, considering that sooner or later it will be substituted by more modern distribution systems. On the other hand, researchers in other countries lack perceptual knowledge of such marketplaces, and have shown almost no interest in this unique economic system thus far.

The precise purpose of this book is to systematically summarize, for the first time, the experience of the specialized markets, the distribution system that has the specialized market as its hub, the industrial clusters that have developed on the basis of the specialized markets, and the numerous dynamic small businesses fostered within the specialized markets.

A brief summary of the contents of the following 11 chapters is given here. Chapter 1 first points out how the appearance of the specialized market is revolutionary through a thorough literature review of SME development.

Chapter 2 presents the framework of the market platform for analyzing specialized markets, distinguishing between the market platform mode clusters and the merchant mode clusters. Basic concepts for specialized market and industrial cluster analysis, including critical mass, indirect network effects, platform governance, and platform competition, are explained. The difference between physical market platforms and virtual market platforms is also discussed.

Chapter 3 overviews the general situation in the specialized markets, using data from 68 markets in 53 industrial clusters in Zhejiang Province. Both the static quantitative characteristics of the specialized markets, and the dynamic process concerning the manner in which the specialized market as a factor of the Wenzhou Model spread to the whole of Zhejiang Province, are clarified in this chapter.

Chapters 4, 5, 6 and 7 form a case study of Yiwu China Commodity City (Yiwu Market). This market is not only the largest daily necessities specialized market in the world, but also the most important innovator in the specialized market system. By focusing on this market, it has been possible to clarify the evolutionary mechanism of the specialized markets in the whole of China.

The fundamental difference between the specialized market and the traditional marketplace is whether the market is being effectively managed and maintained by a platform manager. Chapter 4 points out that the local government has played such a role. The Yiwu government has not only constantly created and fostered new buyers and new sellers for the market, but has also unceasingly established and maintained the transaction infrastructure. As a result, Yiwu Market has overcome various problems that have often occurred in the physical market platform, and has thus become a pioneer market in China's specialized market system.

Chapter 5 investigates the domestic linkages of the Yiwu Market. Based on the data of a large-scale survey carried out by a local newspaper in Yiwu, this chapter demonstrates that a powerful distribution system for daily necessities has been formed between the industrial clusters, the Yiwu Market, and the markets in China's main cities. The role of Yiwu merchants in the formation of this system is also discussed in depth.

Chapter 6 discusses the overseas linkages of the specialized markets. On the one hand, a large number of foreign buyers have come to make purchases in China's specialized markets, such as Yiwu. On the other hand, a large number of Chinese merchants have begun to open marketplaces in overseas markets, such as in African countries. As a result, a new global distribution system that differs greatly from the well-known global value chains is emerging.

Traditional marketplaces in developing countries are generally dominated by merchants. In Yiwu Market, however, merchants actively take part in the production process and producers are easily able to develop their own marketing means. Chapter 7 describes this unique change in the producer–distributor relationship, and clarifies the factors that caused this change.

Chapters 8, 9 and 10 form a case study of China Changshu Zhaoshang City (Zhaoshang City). This is a latecomer market, and the Changshu apparel cluster where the market is located has no tradition of long-distance trade. In spite of these poor initial conditions, Zhaoshang City has been successful in competition with other platforms and has grown into the largest specialized apparel market in China. The Changshu cluster has also become a leading apparel cluster. Based on the case study of this market, we discuss the mechanism of competition and the logic of upgrading in a market platform mode cluster.

Chapter 8 studies the role of local government in platform competition by tracing in detail the initial stage of the development process of Zhaoshang City. At this time, the local government not only learned a great deal from the pioneer markets in Zhejiang Province, but also devised various measures that were suited to the initial conditions of Changshu. Consequently, this latecomer market was able to become a leading specialized apparel market.

Chapter 9 analyzes the logic of quantitative expansion and qualitative upgrading in the market platform mode cluster. Zhaoshang City has revived and broadened the Landsmann network of its booth-keepers. This network has, on the one hand, attracted a large number of small producers and buyers to the market, and has also, on the other hand, sustained their vitality under great competitive pressure. Consequently, an increasing number of apparel factories appeared in the Changshu cluster, and many leading brand apparel makers have been fostered simultaneously.

Chapter 10 attempts to classify industrial clusters from the perspective of market intermediaries. By analyzing data from 65 apparel clusters in China, we distinguished between three different types of clusters, namely, the specialized-market-based industrial cluster, the export-oriented cluster, and the big-company-dominated cluster.

The Conclusion summarizes the fundamental differences between the specialized market and traditional market, and analyzes the reasons why it was possible for specialized markets to appear in China during the economic transition period. We further discuss the significance of the specialized market in developing economies, and the factors that affect the future of specialized markets.

NOTE

1. Before 2005, "Total Retail Sales of Social Consumer Goods" was the sole indicator reflecting the total transaction scale of goods in China's domestic market. However, this indicator has two limitations. First, it only includes data from so-called "enterprises above a designated size." Second, it only reflects the situation in retail sectors.

1. Specialized markets and small business dynamics in China

Figure 1.1   Bazar-e Bozorg in Tehran, Iran

1.1   THE SMALL BUSINESS MARKETING REVOLUTION IN THE SPECIALIZED MARKETS

The key factor for SME development is how to access the market. In general, small producers are required to sell products to a distant market through the intermediary of "merchants."[1] Within the specialized markets, however, the producers, for the first time, are indeed able to transact directly with distant market buyers, and have realized qualitative developments. This chapter will indicate in what way the appearance of the specialized markets is revolutionary for SME development by means of a search of the literature concerning SMEs and the markets.

We first conduct a horizontal comparison with other countries. With regard to the developed countries, it has been clearly pointed out by Itami, Matsushima and Kikkawa (1998) that in order to respond to rapidly changing and highly segmented demand, small producers generally link with the market through demand carrying firms. These firms are likely to be distributors or assemblers in the manufacturing sector. They may be located either inside the cluster or near the market. In general, however, these are large firms and their number is stable. They play an irreplaceable role in connecting the industrial cluster and the distant market.[2]

A similar situation can also be observed broadly in the developing countries. According to Hayami (2006), in the rural areas of Asia, the merchants are probably smaller and they may not be involved in the production process as much as in the developed countries. In order to carry products to distant markets, there may be a division of labor between different regional merchants. The general pattern by which small producers explore distant markets through merchants, not a large number of unspecific distant market buyers is, however, unchanged.[3]

In developing country distribution centers, there are generally huge wholesale markets that have close linkages with both the SME cluster and distant markets. Even in those markets, however, it remains very rare that small producers operate booths in the marketplaces and trade directly with distant market buyers. We have collected literature related to these wholesale markets in Vietnam, Iran and South Korea. It is surprising that in all three cases, the division of labor between the producers and the wholesale merchants is clear-cut. The small producers have the sole option of selling products through the wholesale merchants in the markets.

Goto (2005) investigated the domestic-market-oriented apparel clusters in Ho Chi Minh City, Vietnam. This study shows that sewing factories play a leading role in the local apparel industry, and primarily sell products to wholesale merchants in the markets in Ho Chi Minh City.[4] However, the sewing factories and wholesale merchants are almost completely separated. No active communication occurs between them. The result is that the apparel cluster is full of imitation goods and shows no signs of upgrading.

Iwasaki (2002) studied the apparel cluster surrounding the Bazar-e Bozorg in Tehran, Iran. The merchants, named Bonak-Dar, privately established a wholesale market as an interface platform that matches the sewing factories with the retailers. They simply sell the products of sewing factories to the retailers on a consignment basis, and never take any part in the production process. Because of the poor cooperation between producers, Bonak-Dar, and the retailers, the apparel cluster thus appeared to lack vitality.

The Dongdaemun Market in Seoul, South Korea is a comparatively successful case. In this market, the wholesale merchants play a leading role in upgrading the apparel clusters. They are engaged in design, promotion, marketing, and provide fabrics for the sewing factories. Wholesale merchants generally maintain long-term cooperative relationships with sewing factories. However, they rarely open or own factories themselves. The sewing factories also never operate booths directly in the Dongdaemun Market (Kim and Abe 2002).

Even in traditional China, the cases where small producers traded directly with distant market buyers were uncommon. Here, the distribution of commodities to a large extent depended on a complicated market-based trading system. The classic studies by G. William Skinner on China's rural marketing activity have clearly described how products manufactured by rural peasants were carried from a standard market town to a city through a hierarchal "marketing system" (Skinner 1964, 1965a, 1965b, 1977). In this system, small producers were capable of trading directly with buyers merely at a local marketplace where commodities are distributed within a narrow geographical scope.

Fu (1956, p. 32) pointed out the influence of the traditional market-based trading system on the development of rural cottage industry in China. According to his study, this system on the one hand maintained the scattered cottage industries and constrained their independence. On the other hand, the system hindered the cottage industry from forming linkages with a distant market. The merchants were able to collect commodities and materials simply by utilizing these countless marketplaces and thus did not need to control the production system directly themselves.

Compared with the above cases, the revolutionary change that occurred in the specialized markets in modern China was that, for the first time, the small producers became easily able to develop their own marketing means. The merchants now also take an active part in the production process. The boundary between producers and distributors has become increasingly ambiguous.[5]

Almost all specialized-market-related literature emphasizes that the specialized market plays a crucial role in providing a *"shared marketing network"* for SMEs (HUFTSED 1996; Zheng et al. 2003, pp. 50, 51; Zhu 2003; Sonobe and Otsuka 2004). This means that the small producers are selling commodities directly in the market and do not rely on wholesale merchants. A number of literature sources also showed that merchants in the specialized market are inclined to open their own factories. Especially in the studies concerning Zhejiang Province, this phenomenon is known as

"First the trade" (Maoyi Xianxing) (Lu, Bai and Wang 2003; Zheng et al. 2003, p. 120; Sonobe and Otsuka 2004). It has also been clarified that most of the small firms connected with specialized markets have accomplished capital accumulation and have developed qualitatively. Leading firms have even made their appearance from among these small firms. They are generally capable of organizing the whole value chain from design and production to marketing (Xie et al. 2001; Sonobe and Otsuka 2004).

In spite of this exciting marketing revolution, however, most of the previous studies have taken it for granted, and did not undertake a deep investigation into its internal mechanism. Some scholars have even emphasized the fact that the surprising lack of powerful merchants in the specialized-market-based clusters, unlike in the early stage of European industrialization, was the weakest point and hindered the further development of industrial clusters in China.[6]

1.2   DYNAMIC SMES WITHIN LOW-END MARKETS

The appearance of the specialized markets brought about two fundamental changes to SMEs. The first change was that small producers were more likely to maintain long-term vitality by trading with the numerous small buyers in the low-end market. This subverted the basic understanding of the demand conditions for SME development.

As previous studies have suggested, in the developed countries market demand is characterized by multi-variety with small batches, rapidly changing information, and high quality standards. This has enabled small-scale, handicraft businesses to maintain their competitiveness vis-à-vis large, integrated manufacturers.[7] Likewise, in the developing countries, only quality-driven marketing channels, either in markets in developed countries or the domestic high-end market, have succeeded in upgrading SMEs in industrial clusters.[8]

Because of this basic situation, most scholars have undervalued the role of the low-end market in SME development. The low-end market oriented industrial cluster growth path is known as the *low road*. Since it is based on low prices, cheap materials, and cheap labor, the low road is regarded as hindering the innovative activities of the *high road* (Sengenberger and Pyke 1991).

According to the author's limited understanding, among existing SME literature, only the Japanese small-scale industrial history research group positively appraised the role of the low-end market (Takeuchi 1996, p. 18). This study emphasized that the huge low-end market in the hierarchal society of Western countries, and the domestic markets in Asian developing countries, where the majority are immature consumers, have strongly boosted catch-up industrialization by latecomer countries such as Japan. However, this study also pointed out that small business in overseas markets generally developed upward from the low-end market to the middle and higher market segmentation.

In contrast to the above-mentioned cases, however, almost all the studies regarding specialized-market-based clusters have shown that, although inter-firm competition is indeed intense and price oriented in low-end markets, SMEs in the specialized market are constantly growing and generally maintaining their vitality (Marukawa 2001, 2007; Zheng et al. 2003; Zhu 2003, pp. 50–52; Watanabe 2004; Fu et al. 2004, Chapter 6; Jin 2004).

Affected by the Western experience, however, few previous studies have made a deep investigation of the sources of this vitality. In contrast, they have concentrated their arguments on whether the SMEs have managed to break away from the low-end market or not. These arguments can be further divided into the following two groups.

The first group admits the fact that the low-end market-oriented SMEs in the specialized-market-based clusters are fast-growing and indeed command a large presence. However, they attribute this to the backwardness of the cluster, and thus states that the cluster must overcome this situation. A typical case is Fu et al. (2004, pp. 59–64). Mainly based on fieldwork in some specialized-market-based clusters in Guangdong Province, this study differentiates cluster development into the *smith stage* and the *chandler stage*. They argue that most Chinese clusters are still in the backward smith stage and need to enter the chandler stage by introducing modern management systems.

The second group focuses on some specific firms in specialized market-based clusters and then arrives at the conclusion that the industrial clusters have broken away from the low-end market. This group basically ignored the immense presence of SMEs in various clusters in China

For example, in terms of the observation of some leading firms in Wenzhou, Xie et al. (2001) assert that a new Wenzhou Model characterized by big business with brand-name goods and a self-sales network has been established.[9] As a further example, based on large-sample questionnaire surveys, Sonobe and Otsuka (2004)[10] argue that several clusters in mainland China have succeeded in transforming from the "quantity expansion phase" to the "quality improvement phase," in a very similar manner to what has occurred in Japan and Taiwan. Some leading firms have entered middle or higher market segmentation and have thus completely broken away from the influence of the specialized market. Meanwhile, a large number of SMEs have been integrated into the production network of the leading firms, or otherwise have been eliminated through competition. However, this study did not present any chronological data concerning the total number of firms in any Chinese clusters to support this viewpoint.

There are naturally a few exceptions. Watanabe (2004) asserts that China's market conditions can allow SMEs to maintain competitiveness over a long period. He summarized the development of Wenzhou enterprises into two directions. The first is that the big mass-manufacturing companies maintain global competitiveness through their dominant power over distribution channels in the huge domestic market. The second direction is that a large number of SMEs in the industrial clusters maintain global competitiveness through a rejuvenation of their early experiences in exploring China's huge domestic market.[11] When discussing the dynamics of SMEs in Wenzhou, Watanabe (2004) laid emphasis on the *scale* of China's domestic market, which refers to both the large quantity of the demand and the multi-layered structure of the market (especially its low-end segment). These two factors provided a large space for SME development. However, this argument still needs to be strengthened from the perspective of the distribution system. This is because, as with China, many developing countries have a huge population and thus have a similarly large potential domestic demand in the low-end market. In most countries (such as India or Indonesia), however, we rarely find a case where SMEs aiming at the domestic low-end market have realized a dynamic form of development. Therefore, in order to understand the relationship between SMEs and China's domestic market, an analytical perspective incorporating the low-end market distribution system must be introduced.

1.3   THE GOVERNMENT-MANAGED OPEN PLATFORM

The second fundamental change brought about by the specialized markets concerns the way in which they provide a platform that constantly creates new small business and fosters their growth into leading enterprises.

Until now, there have been two lines of thought regarding this subject. The first treats the community as the best platform for raising SMEs. On the one hand, some scholars emphasize that the community will help to strengthen the mutual cooperation between merchants and producers. Almost all the studies concerning successful SME clusters have mentioned this point (Watanabe 1979; Takeuchi 1991; Markusen 1996; Ogawa 1998). Sharing the same understanding, some studies have emphasized the necessity of establishing some form of social intermediary such as an industry association or trade association for SMEs in order to gain "collective efficiency" (Schmitz 1995). On the other hand, some scholars focus on the internal mutual constraint function of a community. They believe that opportunistic behaviors in transactions will to a large extend be avoided because of the long-term relationship within a community (Sawada and Sonobe 2006, especially the first chapter by Hayami).

The second line of thought treats big business as the most important platform for fostering SMEs. As the great body of studies concerning the subcontract system in the Japanese manufacturing sector illustrate, big business encourages a number of workers to spin off and deepen the division of labor in a cluster. They also set strict standards and give guidance to the small producers on how to meet the standards (Nishiguchi 1994; Asanuma 1997; Fujimoto, Nishiguchi and Ito 1998). Sharing similar ideas, Markusen (1996) distinguished the hub and spoke industrial district and the satellite industrial platform from the traditional Marshallian industrial district.

With regard to developing countries, most scholars are more pessimistic about whether such a big company can appear within the society. They thus have placed hopes on external actors. A typical study is the "global value chains" approach. It emphasizes the role of a powerful global buyer (such as Wal-Mart) in helping SMEs in developing countries to realize process upgrading and product upgrading.[12]

A similar notion is the flowchart approach (Kuchiki and Tsuji 2005, 2008). As this approach indicated, industrial cluster formation has been facilitated in most East Asian countries through the introduction of a foreign leading firm into an industrial park.[13]

There are also a few exceptional studies that assert that it is entirely possible that such a big company might appear inside a developing country. For example, the above-mentioned Sonobe and Otsuka (2004) mention that big companies have appeared in industrial clusters in East Asian countries. This is known as the "qualitative improvement phase" for a cluster. However, this study did not treat the big company as a platform for SME fostering. It was more inclined to emphasize that the big company would eliminate SMEs through competition.

The specialized-market-based industrial cluster development, however, cannot be explained within any of the above frameworks. Thousands of small producers and small merchants may participate in a specialized market and it is generally vital to invite booth-keepers from non-local areas in order to sustain the development of a market (Ou and Xiao 2007, pp. 185–93).[14] Fu et al. (2004, pp. 51, 52, 190, 191) reported that these non-local booth-keepers have even become leading firms in specialized-market-based clusters. Given this situation, it would be very difficult indeed to establish a community-based cooperative relationship between all of the members of the cluster, or for all of these firms to be controlled by a single big company.

Up until now, however, there has been little investigation in the litera-ture concerning non-local firms in the specialized market. On the other hand, most literature has focused on the role of local government in raising SMEs in the specialized market. Chen (1999, pp. 315–16, 336–45) pointed out that local government has played an important role in deregu-lating private small business and building up a management system in spe-cialized markets. Zheng et al. (2003, pp. 49–50) pointed out that as a result of government intervention in taxation (cheap tax rates), credit guarantees and so on, the specialized market has become a "Special Market Zone" (Shichang Tequ), which provides a variety of infrastructure and services that support private enterprise. The motivation of local government has also been discussed. It is generally pointed out that in the social back-ground of China's decentralization policy, local governments are strongly motivated to increase taxation for regional development since the reform and opening-up period began (Chen 1999, pp. 315–16, 336–45; Zheng et al. 2003, p. 50; Zhu 2003, pp. 105–106).

In the author's opinion, in order to understand more deeply the features of specialized markets as a platform for fostering SMEs, the discussions concerning local government must be combined with the non-local firms.[15] There are two reasons for this. First, the number of local firms is limited. The local government will not maintain its enthusiasm for intervention in the specialized market unless a large number of non-local firms can be invited to do business in the market. Second, in the specialized market, some non-local firms, such as firms from Whenzhou or Yiwu, have extremely high mobility. As a study on federalism has suggested, *mobile resources* have a tendency to depart from administrative areas that behave inappropriately (thus stimulating competition between local governments) (Qian and Weingast 1997, p. 88). In this sense, non-local firms are there-fore likely to play a key role in interacting with the local government, and stimulating it to improve the business environment in the specialized market.

1.4   UNDERESTIMATION OF THE SPECIALIZED MARKET SYSTEM

As described above, although the specialized market had a great impact on SME development, there are yet few studies that have undertaken a deep investigation of the specialized market and give it a positive evaluation.[16] A similar situation can also been observed in the field of study covering the whole of the specialized market system.

Until now, only Zheng et al. (2003, pp. 5, 35, 74) have pointed out that there is a specialized market network based on the Zhejiang merchant network existing within China's domestic market. However, no hard evidence has been presented for analyzing this phenomenon.[17] In contrast, too much energy has been spent on debating whether the specialized market is a phase in a process of movement from one condition to another or whether it will continue to exist for a long time into the future.

The first opinion can be called the "phased market approach" (HUFTSED 1996; Zheng et al. 2003; Fu et al. 2004). As its representative work, Zheng et al. (2003, pp. 65–7) clarified the marketing channels in an industrial cluster into three types. The first is where local producers directly send salesmen to distant markets for marketing. The second type is where local producers make use of the specialized market system as a shared sales network. The third is where a leading firm directly builds up a sales network. Although the importance of the specialized market system has been emphasized, this study also implied that the specialized market system is merely a marketing channel appropriate for the *initial* and *middle* stages of industrialization.

The second opinion can be called the "market stratification approach." Li (2003) asserts that in China, the specialized market system will be stratified with the modern chainstore retail organizations for a long period. His point concerns demand conditions. Li (2003) notes that a huge low-end demand exists in China's rural areas, inland areas, and among the urban lower class and thus the requirement for the low-end market-oriented specialized market will last for a long time (Li 2003, pp. 69, 112). This study is based on China's fundamental realities and thus is persuasive. Like most of the dual-sector studies, however, it merely treats the specialized market system as a closed system isolated from the modern distribution system. The result is that the active interactions between these two systems have been completely neglected.

Furthermore, although these are two very insightful viewpoints, neither is supported by serious empirical studies. This is because researchers share a common view that the physical marketplace is a primitive and backward institution which deals in low-priced, low-quality and non-brand commodities. The specialized market must be overcome during the process of economic modernization, and thus deserves no careful academic research.[18] This is the general situation for the whole of specialized market research.

NOTES

1. The scope of the definition of "merchants" here is flexible. Merchants may specialize in commodity distribution, may intervene actively in the production process, and may even be a manufacturer. Applying the terminology of political economics, the possibility that merchant capital will transform into industrial capital is sufficiently high. Whether they are pure merchants or manufacturers with distributive functions, however, their roles in linking the small producers within a cluster and the buyers from a distant market are the same.
2. In this book (Itami et al. 1998), the chapter by Takaoka (1998, pp. 103, 104) especially focuses on the functions of demand carrying firms. In her terminology, however, demand carrying firms are called "linkage firms."
3. Hayami (2006)'s empirical evidence is based on the case of agricultural product distribution in Indonesia. However, this study pointed out clearly that the situation in the rural manufacturing sector is similar to that of the agricultural sector (see pp. 34, 35).
4. Although not mentioned in the study, from the context it is inferred that most of these wholesale merchants operate booths in the Ho Chi Minh City marketplaces.
5. Regarding the issue of producer–distributor relationships, the author has benefited significantly from Takeuchi (1996). This study pointed out that a great variety of producer–distributor relationships will form, depending on changes in market conditions. In the Japanese experience, in sectors where demand changes drastically and the market scale is small, the merchants will intentionally treat the small producers as a buffer with which to smooth out the business cycle. In sectors where market demand is stable and large, merchants will try to become producers and actively carry out marketing and product design themselves. In some sectors in which a particular skill is required, the producer is likely to interface directly with the market. This study greatly altered our general understanding that producer–distributor relationships are fixed.
6. Author interview with some Chinese industrial cluster researchers.
7. For the case of Japan, where SMEs generally have excellent processing abilities and maintain long-term subcontract relationships with big companies, see Watanabe (1979) and Itami et al. (1998); for the case of Italy, where SMEs are aiming at the high-end luxury market, see Piore and Sabel (1984) and Ogawa (1998).
8. See the special issue of *World Development* (1999, Vol. 27, No. 9) regarding industrial clusters in developing countries, especially the case study of Ludhiana woolen knitwear carried out by Tewari (1999), and the case study of the Agra footwear cluster carried out by Knorringa (1999). Both of these clusters happened to be Indian cases.
9. The Wenzhou Model is a typical Chinese rural industrialization model of the 1980s, characterized by the large presence of specialized markets, which have provided a platform that acts as an interface to bring together the large numbers of domestic factories in the Wenzhou industrial clusters and the 100,000 Wenzhou salesmen (tuixiao yuan) in the domestic market.
10. For the English version of this book, see Sonobe and Otsuka (2006).
11. Moreover, as with most Japanese scholars, he did not forget to mention the importance of the manufacturing side, and thus pointed out that the large number of machinery manufacturers in Wenzhou, which provided cheap and simple industrial machines to local SMEs, was a crucial premise for Wenzhou SME development.
12. See the Global Value Chain (GVC) Initiative website: http://www.globalvaluechains. org (accessed 2 October 2006). A noteworthy extension of the GVC approach is the national value chains approach. Schmitz (2006a, 2006b; his presentation at the Fifth International Conference on Industrial Clustering and Regional Development, 2006, Beijing) emphasized many times the role of the "national value chain," citing the cases of Brazil (Bazan and Navas-Aleman 2004) and India (Tewari 1999). We can derive two points from this concept. The first is that using a national value chain is a good way to weaken the control of a single powerful global buyer. The second is that national value chains are generally useful to local producers in realizing functional upgrading.

However, it is noteworthy in the cases of Brazil and India that national chains appear to be only controlled by a few successful leading firms. It seems that no effective distribution system for SMEs has been created as yet.

13. This viewpoint is more clearly reflected in Sonobe (2006, especially p. 70) and Otsuka and Sonobe (2011, p. 19 and Figure 1).

14. This study contains one section that explains in detail the importance of booth-keeper invitations for a wholesale market and the methods of inviting them to participate.

15. Zheng et al. (2003, p. 50) mentioned this point in passing. However, the argument is made from the perspective of the elimination of discrimination against non-local firms.

16. Studies concerning Yiwu China Commodity City are minor exceptions (Zhang et al. 1993; Lu et al. 2003; Fah 2008).

17. This study presented survey data from a questionnaire conducted at four markets in Hangzhou City (see pp. 76–84). However, it did not analyze the linkages between these markets and the specialized markets in the industrial clusters.

   Regarding the specialized market system, based on fieldwork in Changshu (from 2001) and Yiwu (from 2002), the author gradually came to a basic understanding concerning this system. Following that, using the data from a large-scale survey carried out by a local newspaper in Yiwu, the author independently clarified the features of the specialized market system (see Chapter 5).

18. This viewpoint is undoubtedly affected by the experience of developed countries. As the classic study by Mills (1951, pp. 20–28) shows, in the first half of the twentieth century, most small American merchants were eliminated through competition with modern big business (supermarkets, department stores, big manufacturers with their own brands, and so on) or dominated by them (cited from Huang 2008).

2.   Analytical framework

Figure 2.1   A leading sock company established by a former Yiwu Market booth-keeper

2.1   A FRAMEWORK FOR THE ANALYSIS OF THE SPECIALIZED MARKET: THE MARKET PLATFORM

There is a large imbalance between the thriving development of the specialized market and the underestimations of the specialized market studies. In the author's opinion, this has primarily resulted from a lack of an appropriate analytical framework. Hagiu (2007) was the first to combine the literature on market microstructure and intermediation

(Rubinstein and Wolinsky 1987; Stahl 1988; Biglaiser 1993; O'Hara 1995; Spulber 1996a, 1996b; Rust and Hall 2003), and the literature on two-sided markets, which is an important field of the platform studies (Schmalensee 2002; Caillaud and Jullien 2003; Rochet and Tirole 2003, 2006; Evans 2003; Armstrong 2006; Hagiu 2006a, 2006b). He pointed out that there are two polar strategies for market intermediation, namely the merchant mode and the two-sided platform mode.[1] In order to understand specialized markets, we must first realize that their nature is nothing but a two-sided platform.

The general differences between the merchant mode intermediary and the two-sided platform mode intermediary are as follows. In the merchant mode, sellers sell goods to the merchants and then the merchants sell goods to the buyers. In this process, the ownership of the goods changes hands from the sellers to the merchants, and then to the buyers. Wal-Mart can be regarded as a typical merchant mode intermediary.

On the other hand, a pure two-sided platform consists of the following factors, namely, sellers, buyers, a platform, and a platform manager.[2] In the two-sided platform mode, buyers and sellers are affiliated with the platform and transact with each other directly. In the transaction, the ownership of the goods does not pass through the hands of the platform manager.

The two-sided platform is a typical market intermediary with the nature of a two-sided market. As platform users, sellers and buyers are two heterogeneous groups. The more sellers that are affiliated with a platform, the more buyers there are who will be willing to use the platform for purchasing, and vice versa. Such interaction is the key for the development of a two-sided platform, and is known as the "indirect network effect."[3]

In reality, in addition to buyers and sellers, there may be third parties or even further user groups on a platform. Whether the platform is two-sided or multi-sided, indirect network effects will be exhibited through their interactions. The essential function of all these platforms is to promote efficient market transactions between different user groups. In this book, I define both the two-sided platform and the multi-sided platform as a *Market Platform*. In order to emphasize the roles of buyers and sellers as the major actors, in some cases the term *two-sided platform* will be used alternatively.

A market platform exhibits an indirect network effect only after the total number of users (buyers and sellers) exceeds a minimum network size, namely the *critical mass* (Economides and Himmelberg 1995; Economides 1996; Evans 2009). When the total benefits of using a platform exceed the costs, the platform will achieve a critical mass. The benefits of using a platform depend on the number of platform users. The costs of using a

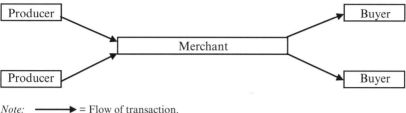

Note: ——▶ = Flow of transaction.

Source: Based on Hagiu (2007, p. 116). Revised by the author to show the situation in industrial clusters.

Figure 2.2   The merchant mode industrial cluster

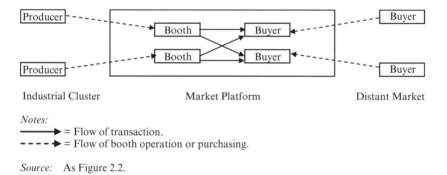

Industrial Cluster   Market Platform   Distant Market

Notes:
——▶ = Flow of transaction.
- - - -▶ = Flow of booth operation or purchasing.

Source: As Figure 2.2.

Figure 2.3   The market platform mode industrial cluster

platform include not only the membership fees and/or usage fees paid to the platform manager, but also various transaction costs and other costs concerning use of the platform. Even if strong indirect network effects are being exhibited in a platform, they could disappear again if the platform manager acts inappropriately and the costs of using the platform exceed the benefits.[4]

In terms of the different market intermediaries by means of which the cluster and the market are connected, industrial clusters can be classified into two types, the merchant mode industrial cluster (Figure 2.2) and the market platform mode industrial cluster (Figure 2.3).

In Figures 2.2 and 2.3, on one side is a set of producers – the industrial cluster – and on the other side is a set of buyers – the distant market. In the pure merchant mode cluster, the producers in an industrial cluster sell products to the merchants, and then the merchants resell the products to the buyers in the distant market at their own risk. The merchants here can be either a few big companies or a number of small merchants. They may either specialize in the distribution sector as a wholesaler or a retailer, or may be an assembler engaged in organizing the production. The merchants can be located either inside an industrial cluster, or outside a cluster but near a distant market. All the merchants, producers, and buyers are respectively homogeneous, but are heterogeneous with respect to each other. The producers in an industrial cluster and the buyers in a distant market are completely separated. No indirect network effect arises, and thus no information or knowledge is exchanged between them.

In the pure market platform mode cluster (Figure 2.3), the platform can be either a specialized market or other intermediaries with the nature of a two-sided market (trade fair, e-commerce platform and so on). The producers in an industrial cluster operate booths in the market platform, and the buyer comes from a distant market for purchasing. They trade directly with each other within the platform. All the producers and buyers are respectively homogeneous, but are heterogeneous with respect to each other. An indirect network effect is generated between buyers and sellers as long as the market platform reaches a critical mass. The larger the number of producers in a platform, the more intense the competition, which brings about cheaper prices and more varieties of goods for buyers. Consequently, an increasing number of buyers will be attracted to the platform. On the other hand, the larger the number of buyers in a platform, the lower the sales risk becomes and the richer will be the market information brought to the producers. As a result, an increasing number of producers will be attracted to the platform.[5] In general, a stronger indirect network effect is more likely to arise in the low-end segmentation in a market, as the barriers to entry and exit there are lower, and there are thus more potential buyers and producers.

It is necessary to clarify here the difference between merchants in a merchant mode industrial cluster and buyers in a market platform mode industrial cluster. In many merchant mode industrial clusters, the merchants may come from a distant market and their size may not be so large. Merely from appearances, there seems to be no difference between them. Here, the concept of the indirect network effect will help to distinguish between these two groups more precisely. Generally, in a market platform mode industrial cluster, the market platform exhibits a strong indirect network effect. The number of buyers will change *flexibly* along with changes in the number of producers. In contrast, in a merchant mode cluster, there is no indirect network effect. The number of merchants will be more *steady* and not increase or decrease along with the number of producers. This is the fundamental difference between these two groups.

2.2 TWO-SIDED MARKET THEORY AND THE DEVELOPMENT OF THE PHYSICAL MARKETPLACE

In order to analyze the specialized market in depth in the framework of the market platform, it is necessary to link the great body of literature on two-sided markets with specialized market studies. As a monograph in the field of area studies, my basic stance is to obtain some clues for understanding specialized markets through a dialogue with two-sided market theory. In the author's opinion, two-sided market theory is extremely instructive for specialized market study in the following two aspects.

First, two-sided market theory treats primarily virtual digital economies as its research subject. The features of digital economies clarified by this theory are helpful in understanding the characteristics of the specialized market as a physical marketplace.

Second, a key factor in the two-sided market theory is the two-sidedness. Until now, the argument concerning industrial clusters has concentrated on one side. The emphasis on two-sidedness can thus enrich our understanding of industrial clusters.

This section first discusses the former point. One fact needs to be emphasized again. The specialized market described in this book, namely a marketplace where small producers trade directly with distant market buyers, has never before existed in economic history. In Europe, the marketplace appeared extensively on the eve of the industrial revolution, but eventually disappeared. By checking the cases introduced in Braudel (1992), we can find that the distant market-oriented large-scale markets were generally dominated by merchants, and only in the markets for intra-regional trade were the small producers able to become the main actors. In developing countries, marketplaces still command a large presence in the economic system. However, most of them tended to be part of a large informal sector (ILO 1972; Geertz, Geertz and Rosen 1979; Ikeno and Takeuchi 1998).

From the above facts, we can judge that in the real world, there are many factors that hinder the marketplace from developing into a pure market platform. The marketplaces in China, however, because of a number of unique social and economic conditions during the transitional period, overcame these obstacles smoothly. Therefore, although it is a physical market, the specialized market achieved a dynamic development that can otherwise be observed solely in the virtual digital world. Two-sided market theory can simply provide a good reference system for clarifying these conditions. By analyzing carefully the features of the virtual digital economies (credit cards, video games, e-commerce platforms and so on) indicated by the two-sided market literature, we will very conveniently discover various factors that affect the development of physical markets.

2.2.1   Restraints on a Platform Manager

In two-sided market theory, the platform manager is assumed to be an omnipotent actor who is not restrained by any factors in the brick-and-mortar world, and can easily attract sufficient numbers of buyers and sellers to a platform simply through appropriate setting of the price structure (by charging one side or both sides of the platform, the types of fees imposed, etc.) (Armstrong and Wright 2008). The platform manager of a physical marketplace, however, will inevitably encounter various restraints.

The first restraint the platform manager often encounters is barriers to trade. In the real world, because of various institutional and informational restraints, not every buyer can move freely from a distant market to an industrial cluster. The producers also may not be allowed to access the market smoothly. It may therefore not be possible for the marketplace to exceed the critical mass for a market platform. Even if this point is exceeded, the indirect network effect will not necessarily arise between the two sides of the market. Thus, a successful physical market manager must help SMEs to remove these trade barriers.

The second restraint for a platform manager in the brick-and-mortar world concerns the platform itself. Almost all the two-sided market literature assumes that information will flow smoothly and no physical infrastructure problem exists in a marketplace. They have thus concentrated discussions on the *market*, but have completely ignored the importance of *place*.

In the brick-and-mortar world, however, the *place* will result in two types of costs. The first concerns the costs of using real estate. For a physical market manager, in order to efficiently accept all potential buyers and sellers, not only do the transaction facilities need to be substantially enlarged and improved, but flexible transactions of the ownership and use rights of the real estate regarding the market must also be possible. Otherwise, the transaction space will become increasingly narrower and the congestion costs will become increasingly larger.[6] Eventually, the number of sellers (as booth-keepers) may not be capable of adjusting flexibly in line with the increase or decrease in the number of buyers, and the indirect network effect will disappear.

The second concerns transaction costs. A physical market can save on the traveling costs of buyers and sellers searching for each other through centralized transactions. However, as Figure 2.3 illustrates, there will be no savings on the total number of searches and transactions in a market, which remains m (number of buyers) × n (number of sellers).[7] Thus, along with the expansion of transactions, the transaction costs in the physical market will show a surprising rise. Therefore, a successful physical market manager must work out various ways of reducing these costs and improving transaction efficiency.[8]

2.2.2 Mobility of Traders

Two-sided market literature assumes that both buyers and sellers have a high mobility. As long as the platform exhibits an indirect network effect, an increasing number of buyers and sellers will constantly gather on the platform. It must be noted, however, that the mobility of traders in the real world differs considerably by region. Producers from some regions have a strong desire to access the market, but from others may be completely separate from the market. Merchants from some regions delight in long-distance trade and never fatigue. Merchants from other regions may have a narrow activity radius and never take the initiative in exploring distant markets. These producers and merchants from different regions thus play a different role in the development of a physical marketplace. When analyzing the specialized market, we must thus take the social and economic background of the traders into full account.

2.2.3 The Mixed Mode of the Market Platform and the Merchant

Among the literature on the two-sided market, Hagiu (2007, p. 129) has paid particular attention to economic realities. He not only distinguishes between the two types of market intermediaries, but also points out that in reality these two types are a continuum between the pure two-sided platform and the pure merchant. The two are not either one or the other, but are mutually intermixed. In addition to the indirect network effect, this study lists a number of fundamental economic factors (asymmetric information between sellers and the intermediary; investment incentives; and product complementarities/substitutability) that determine the two modes.

It is very insightful to notice the mixed mode of these two market intermediaries. However, an important premise of this study is that there is a powerful economic actor who can simultaneously engage as both a two-sided platform manager and a leading merchant, and can transform freely from one mode into the other in accordance with his strategic needs. We must recognize that this assumption does not comply with the reality in developing countries. This is because most market intermediaries in low-end markets in developing countries do not have sufficient organizational capability. Market platform mode intermediaries, such as the manager of a marketplace, are incapable of buying up a large number of commodities efficiently and further distributing these efficiently to the large numbers of small merchants in a distant market, at least in the initial stages. Merchant mode intermediaries, such as small retailers, are incapable of providing a large transaction platform and providing for effective transactions between such large numbers of buyers and sellers. In most cases, the form of intermediaries in developing countries is highly path dependent, being affected by various institutional factors such as the form of traditional commercial capital, and the land use system.

Since it is difficult for a market platform manager or a merchant to transform into one another in developing countries, we should therefore treat the mixed mode problem from another perspective. As stated in Chapter 1, in wholesale markets in the industrial clusters of many developing countries, producers and wholesale merchants in the markets are completely separated. Producers cannot access the market and are required to sell products through the merchants.[9] For the small producers, these wholesale merchants are undoubtedly typical "merchants." On the other hand, in China, producers have a large potential for operating booths directly in the market. For these producers, if their share in the total number of booths is increasing, the marketplace is transforming towards a pure market platform. In contrast, if the share of merchants is increasing, it will become a merchant mode intermediary. Therefore, the appropriate research perspective for the discussion of the mixed mode of merchant and market platform is not the *manager* of the marketplace itself, but the *seller* within the marketplace.

2.3   THE LOGIC OF MARKET PLATFORM MODE INDUSTRIAL CLUSTER DEVELOPMENT

We then discuss the impacts of two-sided market theory on industrial cluster studies. Until now, most arguments related to industrial clusters have concentrated on the production side.[10] Two-sided market theory, however, tells us that the other side of an industrial cluster could be important as well.

2.3.1   Externalities

The economic effect of an industrial cluster to a large extent results from externalities. According to Marshall (1920, p. 271), a firm located in an "industrial district" may have advantages in obtaining technological information, the use of specialized machinery, employing specially skilled laborers from a local market, and so on.

Although Marshall (1920) did not mention it, the industrial clusters that he refers to are simply in the merchant mode. Thus, his arguments concentrated on the externalities existing between producers. Affected by Marshall's classic study, most of the contemporary industrial cluster literature has discussed the economic effect of industrial clusters primarily from the same perspective (Watanabe 1979; Piore and Sabel 1984; Krugman 1991; Schmitz 1995; Sonobe and Otsuka 2004).

Two-sided market theory, however, indicates that through the intermediation of a market platform, externalities (indirect network effects) are likely to exist between local producers and distant market buyers.[11] When indirect network effects arise, the number of producers and buyers will become increasingly larger. This will cause a constant expansion of production scale and market size. On the other hand, because of the active interaction between producers and distant market buyers, the producers are able to obtain demand information on distant markets immediately; buyers can also easily obtain information on various producers and products. In this situation, even though no transaction relations exist, simply based on the expectation concerning the increasingly expanding demand, and the availability of sufficient information, producers and buyers will obtain great opportunities for growth and will formulate unique business strategies.

2.3.2 Inter-Platform Competition

In the merchant mode, competition between industrial clusters occurs on only either the buyer side or the producer side. In the former case, producers in different industrial clusters compete with each other in the scramble for buyers (customers) through the intermediation of merchants. In the latter case, there is generally an industrial park. The managers of industrial parks in different clusters compete with each other in the scramble for powerful producers who have their own marketing channels.

Compared to this, in the market platform mode, competition between industrial clusters is essentially competition between platforms. Because platform managers can benefit from both sides, both buyers and producers will become the target of competition. Theoretically, since buyers and producers are mutually attracted because of the indirect network effects, a platform will be successful in the competition as long as sufficient numbers of traders are attracted to one side of the platform. In reality, however, compared with buyers, it is more difficult to attract sufficient numbers of producers. On the one hand, the number of local producers is limited. On the other hand, producers generally bear higher fixed costs, and their mobility is lower than that of buyers. Therefore, in most cases, attracting a large number of highly mobile producers (or merchants as their reserve army) from non-local areas will be a crucial factor for the development of a market platform mode cluster.[12]

Platform competition can greatly stimulate the evolution of platforms, such as traditional marketplaces. In order to ensure sufficient numbers of buyers and sellers, a platform manager will be forced to devise various innovations. Transaction infrastructure will be improved, a credit system will be built, and the market user fees will be reduced. Through this kind of fierce competition, a successful marketplace is eventually likely to attract most of the potential buyers and sellers, and thus became a dominant power in the market. The industrial cluster in the area where the market is located will then accordingly become a production base with a dominant share in the industry.

2.3.3   Upgrading and Governance

Two patterns of upgrading
When an indirect network effect arises, increasing numbers of producers will appear in the platform, stimulating intense intra-platform competition, which inevitably exerts a strong pressure on firms to improve productivity and upgrade. In the market platform mode, the crucial point for determining a firm's upgrading strategy is the interaction between the industrial cluster and the markets, namely, the interaction between producers and distant market buyers. Concretely, two upgrading patterns have been recognized.

The first upgrading pattern is to make progress in the fields of design and branding, the well-known functional upgrading (Schmitz 2006a, 2006b). In a market platform mode cluster, a large non-stop flow of buyers will come to the market platform for purchasing. Simply by communicating with these buyers, or watching the salability of the goods in the market, producers can easily understand the changes that are taking place in market conditions, and thus develop various products suited for market needs.

In the initial stage, the market structure in the industrial cluster is a perfect competition-like market. Producers in the clusters provide undifferentiated goods by either imitating goods in the middle and high-end market or by imitating each other. On the other hand, buyers are both price takers and design takers, having no bargaining power and design abilities. Any products, even though they may be imitation goods, will be accepted by them as long as they are cheap.

When the indirect network effect arises, an increasing number of buyers are attracted to the market platform, which brings about abundant heterogeneous market information and a large number of orders for the producers. As a result, the per unit cost of design and brand differentiated goods for producers becomes increasingly cheaper, and the opportunities for trial and error become increasingly larger. Eventually, the system will nurture a number of leading producers who are adept at design and branding.

The second pattern of upgrading is to enter the upstream sector of an industry. Economically, the effects of backward linkages are defined as the effects through which demand expansion in the downstream of an industry will stimulate the development of the upstream sector, which is generally more capital-intensive and technology-intensive (Hirschman 1957). In a market platform mode cluster, distant market buyers are constantly flowing into the cluster. Although orders placed by each buyer may be small, the total quantity of orders is sufficiently large. As a result, merchants as booth-keepers in the market are likely to take on the risks of entering the manufacturing sector, and producers engaging in the production of final goods are likely to take on the risks of initiating the production of intermediate goods. A large number of new firms also have incentives for entering these upstream sectors. Eventually, a complete value chain will be formed in the cluster.

Platform governance
Appropriate platform governance is necessary for the realization of the two upgrading patterns mentioned above.[13] As mentioned in section 2.2, the physical marketplace has its own difficulties. The purpose of governance for a market platform is precisely to overcome these difficulties, acquire sufficient numbers of platform users, and reduce the various costs on the platform to ensure efficient transactions and smooth information flows between industrial clusters and markets.

Governance of the physical marketplace concerns both the *market* and the *place*. With regard to markets, a platform manager is required to lower the barriers to trade and cultivate buyers and sellers. Concerning place, on the one hand the platform manager needs to provide sufficient land and transaction infrastructure to reduce congestion costs on a platform. On the other hand, the platform manager must also build up an efficient transaction system to lower increased transaction costs.

According to Humphrey and Schmitz (2000), previous studies primarily referred to two types of approaches concerning industrial upgrading and governance for firms in developing countries, namely, the industrial cluster approach and the global value chain approach. By comparing these two approaches, we can more clearly recognize the unique features concerning upgrading and governance of the market platform approach (see Table 2.1).

Table 2.1   Governance and upgrading: clusters, value chains vs. platforms

	Clusters	Value chains	Platforms
Governance within the locality	Strong local government characterized by close inter-firm cooperation and active private and public institutions. Risks attenuated by local mechanisms for risk-sharing.	Not discussed. Local inter-firm cooperation and government policy largely ignored.	Emphasis on the role of a strong platform manager capable of fostering traders, and lowering transaction and congestion costs. Inter-firm competition is more important than inter-firm cooperation.
Relations with the external world	External relations not theorized, or assumed (by default) to be based on arm's length market transactions.	Strong governance within the chain. International trade increasingly managed through inter-firm networks based on quasi-hierarchical relations. Risks attenuated by relationships within the chain.	Weak governance within the chain. Major buyers are small buyers from the developing world. Indirect network effects matter more than direct transaction relations.
Upgrading	Emphasis on incremental upgrading (Learning by doing) and the spread of innovations through interactions within the cluster. For discontinuous upgrading, local innovation centers play an important role.	Incremental upgrading made possible through learning by doing and the allocation of new tasks by the chain's lead firm. Discontinuous upgrading made possible by "organizational succession" allowing entry into more complex value chains.	Active interactions between increasing numbers of buyers and producers stimulate functional upgrading and upgrading by entering the upstream capital-intensive and technology-intensive sectors.

Table 2.1   (continued)

	Clusters	Value chains	Platforms
Key competitive challenge	Promoting collective efficiency through interactions within the cluster.	Gaining access to chains and developing linkages with major customers.	Promoting inter-platform competition and intra-platform competition by attracting highly mobile producers (or merchants as their reserve army). Inter-platform competition enhances platform evolution, and intra-platform competition enhances the nurturing of leading firms.

Source: Revised by the author based on Humphrey and Schmitz (2000, Table 3). Reproduced by permission.

NOTES

1. According to Hagiu (2007), the literature on market microstructure and intermediation focuses primarily on the merchant mode market intermediary, and the two-sided market related literature discusses the two-sided platform mode market intermediary.

    As a monograph in the field of area studies, this book has simply applied Hagiu's framework for the analysis of specialized markets. As stated below, in view of the realities of developing countries, we accept his classification but do not accept his analysis of the mixed form of these two modes.

2. Existing literature often uses the terms "platform owner" or "platform provider." In view of the importance of platform governance (see below), however, this book has chosen to use the term "platform manager."

3. In other two-sided market literature, it is known as *cross-group externality* or some other term.

4. My understanding of the determination of critical mass has benefited greatly from discussions with my colleague, Toshitaka Gokan.

5. The mechanism of indirect network effects in a market platform has also been mentioned in Ding and Pan (2011).

6. Concerning the discussion on congestion cost, see Fujita, Krugman and Venables (1999).

7. Some scholars assert that the total number of transactions in the specialized market is $m + n$ (see Jin and Ke 1997). They have clearly confused the merchant mode and the two-sided platform mode.

8. To be precise, transaction costs caused by opportunistic behaviors also exist in virtual platforms. Except for Boudreau and Hagiu (2009), however, most two-sided market literature has ignored this point.

9. This situation is impossible in the virtual e-commerce platform. Since it is not physically restrained by infrastructure at all, the situation where producers cannot enter the platform will never occur.

10. An exception is the IDS research group, Sussex University, UK. Since Schmitz and Nadavi (1999), they have emphasized the importance of external linkages for an industrial cluster. The latest research outputs of this group are the above-mentioned GVC and NVC studies. A difference between this group and the author is that they focus on the transaction relations between the producers and buyers, but I pay more attention to the externalities between them.

11. The two-sided market literature also discusses the own group externalities, namely externality existing on one side of a platform, but primarily emphasizes the negative effect of externalities. For example, it asserts that an increasing number of sellers from the same side will justify a higher price for a platform (Wright 2004).

12. In spite of this, existing two-sided market literature discusses only the case where buyers select just one platform (singlehoming), and sellers select all the platforms (multihoming, Armstrong and Wright 2008). This is based on the assumption that sellers are more powerful than buyers and are capable of multihoming. Under this assumption, inter-platform competition merely lays emphasis on the scramble for buyers. This book will suggest that there are not only large numbers of singlehoming buyers, but also a large number of singlehoming sellers (producers) in China, who have sufficient mobility, and thus have became the main driving force in promoting inter-cluster competition.

13. Two previous studies have inspired the author to recognize the importance of platform governance. Boudreau and Hagiu (2009, pp. 165, 184, 185) pointed out that various factors may cause market failures in a multi-sided platform, including externalities, information asymmetries, non-pecuniary motivations, and uncertainties. Regulations on platform access and regulations on interactions in a platform are therefore necessary. However, this study laid emphasis on private regulation, and intentionally avoided the significance of public regulation for platform governance.

On the other hand, McMillan (2002) argued that for a market to function well, it is necessary to design a platform that has five elements. Namely, that information flows smoothly; property rights are protected; people can be trusted to live up to their promises; side-effects on third parties are curtailed; and competition is fostered. McMillan further emphasizes that help from the government is essential if the market is to reach its full potential (McMillan 2002, p. 13). A problem with McMillan's study is that it ignored the importance of critical mass for a platform. As Evans (2009) pointed out, a platform will not survive for long if the total number of traders on a multi-sided platform are not able to reach some minimum number, the critical mass.

3. The general situation in the "Province of Markets"

Figure 3.1   A booth in Shaoxing China Textile City

3.1   INTRODUCTION[1]

The specialized market first made its appearance in Wenzhou, Zhejiang Province in the 1970s. As one of the main factors of the Wenzhou Model, a typical model of China's rural industrialization, specialized markets have provided a platform that acts as an interface to match the large numbers of domestic factories in the industrial clusters in Wenzhou with the 100,000 Wenzhou salesmen,[2] who are dispersed throughout various locations in China (Yuan 1987; Fei and Luo 1988; Zhang and Li 1990; Komagata 2004).

From the 1980s, the specialized markets expanded rapidly from Wenzhou to the whole of Zhejiang Province. Between 1978 and 2003, the total number of marketplaces in Zhejiang, including specialized markets and other markets, increased from 1322 to 4036 (ZUESRG 2007, p. 35). Accordingly, the domestic retail share of products originating from 52 Zhejiang industrial clusters amounted to over 30 percent of China's total retail volumes for those products in 2002 (Jin 2004, p. 13).[3] Almost all of these industrial clusters formed strong links with specialized markets. Zhejiang was thus called the "Province of Markets."

This chapter attempts to overview the general situation in the specialized markets of Zhejiang, and thus clarifies the characteristic features of the development of China's specialized markets. The first half will indicate the characteristics of some of the basic factors of Zhejiang's specialized markets in 1998. The second half of this chapter attempts to clarify the mechanism through which the specialized markets have spread from Whenzhou to the whole of Zhejiang Province.

3.2   DATA SOURCE

This chapter utilizes *Zhejiang Sheng Shichang Zhi* [Zhejiang Province Market Chronicle] (ZPMC) as the main data source. As part of the *Zhejiang Shengzhi Congshu* (Zhejiang Provincial Chronicle Series), ZPMC was co-edited by the Zhejiang Chronicle Office and researchers at the Zhejiang Academy of Social Sciences between 1999 and 2000. The Administration for Industry and Commerce (AIC) at each administrative level of Zhejiang Province provided necessary information for the book (ZPMC, p. 3 and postscript). In China, marketplaces have been controlled by the AIC since the socialist planned economy period.[4] Thus, the information provided by the AIC is the most comprehensive and the most credible data.

Before analyzing ZPMC, however, we need to be aware of the following four constraints of this material. The first is that although ZPMC covers all 3953 marketplaces in Zhejiang (except for the markets in Longwan District and Ouhai District in Wenzhou), only information concerning the most typical markets is published in detail in this material. Of this, the information concerning specialized markets, which are located around the industrial clusters, is more limited. Consequently, this chapter will narrow the focus down to 68 specialized markets in 53 industrial clusters (Table 3.1).

The second constraint is that the information concerning specific indices varies widely in ZPMC. The *Fanli* (Guide) to ZPMC states that the following seven factors are given for each typical market: (1) the name of the

Table 3.1 Specialized markets in Zhejiang Province (1998)

Region	Northeast Zhejiang			Central Zhejiang 1		Central Zhejiang 2			Southeast Zhejiang	
City	Hangzhou	Jiaxing	Huzhou	Shaoxing	Ningbo	Jinhua	Quzhou	Lishui	Wenzhou	Taizhou
Population (10,000 persons)	611.4	329.91	254.81	430.04	535.27	442.96	240.13	246.16	717.89	539.51
No. of clusters	2	5	6	8	5	5	1	1	13	7
No. of markets	3	6	6	11	7	8	1	1	17	8

Note: The regional classification of Zhejiang Province is based on the division of labor between the writers in ZPMC (see postscript).

Sources: Data for population: *Zhejiang Statistic Yearbook 1999*; other data: compiled by the author based on data from ZPMC.

market; (2) the location; (3) the development process; (4) the features of the market; (5) the commodities; (6) the extent of geographical coverage of the market (including the geographical distribution of non-local booth-keepers and the geographical range of circulation of the commodities of the market); and (7) basic data for the market, including transaction volume, taxes, and so on. However, the actual situation is that a full set of these seven factors is not included for all of the typical markets, whereas some important information going beyond the scope of these factors is included in a considerable number of cases.

The third constraint is that the information concerning typical markets was described in the form of prose articles. We thus had to derive a great deal of information from ZPMC on the basis of subjective judgments.

The fourth constraint is that the information in ZPMC covers only the period up to 1998. Following that, some specialized markets have drastically changed under the influence of globalization. We will present the information concerning the effects of globalization through case studies in this book.

Because of the above constraints, the focus of the analysis in this chapter is not to describe precisely the features of Zhejiang's specialized markets through exact numerical values, but simply to describe important points for understanding specialized markets.

3.3   TRANSACTIONS IN SPECIALIZED MARKETS IN ZHEJIANG

3.3.1   Commodities

As a starting point for our analysis, the following two sections focus on the basic factors of specialized markets in Zhejiang. We first discuss what kinds of commodities the specialized markets were dealing in. As Table 3.2 shows, of 68 markets, except for 11 intermediated goods markets, 57 markets sell the same commodities as produced by the local cluster. From the context, we can judge that all of these 57 markets deal in local commodities. The most important function of the specialized markets is to support the local firms in their marketing efforts.

Examining the content of the commodities in these 57 markets, 53 are dealing in consumer goods. Concretely, 25 markets are dealing in daily necessities, 21 markets in textiles and apparel, and seven in hardware.

On the other hand, 39 markets are dealing in raw materials, machines, parts and other inputs necessary for the production of these commodities. Of these, 11 markets specialize in the sales of these intermediate goods.

Table 3.2 Commodity types in Zhejiang specialized markets (1998)

Commodities	1	2	1 + 2	1 + 3	2 + 3	1 + 2 + 3
Number of markets	19	11	23	10	0	5
Northeast Zhejiang	3	0	9	3	0	0
Central Zhejiang 1	4	3	8	0	0	3
Central Zhejiang 2	0	2	5	3	0	0
Southeast Zhejiang	12	6	1	4	0	2

Notes:
1 = Local commodities and commodities similar to local commodities.
2 = Raw materials, machines, parts and other inputs necessary for the production of finished products.
3 = Commodities unrelated to local commodities.

Source: Compiled by the author based on data from ZPMC.

Because of the presence of both finished goods markets and intermediate goods markets, a complete value chain has been formed within the industrial clusters. Of 53 clusters, 51 either have both finished products markets and intermediate products markets, or have markets that carry both of these two types of products simultaneously.[5]

Following that, we examine the commodities of specialized markets by regions. As Table 3.2 shows, in southeast Zhejiang, most markets specialize in the sales of finished products or intermediate products. Compared to this, most of the markets in other regions are dealing in finished goods and intermediate goods simultaneously. This is because in southeast Zhejiang, especially in Wenzhou, most of the specialized markets were formed spontaneously. In contrast, the specialized markets in other regions were mainly built by local governments. As latecomers, the local governments in these regions intentionally integrated a complete value chain of local commodities within the specialized markets. We will further analyze this point in section 3.5.

An interesting point derived from Table 3.2 is that there is little restriction on the sales of commodities in specialized markets. Of 68 markets, there are 29 that clearly deal in both local commodities and similar types of commodities purchased from other regions. Fifteen markets deal in commodities completely unrelated to local commodities, while simultaneously dealing in local commodities and/or their inputs. As will be shown in the case studies, because of this feature, the accessibility of specialized markets improved continuously, and small booth-keepers were thus able to move around between the various markets more easily.

Table 3.3   Transaction volumes of Zhejiang specialized markets (1998)
          (billion yuan)

Transaction volume	< 0.1	0.1 to 1 exclusive	1 to 5 exclusive	5 to 10 exclusive	10 or more	Unknown
Number of markets	11	25	14	7	3	8
Northeast Zhejiang	1	6	6	2		0
Central Zhejiang 1	0	4	5	4	1	4
Central Zhejiang 2	6	0	1	0	1	2
Southeast Zhejiang	4	15	2	1	1	2

Note: This table shows the maximum transaction volume up to 1998.

Source: As for Table 3.2.

3.3.2   Sellers

ZPMC does not show the exact number of sellers in each specialized market. Instead, we make a tentative estimation of this by examining the number of booths.[6] Of the 56 markets for which information is available, the number of booths in 35 of them is between 100 and 999, the number in 14 markets is between 1000 and 4999, and the number in seven markets is over 5000.[7] These data combined with the data for transaction volume (Table 3.3) confirmed that the majority of sellers in Zhejiang's specialized markets are SMEs.

It is difficult to judge whether these sellers are producers or distributors. According to the limited information in ZPMC, we find that pure producers clearly operate booths in 17 markets and pure merchants clearly operate booths in seven markets. Of these seven markets, only two have merchants but no producers. The ambiguous boundary between producers and distributors is in itself a distinctive feature of specialized markets.

Although ZPMC does not give clear information on every market, it is natural that local firms (whether producers or merchants) are selling products in these markets. On the other hand, there are at least 15 markets that have non-local booth-keepers. Concretely, the sellers in 12 of these markets are from other provinces of China and in three markets the sellers are from foreign countries.[8] This suggests that non-local booth-keepers are a large factor for understanding specialized markets.

There are ten markets where big domestic and overseas companies, which deal in brand-name or other high value added goods, operate booths directly in the specialized markets or have arranged to have agents in the markets. This fact is contradictory to the general understanding of the Phased Market Approach and the Market Stratification Approach, which assert that these firms never utilize the specialized market as a marketing channel. This paradoxical phenomenon will be further discussed in the case studies.

3.3.3 Buyers

There are a large number of buyers who make their purchases in specialized markets. Of 68 markets, according to the limited data, there are two that have 100,000 buyers visiting per day.[9] Additionally, there are five markets visited by 50,000, 15,000, 10,000, 8000 and 50 buyers, respectively, per day.[10]

The information on buyers can also been indirectly derived by examining the geographical scope of the commodities. In 1998, among the 68 markets, 45 sold commodities to China's domestic market, 21 sold to developing countries, and 15 sold to developed countries. The buyers in developing countries appeared to prefer to make purchases at the specialized markets.

From the descriptions in ZPMC, we can discover three reasons for understanding why these specialized markets in Zhejiang were able to attract such a large number of buyers from such a broad geographical area.

The first reason is that there are a large number of local SMEs engaged in the sales of local commodities to distant markets. Table 3.4 contains five such cases. As indicated in the table, the owners of these SMEs, most of whom were originally peddlers or itinerant craftsmen, are doing business in domestic markets, or in China's neighboring countries.

The second reason is that the specialized markets have built extensive sales networks with distant markets. Thirteen such cases can be found in ZPMC (Table 3.5). All these sales networks are distributed over a wide geographical area outside Zhejiang Province. Of these, the sales networks of three markets have spread to overseas markets.

It is noteworthy that most of the sales outlets of these networks are similarly marketplaces. Four specialized markets formed links with existing markets and three established their own branch markets. In overseas business especially, branch markets are established in every case. Only one market formed a link with department stores, which are recognized as a higher rank distribution system than the market.

The third reason is that some markets began to hold trade fairs from the 1990s. The data we obtained from ZPMC are as follows:[11]

Table 3.4 Long-distance trade activities of SMEs in Zhejiang clusters

Clusters	City	Commodities	Markets	Trade scope	Trade activities	No. of local firms or persons
Yongkang	Jinhua	Hardware	China Science and Technology Hardware City	Various locations in China	Production, distribution and repair of hardware	100,000 (after 1990s)
Yiwu	Jinhua	Daily necessities	China Commodity City	Various locations in China	Peddling, operating booths in marketplaces	7000 merchants (1990)
Qiaotou, Yongjia	Wenzhou	Buttons and zippers	Qiaotou Button Market	Over 200 large and medium cities in China	Operating booths in department stores	10,000 (after 1986)
Duqiao, Linhai	Taizhou	Eyewear	Zhejiang Eyewear City	Various large and medium cities in China. The border with the Former Soviet Union, India and Vietnam	Opening eyewear shops	Over 5000 shops (1998)
Zeguo, Wenling	Taizhou	Shoes, suitcases	Zhejiang Zeguo Leather and Shoes City	Various locations in China, Russia, Ukraine	Selling the market's commodities	Over 10,000 persons (1998)

Sources: Data for Yiwu and Yongkang: author fieldwork; other data as in Table 3.2.

Table 3.5   Sales network of Zhejiang specialized markets (1998)

Markets	Geographical distribution of the market's formal network	Sales outlets
Lin'an Silk Markets	Wuhan	Hanzhengjie markets
Honghe Woolen Sweater Markets	Various locations in China	Marketplaces
Zhejiang Leathers Apparel City	Kazakhstan	Branch market
Zhejiang Datang Socks City	Various locations in China	–
Sonxia Umbrella and Parts Market	50 or more large cities in China	Wholesale outlets of this market
China Necktie City	Various locations in China	Department stores, large-scale markets
Yuyao Lighter World	Yiwu	Yiwu China Commodity City
Lanxi Towel Wholesale Market	Kunming, Chengdu, Chongqing, Wuhan, Liuzhou, Beijing, Shanghai	–
Yiwu China Commodity City	45 locations in China, overseas markets (2000)	Branch markets
Oubei Mechanical and Electrical Valves Market	No less than 1000 locations in China's large and medium cities, of which 300 locations are in Shanghai	Joint operation shops (in the case of Shanghai)
Cangnan Textile Products Market	Over 20 provinces are in China	–
China Daily Necessities City (Luqiao)	South Asia, Hong Kong, Guangyuan in Sichuan, Harbin, Suifenhe, Tianjin	Branch companies, branch markets
Zhejiang Zeguo Leather and Shoes City	Wuhan, Chengdu, Xi'an, Shijiazhuang, Tianjin, Nanjing, Wuxi, Changshu, Urumqi, Heihe	–

Sources: Data for Yiwu: author fieldwork; other data as in Table 3.2.

Zhejiang Leather Clothing City began to hold National Leather Clothing Annual Fairs from 1994. In 1996, 1200 firms (including overseas firms) participated as exhibitors.

Zhejiang Nanxun Building Materials Markets began to hold National Veneer Board Annual Trading Fairs from 1996.

Puyuan Woolen Sweater Markets held National Wool and Woolen Sweater Fairs in 1995 and 1997.

Shaoxing (China) Dyes City held trading fairs in 1996 and 1997. Over 1000 buyers and exhibitors participated from the Netherlands, Germany, Korea and over 20 provinces of China.

Shaoxing China Textile City Textile Machinery Markets held the 8th and 9th Zhejiang International Textile Machinery Trading Fairs in 1997 and 1998. Over 150 exhibitors from France, Germany, Switzerland, Italy, and various locations in China exhibited goods at the 8th fair.

As the above data show, there are at least two markets that hold fairs annually and three markets where overseas firms participate in the fairs as exhibitors. The majority of them are from advanced countries.

3.4   MANAGEMENT OF SPECIALIZED MARKETS

3.4.1   Establishment of Specialized Markets

As most previous studies have pointed out, active intervention from local government is the most important characteristic feature of the specialized market. Table 3.6 clearly indicates this fact. Of Zhejiang's 43 markets for which data are available, 38 were established by local governments and only five were established by private firms.

The AIC has historically taken charge of the management of markets since the socialist planned economy period. However, as Table 3.6 indicates, in Zhejiang Province, in addition to the AIC, there are also various government departments, such as village, town, county and city governments, that have been very keen to establish specialized markets. The most general cases are those in which several government departments jointly establish a market. We can find 14 such markets in Table 3.6. This is because market construction requires large amounts of funds and land, and this requires cooperation between multiple government departments. This point will be discussed in the case studies in this book.

In addition to local governments, enterprises have also gradually come to play a part in the establishment of specialized markets. Concretely, of 43 markets for which data are available, five were established by purely private enterprises, five were jointly established by enterprises and government departments, and four were initially established by

Table 3.6   Organizations in charge of establishment of Zhejiang specialized markets (1998)

Organizations	AIC	V	TG	CG1	CG2	G + G	G + E	G → E	E	Unknown
Number of markets	6	5	1	2	1	14	5	4	5	25

Notes:
AIC = Administration for Industry and Commerce.
V = Village.
TG = Town government.
CG1 = County government.
CG2 = City government.
G + G = Multiple local governments or government departments jointly establishing a market.
G + E = Local governments and enterprises jointly establishing a market.
G → E = Local government transferred authority to an enterprise after establishing and managing the market for some time.
E = Enterprises.

Source: As for Table 3.2.

governments, but the rights of management were later transferred to enterprises.[12] Particularly noteworthy is China Textile City (Shaoxing), China Commodity City (Yiwu) and China Daily Necessities City (Luqiao), which have successively become joint-stock companies. Of these, China Textile City listed their stocks on the Shanghai stock exchange in 1997 and China Commodity City listed its stocks on the Shenzhen Stock Exchange in 2002.

3.4.2   Construction of Specialized Markets

This subsection discusses the construction of specialized markets in Zhejiang. As the construction of a market involves land use and fundraising problems, local governments play an irreplaceable role.

We first analyze the siting of specialized markets. Of the 44 markets for which data are available, 24 are located near a state road, nine are near ordinary roads, seven are near railways, six are near airports, four are near highways,[13] three are in downtown locations, two are near bus terminals, two are near the borders of multiple regions, and one is near a canal. The above data indicate that specialized markets are generally established in logistically convenient locations. In the 1990s, only local governments had the power to arrange such locations for these markets.

Next, we discuss the land areas of specialized markets. Of the 57 markets (1998) for which data are available, the area of two markets is no less than 500,000 square meters; 15 markets are between 100,000 and 500,000 square meters; 30 are between 10,000 and 100,000 square meters; five are between 5000 and 10,000 square meters, and five are 5000 square meters or less. We can clearly understand how large these areas are by making an international comparison. Nam Daemon Market, as one of the largest markets in South Korea, with more than 10,000 booths, has an area of only 42,225 square meters.[14] In China, the large areas covered by specialized markets can naturally only be provided by local governments.

Following that, we discuss the financial issues concerning specialized market construction. Of the 42 markets for which data are available (1998), the amounts invested in six markets were less than five million yuan; seven markets had investments of between five and 10 million yuan; 16 had between 10 and 50 million yuan, four had between 50 and 100 million yuan, and nine had 100 million yuan or more. In the 1990s, it was absolutely impossible for private enterprises to put up this level of investment. According to the China Industry and Commerce Association (CICA 2007, p. 116), at the end of 1999 the median value of actual funds[15] (Shiyou Zijin) of a sample of 3073 private real estate firms in the whole of China was a mere 10.5 million yuan. Thus we can confirm that only local governments can provide the kind of financial support required for specialized market construction.[16]

It is noteworthy that the local governments were able to *continually* provide the land and funds necessary to respond to the constant expansion of the transaction scales and the increase in numbers of traders. As Table 3.7 shows, of Zhejiang's 68 specialized markets, at least 36 expanded or relocated their transaction buildings. Of these, 21 markets expanded or relocated their buildings multiple times. Chapter 7 will argue in detail that this point has become the very premise for a specialized market to exhibit a strong indirect network effect, and thus transform into a pure market platform.

3.4.3 Management of Specialized Markets

From fragmented data in ZPMC, we can derive three features of specialized market management in Zhejiang Province.

The first is that the government generally introduces various service organizations into the markets for supporting market transactions. We can discover 39 such markets that have introduced such organizations, including financial institutions, insurance companies, telecoms, logistics, warehouses, water and electricity supply systems, parking areas, post offices, fire stations, private securities firms, information centers, museums, exhibition centers, restaurants, hotels, amusement facilities and hospitals.

The second feature is that besides the founders of the specialized market, other government departments have also intervened heavily in the management of specialized markets. Of 44 markets for which data are available, at least 18 have established local government branches, including the AIC, the Tax Bureau, the Quality and Technical Supervision Bureau (QTS), the Police Bureau, and so on. We also find that at least seven markets have established social intermediaries in order to manage the numerous private SMEs effectively. Generally, these intermediaries are under the control of AIC. They are expected to coordinate the relationships between the government departments and the private booth-keepers.

The third feature is that the managers of specialized markets have classified the large quantities of commodities by industry and location in some large-scale markets in order to improve transaction efficiencies. In 1998, of Zhejiang's 68 specialized markets, at least 18 had their commodities classified by industry and location. Of these, the transaction volume of five markets amounted to between 100 and 1000 million yuan. The transaction volume of 13 markets exceeded one billion yuan. We will analyze this issue in detail in the case study of Yiwu China Commodity City.

Table 3.7   Number of extensions or relocations of specialized market transaction buildings in Zhejiang (1998)

Times Region	0	1	No less than 1	2	No less than 2	3	No less than 3	No less than 4	Planned	Unknown
Number of markets	12	10	6	2	9	1	3	5	2	19
Northeast Zhejiang	2	1	2	1	3	0	1	3	0	2
Central Zhejiang 1	4	1	0	0	2	0	0	1	2	9
Central Zhejiang 2	3	2	0	0	3	1	1	0	0	0
Southeast Zhejiang	3	6	4	1	1	0	1	1	0	8

Note: As the Zhuji Pearl Market (Central Zhejiang 1) has plans for a fourth extension, and has already expanded its scale three times, its data were double calculated.

Source: As for Table 3.2.

3.4.4 Government Incentives

Lastly, we explain why local governments are so keen to intervene in specialized market development. By examining the limited data in ZPMC, we find that government departments concerned with 13 markets levied taxes and/or fees from booth-keepers, including booth rents, management fees and quality control fees. The background to this situation is that in the 1980s, most of China's government departments were troubled by budget shortfalls. The central government thus permitted these departments to levy various kinds of fees for maintaining infrastructure, to cover administrative costs, to buy office supplies and improve the welfare of employees. Most of these fees were not under the control of the budget framework, and the government department itself was allowed to decide the use of these fees. Government departments were thus strongly stimulated to become involved in specialized market development.

However, it is interesting that the level of both the taxes and the fees is very low. We calculated the shares of taxes and/or fees in the total transaction volume of the 13 markets for which data are available. The result shows that the shares are less than 0.1 percent in two markets; between 0.1 and less than 1 percent in seven markets; between 1 and less than 5 percent in three markets; and 5 percent or more in only one market. Compared to general tax rates in China, these values are at an extremely low level. We will discuss why the local governments were willing to accept such a low level of taxes and fees in the case studies.

3.5 THE DYNAMIC PROCESS OF SPECIALIZED MARKET DEVELOPMENT IN ZHEJIANG PROVINCE

3.5.1 Periods of Industrial Cluster Formation and Specialized Market Establishment

Section 3.5 focuses on the specialized market development in Zhejiang Province from a dynamic perspective. As a starting point, we will discuss the formational period of the industrial clusters and the specialized markets.

As Table 3.8 shows, among the 42 clusters for which data are available, more than half (22 clusters) were formed before the People's Republic of China (PRC) was established, including 16 textile or apparel clusters, two leather clusters, one daily necessities cluster, one furniture cluster, one

Table 3.8   Periods of industrial cluster formation in Zhejiang

Period / Region	Before 1949	1960s	1970–83	After 1984	Unknown
Number of clusters	22	4	14	2	26
Northeast Zhejiang	9	0	2	0	4
Central Zhejiang 1	5	2	2	0	9
Central Zhejiang 2	1	0	0	2	7
Southeast Zhejiang	7	2	10	0	6

Note: The formation period of the Changqiao cluster (Ruian, Wenzhou) is given as "1998" in ZPMC. From the context, however, we judge that this is a misprint for "1968."

Source: As for Table 3.2.

hardware cluster, and one wooden bead cluster. This suggests that local tradition is the largest factor contributing to cluster formation.

Twenty clusters were formed after the PRC was established. Of these, 18 were formed before 1983. During that period, the circulation of commodities and the interregional movement of people were severely restricted in China (Zheng et al. 2003, pp. 163–4). As the development of heavy industry was given priority, the development of the consumer goods industry was restrained. Within this social background, except for central Zhejiang 2 region, all the regions of Zhejiang acquired opportunities to foster their own SME industrial clusters for the production of consumer goods (see Table 3.8).

A typical case is the southeast Zhejiang region (Wenzhou being the core city), where 12 clusters appeared between the 1960s and 1983. Being distant from the control of the central government, the itinerant craftsmen of this region were allowed to travel around various locations inside China. They captured market information and transmitted it back to their hometowns, thus causing numerous small businesses to engage in the production of consumer goods.

Compared with the formation of industrial clusters, the establishment of specialized markets came much later. Table 3.9 divides the timing of the establishment of specialized markets in Zhejiang into three periods. The first is from 1970 to 1983, when only 15 markets were established. The second period is from 1984 to 1991. As a turning point for the development of specialized markets, the peasants of China were first allowed to engage in trade in 1984. Thus, there were 18 markets established during this period. The third period is after 1992, when China completely liberalized its consumer goods market. As a result, the development of

Table 3.9   Year of establishment of specialized markets in Zhejiang

Period Region	1970–83	1984–91	After 1992	Unknown
Total	15	18	31	4
Northeast Zhejiang	2	6	7	0
Central Zhejiang 1	2	2	12	2
Central Zhejiang 2	2	4	4	0
Southeast Zhejiang	9	6	8	2

Note: Some specialized markets were formed spontaneously and then formally established by local governments or other organizations. In this case, the year of establishment is calculated from the point in time when the markets were formed spontaneously.

Source: As for Table 3.2.

specialized markets was accelerated. More than half of the markets were established during this period.

Indeed, local governments in Zhejiang simply treated the establishment of specialized markets as an effective industrial cluster policy. We can find the ringing slogan, "Jian yige shichang, dai yipian jingji, xing yifang chanye, fu yifang qunzhong" [By establishing a specialized market, we can enliven local economies, stimulate the development of local industries, enrich the local people] everywhere in ZPMC. In this book, we will show in detail how specialized markets stimulated industrial cluster development, and thoroughly analyze the mechanism of that development.

3.5.2   Mutual Learning for Specialized Markets

In last two subsections, we discuss the mechanism by means of which specialized markets as one factor of the Wenzhou Model spread to the whole of Zhejiang. By examining the data in Table 3.9, we can discern a clear trend showing that specialized markets first appeared in southeast Zhejiang, and then gradually expanded to the whole of the province.[17]

Generally speaking, government departments at the central government level and the Zhejiang provincial level took various measures to stimulate mutual learning between local governments at the lower level, which eventually resulted in the widespread construction of specialized markets in the whole of Zhejiang.

The *Dashi Ji* (Main Events) of ZPMC contains a certain amount of useful information concerning this issue (Table 3.10). By analyzing the information, we can summarize the roles of these government departments in terms of the following five points.

Table 3.10 Main events concerning specialized markets and other markets in Zhejiang

Date	Events
December 1984	State Councilor Chen Muhua made inspection tour of Qiaotou Button Market
1 September 1985	Zhejiang Province AIC held a city and local region AIC directors' meeting and a meeting to exchange experiences on specialized markets in Hangzhou. A member of Zhejiang Province Standing Committee, Vice-Governor Shen Zuluo attended the meeting and gave a speech
29 November 1985	Prime Minister Zhao Ziyang made an inspection tour of Qiaotou Button Market
8 April 1986	Vice-Premier Wan Li and a Member of the Secretariat of the Communist Party Committee Central Committee, Hao Jianxiu, made an inspection tour of Qiaotou Button Market
31 May 1986	Minister of Civil Affairs, Cui Naifu, made an inspection tour of Qiaotou Button Market
16 June 1988	Zhejiang Province held a meeting to commend the "Five-Virtues Markets" in Hangzhou; 51 markets (Zhuji Donghu Agricultural Market, etc.) were selected as provincial-level "Five-Virtues Markets"
25 June 1990	Zhejiang Province government issued a notice on further improvement and rectification of Yueqing County Low Voltage Apparatus Market and a resolute crackdown on the production of non-licensed, counterfeit and shoddy products
15 July 1991	Zhejiang Province government issued a notice on further facilitating the development of city and rural markets
25 September 1991	Zhejiang AIC printed and distributed the trial implementation of registration and management of markets in cities and rural markets in Zhejiang
22 February 1992	Zhejiang Province government issued a notice on the strict crackdown on the production and sales of counterfeit and shoddy products
27 May 1992	The China Mayors' Association held a symposium concerning the development of a city commodity market in Yiwu. This symposium proposed the famous opinion, "The mayors must take charge of the management of the markets."
5–9 December 1993	Vice-chairman of the Standing Committee of the National People's Congress (NPC), Li Ximing, made an inspection tour of Wenzhou Industrial Products Market and wrote an inscription for Wenzhou Trading City

7 September 1994	Zhejiang AIC issued an urgent notice on strengthening law enforcement, strengthening monitoring and management, preserving normal market order
24–29 October 1994	The third meeting of the eighth session of the Standing Committee of the People's Congress of Zhejiang Province passed the regulations on the management of Zhejiang Province Commodity Transaction Market
May 1995	Zhejiang Provincial AIC issued the notice on the separation of market management (as administrative work) and market operation (as a business)
22 August 1995	Zhejiang AIC printed and distributed the measures for the registration and administration of the naming of markets as *Zhejiang . . . Market*
4 October 1995	Zhejiang Provincial AIC printed and distributed the action plan on the crackdown on counterfeit products and preservation of brand-name products in the whole of the province
1997	Zhejiang AIC began a campaign for extensive establishment of the star standard markets in the province
1998	Zhejiang Provincial Government issued a notice on facilitating sustainable development of commodity transaction markets
1998	Zhejiang Provincial Government General Office forwarded a notice on an overall acceleration of the construction of physical markets, issued by the Department of Construction of Zhejiang Province and Department of Supervision of Zhejiang Province
8 October 1999	Vice-Chairman of the NPC, Jiang Chunyun, Vice-Chairman of the National Committee of the Chinese People's Political Consultative Conference, Sun Fuling, etc. participated in the opening ceremony of the 1999 China Commodity Fair. Secretary of the Zhejiang Province Committee of the Communist Party, Zhang Dejiang, declared the opening of the fair
8 November 1999	The 99th China Daily Necessities Trade Fair & Economy, Technology Negotiation Conference was held in China Daily Necessities City (Luqiao District, Taizhou). Vice-Chairman of the NPC, Jiang Zhenghua, a member of the Zhejiang Province Standing Committee of Communist Party, Wang Guoping, etc. participated in the opening ceremony

Source: As for Table 3.2.

First, these government departments issued various notices or other government documents to encourage local governments to intervene in the development of specialized markets and other markets.

Second, they held various meetings and symposiums for spreading the experiences of successful specialized markets and other markets to local governments.

Third, these government departments issued various notices and public documents in order to urge local governments to take countermeasures against the counterfeit goods problem.

Fourth, they held various market contests at the Zhejiang provincial level in order to stimulate competition between local governments.

Fifth, these government departments arranged for various top-tier officials to visit the specialized markets and other markets in order to confirm their legitimacy (especially in the early period) and publicize successful markets.

3.5.3   Inter-Market Competition

The above measures taken by government departments clearly stimulated the dissemination of information concerning specialized markets and other markets to local governments in Zhejiang Province. As a result of mutual learning, competition between the specialized markets was greatly stimulated. Two sets of data support this point.

The first is that the transaction volumes of specialized markets vary by regions (Table 3.3). Generally speaking, southeast Zhejiang has lagged far behind other regions in spite of the fact that it was the first to establish specialized markets. This is because, compared with local governments in other regions, the Wenzhou government failed to work out an efficient policy for the facilitation of specialized market development. This point will be mentioned again in the case study on Yiwu China Commodity City.

The second set of data is that both "winner" markets and "loser" markets have appeared simultaneously in Zhejiang.[18] The winner markets have occupied very important positions in China's commodity circulation. In terms of data given in ZPMC, ten markets have the largest transaction volume in China. Five markets account for 10–49 percent of China's total transaction volume, one market accounts for 50–100 percent of China's total transaction volume, and there is even one market that has the largest transaction volume in Asia. On the other hand, transaction volumes decreased in four loser markets. In two markets, volumes decreased dramatically to one-tenth of their previous maximum.

Beside government intervention, two further factors explain why competition intensified. The first is that many specialized markets in Zhejiang are dealing in the same type of commodities. Buyers can thus choose the most appropriate market for purchasing. The second factor is that booth-keepers can travel around the various markets in search of better market opportunities since they are from regions that have a tradition of long-distance trade. The second factor will be thoroughly examined in the case studies.

NOTES

1. A draft version of this chapter was presented at the Fifth International Conference on Industrial Clustering and Regional Development in Beijing, July 2006.
2. In the case of Wenzhou, the salesmen are essentially itinerant craftsmen (see Chapter 7).
3. Two indirect pieces of data support this point. The first is that according to statistics of the State Economic and Trade Commission, of 532 products in China, 154 Zhejiang products held the top three positions in retail volume in 2001. The second is that according to statistics of the Zhejiang Economic and Trade Commission, 232 Zhejiang products held the top position for retail volume in the whole of China; 160 Zhejiang products accounted for a share in retail volume exceeding 40 percent of those products for the whole of China in 2001 (Zheng et al. 2003, p. 22).
4. In China, the AIC generally has the following functions: (1) maintaining order in transactions; (2) administrating self-employed enterprises and private enterprises; (3) examining and registering new enterprises; (4) registration of trademarks; and (5) super-vising the activities of enterprises in the distribution sector (www.saic.gov.cn, accessed 1 August 2002). The AIC is an important factor for understanding SME development in China. Regarding the development history of the AIC, see Shi (1993, pp. 123–6).
5. Two clusters have only intermediate products markets. They are both located in Wenzhou.
6. In the specialized market, one booth may be shared by several persons, or one person may own several booths, but this will not be taken into account in this chapter.
7. Regarding the number of booths, we selected the largest number up to 1998.
8. All three sellers were selling raw materials.
9. This is the maximum number.
10. These are the maximum numbers.
11. We also confirmed from other data sources that Yiwu China Commodity City and Yongkang China Science and Technical Hardware City began to hold annual trading fairs from 1995 and 1996, respectively.
12. It is not very clear whether these enterprises were owned by the public sector or the private sector.
13. In 1998, highways were still not yet widely constructed in China.
14. Seoulkankou.com, accessed 29 January 2009.
15. Shiyou Zijin is a very Chinese concept in the country's accounting system. Generally, the value of this index is equal to the net assets.
16. Local government generally requested state-owned banks or state-owned enterprises to invest in specialized markets. In the 1980s, however, considerable funds for specialized market construction were also collected from booth-keepers (see Chapter 8).
17. Complementary data show that of 14 markets that were formed spontaneously, nine were located in southeast Zhejiang and only five were located in other regions.
18. An indirect fact supporting this point is that the total number of markets in Zhejiang (including both specialized markets and other types of markets) began to decrease from 1999 (ZUESRG 2008, p. 35).

4. Local government and platform governance in Yiwu

Figure 4.1 A campaign called "Establishing Credibility as an Exemplary Market" in Yiwu Market

4.1 INTRODUCTION

Chapters 4, 5, 6 and 7 investigate the basic structure of the specialized markets by use of a case study of Yiwu China Commodity City (Yiwu Market). Through the interaction between local government, regional groups of merchants and countless small firms, Yiwu Market has grown into the largest specialized market in the world, and has become the most important innovator in the specialized market system. By focusing on this market, it has been possible to clarify the evolutionary mechanism of the specialized markets in China.

Chapter 4 first focuses on the role of local government in the development of Yiwu Market. As has been pointed out in Chapter 2, although existing two-sided market literature assumes an omnipotent platform manager, it is actually faced with various difficulties in the real world. The first difficulties are the barriers to trade, which are caused by various institutional and informational factors. The second difficulty concerns the *physicality* of a platform, which is caused primarily by real-estate-related institutions and transaction costs. Appropriate platform governance is indispensable for overcoming these difficulties. Regarding this issue, previous studies have suggested that the local government is a key actor. The role of local government in deregulating the private sector, guaranteeing credibility and so on has been mentioned briefly (see Chapter 1). This chapter will, for the first time, systematically analyze the role of local government within the framework of platform governance through careful tracing of the growth trajectory of Yiwu Market.

4.2 YIWU CHINA COMMODITY CITY

As a county-level city, Yiwu is located within Jinhua City, in the center of Zhejiang Province, and has a total population of over 1.6 million people. Until the end of the 1970s, Yiwu was still an impoverished rural area. From the 1980s, however, it embarked on a surprising episode of rapid economic growth. The GDP of Yiwu exploded from a mere 128 million yuan to 35.206 billion yuan during the period from 1978 to 2006, and of this the total share of the non-agricultural sector increased from 42.6 percent to 97.4 percent (ZUESRG 2008).

The rapid development of a huge specialized market, Yiwu China Commodity City, resulted in this drastic transformation.[1] The local government formally established Yiwu Market in 1982. At first, it was a small market with only 705 booths, but it developed rapidly. Since 1991, this market has held the top position as China's largest industrial products market. By 2006, the number of booths in Yiwu Market had reached 58,000. Along with this expansion, the transaction volume of Yiwu Market increased from 3.92 million yuan to 31,503 million yuan during the period 1982 to 2006 (Table 4.1). In 2010, the number of booths in Yiwu Market had increased to 62,000, dealing in over 1,700,000 commodities in 4202 categories from 16 industries. Of these, jewelry, toys, crafts, daily hardware, socks and zippers accounted for over 30 percent share of the

Table 4.1   Basic data on Yiwu Market

Year	Number of booths	Transaction volume (100 million yuan)
1982	705	0.0392
1983	1050	0.1444
1984	1870	0.2321
1985	2847	0.619
1986	5500	1.0029
1987	5600	1.538
1988	6131	2.65
1989	8400	3.9
1990	8900	6.06
1991	8900	10.25
1992	16,000	20.54
1993	16,000	45.15
1994	24,600	102.12
1995	34,000	152
1996	34,000	184.68
1997	34,000	145.11
1998	34,000	153.4
1999	34,000	175.3
2000	34,500	192.89
2001	34,500	211.97
2002	42,000	229.98
2003	42,000	248.3
2004	42,000	266.87
2005	42,000	288.48
2006	58,000	315.03

Source: ZUESRG (2008, p. 11).

domestic market.[2] It is even reported that 80–90 percent of the world's Christmas gifts are purchased from Yiwu.[3]

Two important actors have played crucial roles in the development of Yiwu Market. The first is the local Yiwu merchant, who has a long tradition of peddling dating back to the beginning of the Ching Dynasty (1644– 1911). At that time, in order to acquire rooster feathers for compost, a few peasants in Yiwu began to travel around neighboring rural areas, selling brown sugar in exchange for feathers. Their trading area gradually expanded to cover seven provinces and their range of merchandise also expanded to include many different kinds of daily necessities. Gradually, a peddler's organization, Qiaotang Bang, was formed. At its peak in the second decade of the twentieth century, Qiaotang Bang had 7000 to 8000 members (ZPZHDC 1997, pp. 301–03). After the PRC was established, Qiaotang Bang was dissolved and its peddling activity was discontinued for some time. However, it began peddling again at the latest in 1963 (Wu 2004).[4] The role of Qiaotang Bang in the development of Yiwu Market and in the industrial cluster formation in Yiwu will be thoroughly analyzed in Chapters 5, 6 and 7.

The second important actor is local government. By establishing a powerful management system, the Yiwu government succeeded in conducting outstanding platform governance and greatly simulated the expansion of Yiwu Market. We first introduce this management system.

This system consists of three levels. The first is the Yiwu Market Managing Committee, which is in charge of the strategic decision-making concerning the development of Yiwu Market, and deals with various administrative matters. The Yiwu government established this committee in 1986. In 1999, the Yiwu Market Trade Development Bureau (YMTDB) was established. Thereafter, most of the functions of the managing committee were transferred to this bureau.[5]

The second level of this system consists of various government departments and economic organizations relating to Yiwu Market. It includes the Yiwu Administration for Industry and Commerce (AIC),[6] the Tax Bureau, the police, and so on. Of these, the AIC carries out most of the daily management work. In 1994, the AIC established a market-managing company called Zhejiang China Commodity City Group (ZCCC Group), which takes charge mainly of the commercial real estate management in place of the AIC. Meanwhile, the AIC continued to maintain the link with Yiwu Market in the areas of quality control, credibility building and so on.

The third level of the management system consists of various social intermediary organizations, including the Individual Labor Association,[7] the Women's Federation, and so on. Under the control of the AIC, these intermediary organizations assist in coordinating relationships between the public sector and the private sector.

4.3   FIRST THE MARKET (XIAN YOU SHI)

As explained in Chapter 2, a market platform only exhibits indirect network effects after the total number of users has exceeded a critical mass. In the case of a specialized market, this means sufficient buyers and sellers must be secured when a marketplace is established. Yiwu government may not be aware of this economic principle, but they have indeed practiced it in their daily work. Every time Yiwu government officials introduce Yiwu

Market's successful experiences, they consistently emphasize the slogan "Xian you shi, hou you chang" [First the market, later the place].

4.3.1   Reviving the Peddling Tradition

During the period of the planned economy, China's peasants were strictly prohibited from engaging in commerce. In spite of this regulation, however, the Yiwu AIC, along with a number of people's communes and their production brigades, allowed a partial revival of the peddling tradition from 1963, under the pretext that rooster feathers were still important for compost. They issued a large number of licenses to former peddlers. Even as early as 1980, these licenses amounted to 7000 in number (Wu 2004).

Because of this early deregulation, two periodic markets spontaneously appeared in Yiwu in the 1970s. In September 1982, the local government formally designated one market as the regular Yiwu Commodity Market.[8] Shortly thereafter, at the end of that year, the local government formulated the well-known policy of "Sige Xuke" [Four Permissions]. This policy granted Yiwu's peasants permission to engage in four kinds of business, namely: (1) commerce in the city; (2) long-distance logistics; (3) competition with public-owned enterprises; and (4) opening a commodity market (Zhang et al. 1993, p. 35).

The timing of the Four Permissions policy had decisive significance for the development of Yiwu Market. The central government of China strictly prohibited peasants from engaging in any kind of commerce until 1984. The Four Permissions policy was, however, formulated in 1982. Simply because of these two years when powerful competitors were absent from the scene,[9] Yiwu Market enjoyed the benefits of the indirect network effect to the fullest and was able to show rapid development.[10]

After the granting of the Four Permissions, Yiwu peddlers split into two groups. The first group continued to peddle and gradually became the booth-keepers of marketplaces in various places in China. In the early period, members of this group were the largest buyers in Yiwu Market (see Chapter 5). The second group became booth-keepers in Yiwu Market. They traveled to various clusters located in Zhejiang Province, Guangdong Province and other areas of China. Some of them then gradually took part in the manufacturing process and became the main force behind Yiwu's industrialization (see Chapter 7).

The large number of Yiwu peddlers on both the buyers' and the sellers' side has also been very significant. Just because of their common geographical origin, they were readily able to establish relationships of trust with each other, and transactions thus rapidly expanded. As a result, Yiwu

Table 4.2   Number of self-employed enterprises and private enterprises in the manufacturing sector of Yiwu

Year	1992	1993	1994	1995	1996	1997
Self-employed enterprise	7518	8324	8683	8684	8885	10,278
Private enterprise	226	281	431	674	803	738
Year	1998	1999	2000	2001	2002	–
Self-employed enterprise	7273	9955	8424	9686	8765	–
Private enterprise	896	1236	1161	1913	2774	–

Source: Yiwu AIC (2003, Chapter 2, Section 2).

Market was able to exceed the critical mass in a short time. In contrast, as Chapter 8 describes, it would be very difficult for a market to reach this point if it were located in a region that did not have a tradition of long-distance trade.

4.3.2   Fostering Sellers

As the pioneer of specialized markets, Yiwu Market has thus far had sufficient sellers. Throughout the whole of the 1980s, Yiwu merchants were the major sellers. After the 1990s, a large number of non-local merchants moved to Yiwu and gradually formed the majority in the market (see Chapter 7). The Yiwu government did not need to exert itself to *invite* booth-keepers from other regions and has simply taken a number of measures to *foster* existing sellers.

The first measure is the policy known as "Yinshang Zhuangong" [Exhorting merchants to switch from commerce to manufacturing].[11] Before the 1990s, Yiwu merchants mainly purchased goods from other regions and carried out the final stage of processing of semi-finished goods. After trading with Yiwu merchants several times, most buyers tended to go directly to factories in other regions. The profit margins of Yiwu booths gradually declined. Given this situation, the government decided to encourage local merchants to produce Yiwu Market-related commodities themselves in 1993. The Yiwu government provided various kinds of support for the merchants, such as land use,[12] finance and technological upgrading.

This policy greatly stimulated the development of the manufacturing sector in Yiwu.[13] As Table 4.2 shows, since 1993, compared with self-employed enterprises, the number of private enterprises in the manufacturing sector increased markedly. In China, "self-employed enterprises" are non-agricultural small businesses that have no more than five employees, besides family members. On the other hand, "private enterprises" are enterprises that have no fewer than eight employees and are owned by private individuals (Marukawa 2002). Therefore, we can infer from the increase in the number of private enterprises that some modern factories have appeared in Yiwu.

The second measure was the campaign begun in 2002, known as "Shichang Dai Baicun, Baicun Lian Wanhu" [The market links with hundreds of villages, villages link with thousands of households] (*Workers Daily* 11 July 2006). The purpose of this campaign is to help poor peasants in the remote areas of Yiwu to build business relationships with Yiwu Market through a processing business in which materials are delivered to peasant households for processing.[14]

For this purpose, the Yiwu government holds a processing business promotion meeting every year and invites booth-keepers, government officials and organizing agents to participate. Gradually, not only Yiwu peasants but also the peasants from neighboring areas became involved in the processing business. As a result, various processing clusters soon appeared.[15] We will carry out a thorough analysis of this campaign from the viewpoint of the peasants in Chapters 5 and 7.

4.3.3   Creating Buyers

Compared with sellers, the Yiwu government has taken more active measures to create new buyers.

At the beginning of the 1990s, an increasing number of Yiwu people desired to keep a booth in Yiwu Market. Because of the constraints of booth capacity, however, the market could not accommodate all of them. In order to solve this problem, the Yiwu AIC started establishing branch markets in various cities from the second half of 1992 (ZPZHDC 1997, Chapter on He Zhangxing). Branch markets were initially established by the AIC itself. Gradually, merchants originally from Yiwu, but who now work elsewhere became the major establishers and managers of the new markets. The number of branch markets rose to 26 by the year 2000.[16] We will show in detail in Chapter 5 that branch markets helped to disseminate information on Yiwu and stimulated more and more local markets to form links with Yiwu Market. This greatly increased the number of new buyers for Yiwu Market.

From 1995, the Yiwu government began to hold trade fairs in order to attract more qualified buyers from a broader scope. In that year, the Yiwu government and the Zhejiang Provincial AIC jointly held the China Commodity City Excellent Brand and New Commodities Fair, which was oriented towards domestic buyers. In 1996, this fair was renamed the Yiwu

China Commodity Fair. In 2002, in cooperation with the Ministry of Foreign Trade and Economic Cooperation, this fair was further renamed the "China Yiwu International Commodity Fair" (Yiwu AIC 2003, Chapter 4, Section 2). Following that, an increasing number of foreign buyers began to participate in the fair. In 2006, among 103,205 buyers visiting this fair, 16,056 were overseas buyers from 161 countries and regions, and over 50 percent of the overseas buyers were from developed countries.[17]

Stimulated by the China Yiwu International Commodity Fair, various fairs have been held in Yiwu. Between 2001 and November 2005, the annual number of trade fairs in Yiwu increased from 11 to 27. The total transaction volume of these fairs amounted to over 10 billion yuan in 2005, which represented over one-third of the total transaction volume of Yiwu Market (JETRO 2007, pp. 12–30).

From the end of the 1990s, the scramble for domestic buyers by rival markets became increasingly fierce, which caused the margin of Yiwu Market booth-keepers to decline substantially. In order to respond to this situation, the Yiwu government decided to further internationalize Yiwu Market. In 2002, it formulated a strategy named "Jianshe Guoji Shangmao Chengshi" [Construction of an international trade city].[18]

For this strategy, the Yiwu government improved the whole foreigner service system. Various areas of jurisdiction that previously belonged to Jinhua City were devolved to Yiwu. For example, it became possible for government departments in Yiwu to issue visas for foreign residents or visitors, issue employment certificates, and accept applications for establishing a foreign resident office. Yiwu court became the first county-level court able to deal with civil and commercial cases. Yiwu entry–exit administration bureau also became the first entry–exit administration bureau in a county-level city in China. A service center to deal with foreigners was also established.

This internationalization strategy greatly contributed to Yiwu Market's ability to exploit the overseas market. In 2007, exports accounted for 55 percent of the total transaction volume of Yiwu Market. More than ten thousand foreigners from over 100 countries and regions were permanently resident in Yiwu for purchasing, and their resident offices numbered over 1340. At the same time, more than 40 percent of the air passengers to and from Yiwu were foreigners. The total number of foreign passengers passing through Yiwu airport exceeded 500,000 for the first time in 2007. Chapter 6 will analyze the features of these foreign buyers in detail.

4.4   LATER THE PLACE (HOU YOU CHANG)

After attracting a large number of buyers and sellers, the other important part of platform governance for the Yiwu government was to provide a platform to accommodate them and support smooth transactions between them. This is the real economic meaning of *later the place*. Regarding this issue, an advantage of Yiwu is that the Yiwu government is the sole owner of all the real estate related to Yiwu Market.[19] They were thus able to design the market platform as they wished to.

4.4.1   Managing Real Estate in Yiwu Market

Real estate issues form the largest difference between the physical marketplace and the virtual e-commerce platform. With regard to this issue, the Yiwu government took the following three main measures.

First, the Yiwu government continuously expanded or relocated the transaction building along with the expansion of transactions in the market. As Tables 4.1 and 4.3 indicate, not only has the number of booths been increased several times, the transaction infrastructure has also been greatly improved. The current transaction building of Yiwu Market has been established with standard international convention center facilities. As a result, the transaction volume of Yiwu Market has increased smoothly, never being hindered by cramped transaction spaces.

Second, the Yiwu government has intentionally avoided the construction of too many submarkets. In China's marketplaces, as business expands and infrastructure and other constraints became apparent, a new submarket is usually built near the existing market. There are often dozens of submarkets in a marketplace, which makes it difficult for local government to manage all of them effectively and with precision. In the case of Yiwu, however, when a new generation market with better facilities was constructed, the old one was often destroyed.[20] The present one is the fifth generation market (see Table 4.3).

Third, the Yiwu government took flexible measures in allocating the rights of use of the booths. The resale of the use rights and sublease of booths had been prohibited in Yiwu Market until 1992. This hindered entry into the market of a number of qualified enterprises. In order to accommodate these enterprises, Yiwu AIC worked out a new regulation at the beginning of 1993, which first allowed resale of the use rights or subleasing of booths, providing booth-keepers paid 2000 yuan in market construction fees for each occurrence of this kind of activity. This regulation

Table 4.3   Process of establishment of Yiwu Market

Year	No. of submarkets in Yiwu by generation	Location or name of submarkets	Latest facilities
1974	Two periodic markets	Choucheng Town, Niansanli Town	Open-air market
1982	One first-generation market, one periodical market	Choucheng Town, Niansanli Town	Street market
1984	One second-generation market	New street	Square market with fixed booths
1986	One third-generation market	Chengzhong Street	As above
1992	One fourth-generation market	Huang Yuan Market	Transaction building
1995	Two fourth-generation markets	Huang Yuan Market and Binwang Market	As above
2002	Three fifth-generation markets	Huang Yuan Market, Binwang Market and International Trade City	Transaction building established with international convention center standard facilities (air conditioning, Internet facilities, etc.)

Sources: Data for number of submarkets and locations: ZUESRG (2008, p. 12); data for facilities: ZPZHDC (1997) and author's fieldwork.

also allowed several booth-keepers to share one booth simultaneously (ZPZHDC 1997, Chapter on He Zhangxing).

The new regulation had an immediate effect in attracting highly qualified booth-keepers. As Table 4.4 shows, during the period from 1992 to 1997, the share of booth-keepers with an educational background of primary school only sharply decreased. At the same time, the share of booth-keepers with an educational background of junior high school sharply increased. The absolute number of booth-keepers who graduated from senior high school also increased.

Currently, the use rights of more than half of Yiwu Market's booths have been transferred to other persons. In Yiwu's three main submarkets (International Trade City, the Huangyuan Market, and the Binwang Market), the booths for which use rights have been transferred accounts for 59 percent, 57 percent and 55 percent, respectively, of the total (Luo 2005).

Table 4.4   Educational background of booth-keepers in Yiwu Market

Year	No. of booth-keepers	Primary school (%)	Junior high school (%)	Senior high school (%)	Other (%)
1992	16,000	37	39	19	5
1997	24,277	17.20	64.30	17.30	1.2*

Note: * This data refers to booth-keepers with the educational background of undergraduate school.

Sources: Data for 1992: Zhang et al. (1993, p. 60); data for 1997: ZSCMC (1997, p. 23).

4.4.2   Reducing Exogenous Transaction Costs

Applying the framework of Yang and Zhang (2003, pp. 90–91), there are two types of transaction costs, namely: (1) the endogenous transaction cost and (2) the exogenous transaction cost. The endogenous transaction costs are the result of economic distortions caused by conflicts of interest between the decision makers who participate in the transaction.[21] The exogenous transaction cost is the direct or indirect costs incurred in the process of transaction. It consists of information costs, logistics costs and so on.

Subsection 4.4.2 first discusses how Yiwu Market reduced exogenous transaction costs by focusing primarily on the information costs in the market.

In the initial stage, the information costs in the search for commodities in Yiwu Market were high. In 1990, the 8000 booths in Yiwu Market were divided into only four industries (YYLGEO 1992).[22] It was not hard to find any particular type of commodity in spaces designated for other commodities. As a result, the information flow in the market became increasingly poor and it was possible that the same type of commodity was being sold at different prices in different places.

In this situation, Yiwu AIC worked out a plan known as "Huahang Guishi" [the classification of commodities by industry and location] in 1992, which classified Yiwu Market into eight zones. In each zone, the booth-keepers were strictly prohibited from selling a different type of commodity. Thereafter, the classification of commodities was implemented every time a new generation market was established. In 1994, the fourth-generation market was further enlarged. The new market was classified into 13 zones, where the commodities of 21 industries were bought and sold. Currently, as mentioned above, there are over 1,700,000 commodities in 4202 categories from 16 industries. All these commodities are thoroughly classified by industry and location.

Because of the classification of commodities, the information flow within Yiwu Market became increasing smoother. Not only are the buyers able to find the commodities they seek more easily, but the merchants are also strongly motivated to develop newer and better commodities, as the booths that deal in the same commodity are organized in the same area. It is reported that the booth-keepers of artificial flowers develop more than one type of new product almost every day in 1992.

Another important measure for reducing information costs was taken in October 2006. At that time, the Yiwu government and the Ministry of Commerce, China jointly brought out the Yiwu China Commodity Index. This includes a weekly price index, a monthly price index and a monthly business condition index. The basic data for this index are collected from 4330 booths, which deal in over 4000 types of commodities. The Yiwu Index is periodically released through over 20 mass media outlets, such as the business channel of CCTV, the China Economic Daily, and so on.[23]

It is still difficult to evaluate exactly the role of the Yiwu Index. According to reports by various media outlets, the Yiwu government mainly anticipates that the Yiwu Index will have the following three effects:

1. It will weaken the intense price competition usually resulting from inadequate market information.
2. It will help booth-keepers judge long-term market trends.
3. It will strengthen the pricing power of Yiwu commodities in world commodity trade.

The Yiwu government also engaged in activities aimed at reducing information dissemination costs between various major markets in China (Zhang et al. 1993). In 1992, the state AIC established the National Industrial Products Wholesale Markets Association, consisting of 39 member markets. As secretariat of this association, Yiwu Market was in charge of information dissemination between the member markets. The workflow of this system is as follows: At the beginning and the middle of every month, the 39 member markets send price information and demand and supply information to the information center at Yiwu Market. This center then collects and edits this information into a newsletter entitled *Xinxi Fankui* [The Information Feedback]. Lastly, this material is sent back out to the member markets. As Chapter 5 shows, this association, combined with the efforts of Yiwu merchants and the public sectors of other regions, eventually resulted in the formation of a powerful daily necessities distribution system in China.

4.4.3   Reducing Endogenous Transaction Costs

Endogenous transaction costs are caused by opportunistic behavior. In general, opportunistic behavior can be avoided through long-term business relationships (repeated-game). The characteristic point of the specialized market, however, is that new buyers and sellers are constantly entering the market, thus generating a large number of new business relationships, making the formation of long-term business relationships more difficult.[24] A system whereby buyers and sellers will develop mutual trust *quickly* must be established by a third party in order to reduce the endogenous costs generated between the traders.

In Yiwu Market, it has been AIC that has mainly taken charge of measures to reduce endogenous transaction costs. Early on, AIC laid emphasis on improving quality control and trademark awareness of booth-keepers. The AIC staff of Yiwu Market branch bureau informed booth-keepers about what trademarks are and how to judge whether a trademark is genuine or counterfeit. They also held various contests for appraising the most creditable booths and the booths that deal in the best quality products (ZPZHDC 1997, Chapter on He Zhangxing).

The AIC began to seriously work on this issue from the mid-1990s. During this period, an increasing number of booth-keepers became the sales agents of a number of brand-name producers (see Chapter 7). Correspondingly, in 1995, the AIC established the Association for Preserving Brand-name Products. The basic functions of this association were as follows (Luo 2001).

First, in order to have the booth-keepers understand the importance of brand-name products, it publicized widely the product information of member companies in Yiwu Market. Every year, over 50 percent of membership dues were spent for this purpose.

Second, it established a team with a staff of 100 for cracking down on imitation products. This team worked in cooperation with some of the social intermediary organizations, especially the Individual Labor Association.

Third, this association facilitated communications between member companies. In addition to an annual meeting, its staff also regularly visited some of the member companies to exchange views on exposing imitation products.

Table 4.5 shows the achievements of this association for cracking down on imitation goods. We can note that although the number of member companies increased between 1996 and 2007, annual caseloads and amounts of money involved in the counterfeit goods have constantly decreased. This shows that the work of the association has had a sound effect.

Table 4.5   Achievements of the association for preserving brand-name products for cracking down on imitation goods

Year	No. of members	No. of cases	Value of imitation goods (10,000 yuan)
1996	80	352	985
2001	142	272	735
Annual average between 2002 and April 2007*	156**	180	507

Notes:
*   2007 is counted as one-third of a year.
**   Number of members at the end of 2007.

Sources: Data for 1996, 2001: Yiwu AIC (2003, Chapter 9, Section3); data for 2002 to April 2007: *Business Daily* 28 April 2007.

In 1998, the Yiwu government formally began to formulate a strategy known as "Zhiliang Lishi, Xingyu Xingshi" [Quality is the foundation of the city, credibility facilitates the development of the city]. Based on this strategy, Yiwu AIC took various measures to raise the credibility of market transactions. Of these, a typical measure is a campaign called "Chuangjian Xinyong Shifan Shichang" [Establishing Credibility as an Exemplary Market], which began from 2004. During this campaign, the AIC has mainly taken the following three measures.[25]

First, the AIC established a credit monitoring appraisal system. This system classified the credit ratings of nearly 60,000 booths into six levels.[26] According to the data for 5 March 2008, the distribution of levels was AAA (excellent): 1306; AA (good): 3511; A (stable): 46,827; B (fluctuating): 46; C (poor): 46; D (bankrupt, license revoked): 19.[27] Most booth-keepers have a credibility level higher than A.

The AIC staff applied different monitoring methods to booths that have different credit ratings. Booths with a credit rating of A, AA or AAA are monitored once a month. Booths with a B credit rating are monitored no less than once a week. Booths with a C credit rating may be monitored at any time. D-rated booths are expelled from the market.[28]

Second, the Yiwu AIC introduced a system of 24 standards in seven classifications for appraising credit booths. In 2007, 1300 booths were chosen as credit booths. Some booth-keepers who have received this title claim that their business has improved.[29]

Third, the AIC established a brand-name goods inquiry system. The information on every booth-keeper's name, goods and trademarks is stored in this system. This is now being linked with the state AIC trademark registration database. By comparing the two systems, the buyers of Yiwu Market goods can easily check whether a trademark is genuine or counterfeit.

There is no direct evidence that shows the effects of the above three measures taken by the AIC. However, the following two points can be confirmed. The first point is that the Yiwu government attached increasing importance to the establishment of credibility. The second point is that the method applied to establish credibility by the Yiwu government became increasingly precise.

4.5   GOVERNMENT INCENTIVES

The key incentive that stimulates the Yiwu government in intervening in the Yiwu Market, is that, as the owner of the market, the government can obtain various taxes and fees from the booth-keepers. Like most two-sided platforms, Yiwu Market only collects these taxes and fees from sellers (booth-keepers). Booth-keepers in Yiwu Market need to pay a tax, AIC fee, real estate management fees and so on to various government departments. They also need to pay the booth rent to the ZCCC Group, which has Yiwu government as its major share holder, or to the previous keeper if they have subleased a booth. We analyze taxes and booth rents below.[30]

Regarding taxes, in the initial stage, the business tax and income tax were collected on a per-transaction basis. After 1983, since it was technically difficult to ask thousands of booth-keepers to declare their exact sales and profits, the two taxes were combined and levied as a lump tax (ZPZHDC 1997, chapter on Xie Gaohua). In China, this was the first attempt to collect a lump tax from small businesses.

The lump tax on the one hand became an important source of income for the Yiwu government, and to a large extent also reduced the burden of booth-keepers. As Table 4.6 shows, during the period from 1982 to 1992, the share of tax revenue fluctuated in the range of 1.8 percent to 3.8 percent of total transaction volume. Since the central government had fixed the rate of business tax at 3 percent at that time,[31] we can infer that the lump taxes for the small booth-keepers were comparatively low.

The method of fee collection is an important issue for the two-sided market theory. There are generally two types of fees, namely the lump-sum-based fees (membership fee) and the per-transaction-based fees (usage fee). According to the two-sided market literature, the per-transaction-based fees are appropriate for attracting fresh entrants to a newly started platform. After the platform has expanded and the

Table 4.6   Tax revenue and transaction volume of Yiwu Market

Year	Number of booths	Total tax revenue (10,000 yuan)	Tax revenue/ booth (yuan)	Transaction volume (10,000 yuan)	Transaction volume/booth (yuan)	Share of tax revenue in transaction volume (%)
1982	705	15.4	218	700	9929	2.2
1983	1050	32	305	1400	13,330	2.3
1984	1870	60	321	2700	14,439	2.2
1985	2847	135	474	5000	17,562	2.7
1986	5500	283	515	10,000	18,182	2.8
1987	5600	580	1036	20,000	35,714	2.9
1988	6131	986	1608	26,500	43,223	3.7
1989	8400	1487	1770	39,000	46,429	3.8
1990	8900	2148	2413	60,600	68,090	3.5
1991	8900	3000	3371	103,300	116,067	2.9
1992	16,000	3625	2266	205,400	128,375	1.8

Sources: Data for tax revenue: Zhang et al. (1993, p. 41); other data as for Table 4.1.

transaction times increased, however, lump-sum-based fees will lower the average costs of each seller, and attract an increasing number of sellers (Armstrong and Wright 2008). It is clear that the change in the method of levying taxes by Yiwu government is consistent with the two-sided market theory.

One difference with ordinary lump sum fees is that the tax must be levied *after* the sellers have completed their annual business. Therefore, the government was able to continually implement flexible adjustments in the lump tax level in accordance with changes in business conditions. This point can be clearly confirmed from the data concerning average tax per booth in Table 4.6. The government ability to intervene actively in market development was based on just this kind of flexibility.

Booth rent is generated according to the physicality of the specialized market. Reflecting the supply and demand relations, the booth rent in Yiwu Market has continuously increased up to now. According to Luo (2005), the business costs of subsequent booth-keepers (subleasing booths from previous booth-keepers) were higher than the costs of the original booth-keepers (who directly leased their booths from the ZCCC Group) by a factor of between nine and 34. In order to lower the booth rents of the later, non-original booth-keepers, the ZCCC Group took various measures to constrain the resale or sublease of the booths simply for the purposes of speculation. For example, it set an upper limit for the number of times a booth could be subleased.

4.6   CONCLUSION

Physical marketplaces are widespread in developing countries. They are regarded as typical informal economies, and a reflection of the economic backwardness of developing countries. Based on fieldwork with the Suq in Morocco, conducted by Geertz et al. (1979), North (1991, p. 104) has commented appropriately on the central problem of the marketplace:

> What is missing in the Suq are the fundamental underpinnings of institutions that would make such voluntary organizations viable and profitable. These include an effective legal structure and court system to enforce contracts which in turn depend on the development of political institutions that will create such a framework.

Compared to a traditional marketplace such as that of the Suq, the uniqueness of specialized markets is crystal clear. Through the active intervention of local governments, specialized markets have resolved various problems that plague physical marketplaces in a revolutionarily way, and have successfully conducted platform governance. As examined in the case of Yiwu, throughout the development process of Yiwu Market, the role of the local government has been to concentrate on two fields: the active creation and fostering of buyers and sellers; and careful development of the market platform. It is interesting that Yiwu government officials are clearly aware of their role as a platform manager. The secretary of the Yiwu Communist Party Committee emphasized this point as follows:

> The government must know what it should do and what it should not do. What it should never do is intervene in the resource allocation that ought to be coordinated by the market. For example, it should not intervene in the production or the marketing activity of an enterprise. What it should do is intervene sufficiently in the creation and preservation of the market platform. (*Workers Daily* 11 July 2006)

NOTES

1. This market was called the Yiwu Commodity Market until 1992. For brevity, we use the term "Yiwu Market" for both the former and present name in this book.
2. http://www.cccgroup.com.cn/Active.asp?id=1, accessed 8 September 2011.
3. http://www.yw.gov.cn/glb/ywgl/ywkf/2010/cytsp/201105/t20110504_324761.html, accessed 8 September 2011.
4. However, Qiaotang Bang's formal organization has never been revived.
5. However, the managing committee has not yet been abolished.
6. In order to carry out daily work, Yiwu AIC established a branch bureau in Yiwu Market in 1984. The deputy director of Yiwu AIC often doubles as the director of this

branch bureau. In many cases, it is not clear whether the decisions concerning Yiwu Market are taken by Yiwu AIC or by this branch bureau. This chapter will mention this branch bureau only in cases where its role can been clearly confirmed.

7. Individual labor means "self-employed enterprise" in the Chinese context.

8. One periodic market was located in Choucheng Town and the other was located in Niansanli Town. The latter gradually disappeared in the 1980s.

9. The specialized market first spontaneously appeared in Wenzhou, but most of Wenzhou's markets failed to obtain sufficient support from local government, and thus gradually declined.

10. It is often asked why Yiwu and not other markets became the leading market in China, since there are so many other regions that have similar peddling traditions. The answer is indeed that it was these two years that helped to create superiority over other markets at the very beginning.

11. The information on Yinshang Zhuangong is based on an author interview with a government official of the Yiwu Economic Development Bureau (YEDB) in September 2007.

12. To be precise, in 1991, the Yiwu government permitted the compensated use of state-owned land in Yiwu's cities and towns. This was a pioneering reform in Zhejiang.

13. Chapter 7 will show that a structural change among booth-keepers has occurred since this time as well. These factors jointly contributed to the development of the manufacturing sector in Yiwu.

14. Quzhou government has facilitated the formation of links between local peasants and Yiwu since 1999, but the fully fledged development of the processing business began in 2002, when Yiwu started this campaign.

15. Some neighboring provinces such as Anhui and Jiangxi have also been involved. The information on the processing business in Yiwu is from an interview with a staff member of YMTDB in September 2006.

16. According to data from 13 markets, there were 3124 Yiwu merchant households operating 4040 booths in these branch markets in 2000. Most of them were engaged in the sales of daily necessities, garments, shoes and hats. Among these 13 markets, Yiwu commodities accounted for 80 percent of total transaction volume in three markets, 50–70 percent in three markets, 30–45 percent in six markets, and 15 percent in one market (Yiwu AIC 2003, Chapter 4, Section 3). These data indicate that the direct effect of branch markets for the sales of Yiwu commodities was not so remarkable, but their indirect effect should not be underestimated.

17. Yiwu Fair website, http://www.yiwufair.com/cn/about/historyDetails.htm, accessed 11 January 2009. Most of these fair buyers were not permanently resident in Yiwu. In 2006, the top 10 countries or regions that had a resident office in Yiwu are (1) Pakistan; (2) Hong Kong; (3) UAE; (4) Iraq; (5) Korea; (6) Afghanistan; (7) Yemen; (8) India; (9) Russia; (10) Mauritania. The majority of the market's foreign buyers are still from developing countries and regions.

18. Information on the internationalization strategy is mainly cited from Yiwu Fair website (http://www.yiwufair.com/cn/Wizard/Overview.htm, accessed 11 January 2009) and is partially based on an author interview with a Yiwu government official in November 2008.

19. To be precise, Yiwu Market initially collected construction funds from various government departments and booth-keepers, but gradually became the sole owner of Yiwu Market.

20. SDAPCEA website, accessed 11 January 2009.

21. The concept of endogenous transaction costs is cited in the narrow sense of Yang and Zhang (2003, pp. 90–91).

22. For details on Huahang Guishi, see Ding (2010, Section 8.3.2).

23. This information is cited from the Yiwu Index website (www.yiwuindex.com) (accessed 11 January 2009).

24. Detailed data concerning the number of buyers per day in Yiwu Market will be shown in Chapter 5.

25. According to *Market and Consumption News*, 2 November 2007 and an interview with Yiwu AIC carried out by the author in November 2008.
26. The credit rating of each booth is appraised every year. In this system, each booth-keeper has a basic score of 60 points. Bonus points or deductions are decided according to their credibility.
27. The author obtained this information from the computer placed in the International Trade City of Yiwu Market on 5 March 2008.
28. The Yiwu Market AIC branch bureau has a staff of only 50 employees, but has greatly reduced the workload through the introduction of credit ratings for booths.
29. According to an interview carried out by the author in September 2007.
30. We do not have exact data on other fees, but according to Luo (2005), they are very low as a result of government intervention.
31. The rate of income tax is unknown.

5. The specialized market system in the daily necessities industry: an observation from Yiwu Market

Source: The author.

Figure 5.1   Luoshiwan Market: a major sales outlet of Yiwu commodities in Yunnan

5.1   INTRODUCTION[1]

The following three chapters consist of a thorough discussion of the characteristics of all the buyers and sellers in Yiwu Market. As a starting point, this chapter first discusses the traders from the domestic market. We pay particular attention to the way in which SMEs in the industrial clusters, Yiwu Market, the cities and counties became interconnected with each other, and to how an SME-specific distribution system, the Specialized Market System, has been formed in China's daily necessities industry.

Yiwu merchants are a key factor in understanding this issue. As Chapter 4 pointed out, their large presence as both buyers and sellers enabled Yiwu Market to smoothly exceed critical mass in the early 1980s. This chapter further pursues the business activities of the Yiwu merchants. We will clarify the interaction between the Yiwu merchants and various SMEs in the industrial clusters and the cities.

5.2   DATA SOURCES

This chapter attempts to explore Yiwu Market's domestic linkages by primarily using the publication edited by Yiwu Forum Secretariat (2005) known as the *Zhuanye Shichang Yu Quyu Fazhan – Guanzhu Yiwu Shichang Fushequan* [Specialized Markets and Regional Development — Focusing on the Range of Economic Impact of the Yiwu Market (SMRD)]. *Xiaoshangpin Shijie Bao* [Commodities World News] is a newspaper that reports on Yiwu Market. During 2004 and 2005, this newspaper sent a large number of reporters to China's 25 provinces to investigate the business relationship between Yiwu and these areas. The main result of this investigation was published as the SMRD. A few reports have been published on the website of *Yiwu Xinwen Wang* (Yiwu News Net).[2] Since the small producers and merchants related to Yiwu are scattered over an extremely wide area, the SMRD and the information on the website are the most appropriate material for analyzing the traders in Yiwu Market.

The SMRD consists of two parts. The first is entitled "Yiwu Market and Zhejiang's Industrial Clusters" and contains many reports on the clusters in other areas within Zhejiang Province. The second part of the SMRD is entitled "Yiwu Market and the Whole Country." Although it consists of three reports on the clusters in China's other areas, the main content concerns the sales outlets for Yiwu commodities throughout China. Thus, here we narrow down the focus of this study to discuss how the clusters in Zhejiang Province became connected to Yiwu Market and how the buyers in the main cities and a number of counties became connected to Yiwu Market.

5.3 LINKAGES BETWEEN ZHEJIANG INDUSTRIAL CLUSTERS AND YIWU MARKET

As a starting point for exploring Yiwu Market's domestic linkages, we first explore the linkages between Yiwu Market and the industrial clusters in Zhejiang Province that sell commodities to Yiwu Market. Four factors worth noting may be found in Table 5.1, which is compiled based on the first part of SMRD.

First, the clusters that have linkages with Yiwu are widely distributed throughout Zhejiang Province. The clusters of seven of the nine cities of this province, Hangzhou and Zhoushan being the exceptions, are connected with Yiwu. Though data are limited, the share of sales to Yiwu of some industrial clusters as a percentage of the cluster's total sales is considerable. We can infer that Yiwu is becoming a main distribution channel for these clusters.

Second, Yiwu Market is an important channel for selling commodities to both the domestic market and the overseas market. As Table 5.1 shows, among a total of 36 clusters in Zhejiang, 22 use Yiwu Market for accessing both markets. It is difficult to distinguish, however, which kind of market is more attractive. Through careful checking of the reports, we can find a rough trend that the domestic market was definitely crucial in the early stages, and in recent years the overseas market has become increasingly important. This fact is revealed in the export expansion in Yiwu Market since 2002 (see Chapter 4).

Third, there are various methods of establishing business relations with Yiwu Market. It has been mentioned in Chapter 4 that since the 1980s, a large number of Yiwu merchants have traveled to clusters outside of Yiwu for purchasing. In Table 5.1, we can observe at least six such cases. However, many linkages with Yiwu Market are created on the sole initiative of the clusters. As Table 5.1 indicates, in 15 clusters, local firms engaged Yiwu Market merchants for sales on their own initiative. In at least 27 clusters, the local firms themselves opened booths in Yiwu. This suggests that the accessibility of specialized markets such as Yiwu is especially high for producers.

Another interesting point derived from Table 5.1 is that the commodities of leading firms suggest a considerable presence in Yiwu Market.[3] As mentioned in Chapter 1, both the phased market approach and the market stratification approach implied that as economic growth progressed, most of the leading firms would expand their business scale (and work out a brand strategy), and then construct sales networks specific to each firm. As a result, the commodities of these firms would inevitably disappear from the marketplace. However, as Table 5.1 suggests, there are leading firms

Table 5.1 Aspects of linkages of various Zhejiang industrial clusters with Yiwu Market

City of Zhejiang Province	County	Town	Main industry	Ultimate destination*	Method of establishing business relations with Yiwu Market**	Share of sales of cluster***	The presence of commodities of leading firms
Ningbo	Various places		Apparel	D	1,2	–	Yes
	Cixi	Various places	Small home appliances	D, O	1,2,3,4	One of the largest domestic sales outlets	Yes
Shaoxing	Zhuji	19 towns	Socks	D, O	1,2	–	–
	Zhuji	Shaxiahu	Pearls	D, O	2	–	Yes
	Shengzhou	Various places	Neckties	D	2,3	–	Yes
Taizhou	Xianju	Xiage, other towns	Gifts	D, O	2,4	–	–
	Wenling	Daxi	Water pumps	D	3	–	Yes
	Wenling	Various places	Hats	D, O	–	80% (Nanjian Village)	–
	Wenling	Various places	Footwear	D, O	–	Majority	–
	Linhai	Duqiao	Glasses	–	2	–	–
	Luqiao	Various places	Plastic products	D, O (80%)	2	50%	Yes

City	Place		Product				
Wenzhou	Various places		Footwear	D, O	1,2	—	Yes
			Glasses	D, O	2	—	—
			Lighters	D, O	2	—	—
			Shavers	D, O	2	40–50%	—
			Zippers	D, O	1,2,3,4	—	—
	Various places in the city		Stationery	D, O	2,4	—	Yes
	Pingyang	Zhenglou	Gifts, calendars	D, O	2	50%	Yes
	Yongjia	Qiaotou	Plastic parts of accessories	D	2	80%	—
Quzhou	Longyou	Wucun	Buttons	D, O	2,3	—	Yes
			Bamboo wares (bird cages, etc.)	O	3	95% or more	—
	Muchen		Mats	D, O	2,3	—	—
Lishui	Various places		Stationery	D, O	2,3	Nearly 50%	—
	Longquan	Longyuan	Toy snakes	—	3	80% in Zhangcun Village	—
	Various places		Swords	O	2,3	33.3%	—
	Qingyuan		Bamboo chopsticks	D, O	2	Nearly 50%	Yes
	Yunhe		Wooden toys	O	3	Majority	—
	Suichang		Black pottery	—	1 or 3	—	—
Jinhua	Wucheng	Shafan	Chinese knots	—	3	Majority	—
			Crystal crafts	D, O	2,3	10%	—
	Pujiang	Various places	Handmade sewing commodities	D, O	2,1 or 3	—	—

Table 5.1 (continued)

City of Zhejiang Province	County	Town	Main industry	Ultimate destination*	Method of establishing business relations with Yiwu Market**	Share of sales of cluster***	The presence of commodities of leading firms
Jinhua	Dongyang	Huashui	Chinese knots	D, O	2	Majority	–
		Qianxiang	Leather commodities	O (D in early period)	2	Majority	–
		Various places	Apparel	D	2,3	Majority	Yes (in the 1990s)
	Lanxi	Various places	Towels	D, O	1,2,3	50%	Yes
	Panan	Various places	Hair accessories, ribbons, etc.	–	2 or 3	Majority	–

Notes:

*   Ultimate destination.

     D = Domestic market; O = Overseas market.

**   Methods of establishing business relations with Yiwu Market.

     1: Yiwu merchants physically go to clusters to place orders. Some expressions in the SMRD reports are: "*Yiwu Market merchants*."
  However, as the number of merchants who come from other areas is small and they mainly sell their local products in Yiwu, most of the
  "*Yiwu Market merchants*" can be considered to be Yiwu merchants.

     2: Local firms directly open booths in Yiwu Market.

     3: Local firms, on their own initiative, engage Yiwu Market merchants for sales.

     4: Other methods.

***   Share of sales of cluster = Share of the sale of industrial clusters in Yiwu as a percentage of the cluster's total sales.

**** –: No description.

Source: Compiled by the author based on data from SMRD.

from 12 clusters that do not match this view. As shown below, the commodities of leading firms can also be found in other markets.

5.4 LINKAGES BETWEEN YIWU MARKET AND THE MARKETS OF CHINA'S MAIN CITIES

By analyzing the second part of the SMRD, we can roughly divide the flow of Yiwu Market commodities into two stages. The first is from Yiwu Market to China's main cities and the second stage is from those main cities to smaller cities or consumers and so on. Section 5.4 focuses on the first stage. From a close examination of Table 5.2, three interesting facts emerge.

First, as its first stage, most of the Yiwu Market commodities are traded in the markets of China's main cities. As Table 5.2 indicates, 52 sales outlets are geographically distributed among 41 cities in 25 provinces.[4] Of these, 21 are provincial capitals. Of a total of 52 sales outlets, 41 sales outlets are directly named "market" or "the clustering of a few markets."[5] Seven sales outlets are called "street" or "city." In the Chinese context, these can also be considered as markets. Two outlets are named "center." In the case of the "Art Exhibition Center" in Shenzhen, "center" means a market, but in the case of the "Yiwu Commodity Direct Sales Center" in Ningbo, however, "center" refers to a retail shop. There are two non-market cases, namely "various shops in Hohhot, Inner Mongolia" and a "supermarket in Suzhou, Jiangsu." The former is a number of dispersed wholesale shops in the city and the latter is a retail supermarket. This large dependence on the term "market" illustrates that the leading actors dealing in Yiwu commodities in the main cities are small merchants. "Market" provided a good platform for them to seek customers and collect information.

Second, Yiwu commodities command an absolute majority of the commodities stocked in most of the sales outlets. Examination of Table 5.2 shows that of 52 sales outlets, first eliminating 16 sale outlets which have no description, there are 28 sales outlets (of which 26 are markets) where no less than half of the daily necessities or other specific commodities are purchased from Yiwu. At ten sales outlets (all of them markets), though concrete data are not shown, the share of Yiwu commodities in the total sales of daily necessities or other specific commodities clearly accounted for the majority. Section 5.5 will suggest that the geographical sweep of these sales outlets is also very wide. Thus, we can conclude that a powerful market network has been formed between Yiwu Market and the markets in China's main cities. By using this network, a number of SMEs are able to access a huge market.

Table 5.2   Main sales outlets for Yiwu commodities in China

Province	City	Sales outlets	Yiwu commodity	Share of Yiwu commodities in total sales of daily necessities	Methods of connection with Yiwu Market*	Presence of commodities from leading Yiwu firm
Beijing	–	Beijing Yiwu Commodity Wholesale Market	Daily necessities	–	1,2,4	–
	–	Beijing Tianyi Market	Socks, other daily necessities	70% or more (socks)	1,3	Yes
Shanghai	–	Chenghuang Temple Market	Daily necessities	50%	1,2	Yes
Chongqing	–	Chaotianmen General Wholesale Market	Socks, shirts, other daily necessities	80% in the whole Chongqing (socks); 70–80% (shirts)	1	Yes
Inner Mongolia	Hohhot	Tongda Market	National supplies, other daily necessities	–	1,4	–
		Various shops within the city	Underwear, hardware, cosmetics	–	–	–
Liaoning	Dalian	Various markets	Daily necessities	Majority	1,5	–
	Shenyang	Wuai Market	Socks, other daily necessities	70% or more (socks)	1	Yes
Jilin	Changchun	Heishui Road Wholesale Market	Crafts, gifts, clocks, other daily necessities	–	1,4,5	Yes

Zhejiang	Ningbo	Yuandong Wholesale Market	Socks	Almost all	1,4	Yes
		Yiwu Commodity Direct Sales Center	Daily necessities	100%	5	—
Jiangxi	Nanchang	Hongcheng Market	Daily necessities	Majority	3,4	Yes
Jiangsu	Xuzhou	Xuanwu Market	Socks	90%	1,3,4	Yes
	Suqian	Suqian Commodity Market	Daily necessities	Majority	4	—
	Suzhou	Suzhou Yiwu Commodity Direct Sale Supermarket	Daily necessities	100%	5	—
		Qianwanli Bridge Commodity Market	Daily necessities	—	4	Yes
Anhui	Hefei	70–80 wholesale markets in Hefei	Daily necessities	60% or more	1,4	—
	Liuan	Huang Street	Apparel, textiles, other daily necessities	—	1	—
		Dabie Mountain Yiwu Commodity Market	Daily necessities	90% or more	1,2	—
Shandong	Jimo	Jimo Commodity City	Daily necessities	80%	1,2,4	Yes
	Weifang	Weifang Commodity Market	Apparel, knitwear, watches, crafts, other daily necessities	—	4	—
	Weihai	Weihai International Trade City	Daily necessities	—	2,4,5	—
	Heze	Huadu Market	Daily necessities	80%	5	—

Table 5.2 (continued)

Province	City	Sales outlets	Yiwu commodity	Share of Yiwu commodities in total sales of daily necessities	Methods of connection with Yiwu Market*	Presence of commodities from leading Yiwu firm
Henan	Zhengzhou	The clustering of a few markets in Zhengzhou City	Daily necessities	Majority	5	–
	Luoyang	Guanlin Market	Daily necessities	80% or more	1,3,4	Yes
	Kaifeng	Daxiangguo Temple Market	Socks, hardware, toys, suitcases, other daily necessities	50% or more (of which, socks: 80%)	3	Yes
	Xinxiang	Yiwu Commodity General Wholesale Market	Textiles, toys, crafts, apparel, other daily necessities		4,5	–
Shanxi	Taiyuan	Jiancaoping Market	Daily necessities	–	1	–
		Yiwu Commodity Wholesale Market	Daily necessities	–	2,4	Yes
Hubei	Wuhan	Hanzhengjie Market	Cards, accessories, crafts, socks	–	3	Yes
	Yichang	Changjiang General Wholesale Market	Stationery, shirts, socks, crafts, clocks	90% or more	1,3	Yes
Hunan	Changsha	Gaoqiao Market	Knitwear	70%	1,4,5	–
			Stationery, toys	80%		
			Other daily necessities	60%		

Province	City	Market	Products	Percentage		Yes/No
	Zhuzhou	Clustering of more than 40 apparel markets	Shirts, underwear, other daily necessities	Majority	1,3	Yes
Guangdong	Guangzhou	Yide Fine Commodities Street	Christmas gifts	50%	–	Yes
		Dejin Commodity Market	Daily necessities	Majority	5	–
	Shenzhen	Laodongmen Commodity City	Daily necessities	60%	–	–
		Sungang Stationery, Toys Wholesale Market	Daily necessities Of which: lanterns, stationery, artificial flowers	60% 80%	–	–
		Art Exhibition Center	Daily necessities	70% (early period), nearly 50% (now)	1	–
Guangxi	Liuzhou	Feie Market	Leather, apparel, footwear	–	1,4	–
Sichuan	Chengdu	Hehuachi Market	Socks, shirts, accessories, cosmetics	Majority	1	Yes
Yunnan	Yunxian	Yunxing Commercial Street	–	–	1, 2 (under construction)	–
	Dali	Ziyun Market	Socks, other daily necessities	60% of Dali (socks)	1,2	Yes

Table 5.2 (continued)

Province	City	Sales outlets	Yiwu commodity	Share of Yiwu commodities in total sales of daily necessities	Methods of connection with Yiwu Market*	Presence of commodities from leading Yiwu firm
Yunnan	Kunming	Luoshiwan Daily Necessities Wholesale Market	Shirts, socks, rainwear, accessories, crafts, other daily necessities	60% (shirts)	1,3	Yes
Tibet	Lhasa	Bakuo Street	Crafts, Buddhism commodities, other commodities	80% or more	1	–
		Chongsaikang General Wholesale Market	Shirts, socks, other daily necessities	90% or more	1,5	–
	Lingzhi	Qingxiang Market	Daily necessities	80%	1	–
Shanxi	Xi'an	Kangfu Road Market	Shirts, socks, zippers, buttons, children's wear	–	1	Yes
Gansu	Lanzhou	Yiwu Commodity City	Daily necessities	–	1,2,4	–

82

Ningxia	Yinchuan	More than 10 markets	Daily necessities	Almost all	1,2,5	–
Qinghai	Xining	Yiwu Commodity City	Daily necessities	Less than 70%	1,2,3,4	Yes
Xinjiang	Urumqi	Changzheng Wholesale Market	Daily necessities Of which: shirts, socks	90% 100%	1,2,3	– Yes
		Clustering of a few markets around South Station	Socks	Nearly 100%	1,3	Yes

Notes:

* Methods of connection with Yiwu Market.

  1: Yiwu merchants sell Yiwu commodities in the market.

  2: Yiwu merchants open branch markets of Yiwu Market.

  3: Local merchants or merchants from other regions sell Yiwu commodities as agents of Yiwu producers.

  4: A managing committee or managing company took the initiative in establishing linkages with Yiwu.

  5: Others.

  Strictly speaking, some of the methods of becoming connected with Yiwu are not shown clearly in SMRD. However, most of these could be judged from the context.

** Some information is derived from a study of a few individual cases.

*** –: No description.

Source: Compiled by the author based on data from SMRD.

Third, in these main city markets, the methods of becoming connected with Yiwu Market are as various as those found in the industrial clusters of Zhejiang.

Yiwu merchants can be considered the most important contributors to the formation of this market network. In addition to SMRD, we were very fortunate in collecting comparatively complete data for Yiwu merchants doing business outside Yiwu in 1990 (Table 5.3).[6] As this table clearly indicates, in the early stages, the Yiwu merchants were dispersed broadly in 19 provinces (cities) of China.[7] They usually gathered together in great numbers in particular markets. The rough trend that can be confirmed from these data is that the more distant these merchants were from Yiwu, the larger were their numbers. The large numbers of Yiwu merchants not only stimulated the sales of Yiwu commodities, but also helped to disseminate information on Yiwu Market. Consequently, local merchants began to travel to Yiwu.

Here we return to SMRD. Table 5.2 indicates that currently there are 34 markets (no other forms of sales outlets exist) where Yiwu merchants sell Yiwu commodities. By examining the details in SMRD, we find at least 11 markets (no other forms of sales outlets exist) where the number of Yiwu merchants has at some time exceeded 100 and at least 13 markets (no other forms of sales outlets exist) where Yiwu merchants have been the first movers.

However, the mobility of Yiwu merchants was also high. The SMRD shows that in at least five markets (no other forms of sales outlets exist), the number of Yiwu merchants decreased significantly. For example, in the early stages, among 550 booths at the Beijing Yiwu Commodity Wholesale Market, 80–90 percent of traders came from Yiwu or a neighboring area in Zhejiang, but currently the number of Zhejiang merchants has declined to one-fifth of the total. Of these, the number of Yiwu merchants fell to below 30. On the other hand, their number increased surprisingly in other markets. As an extreme example, from 1990 to 2005, the number of Yiwu merchants in Chengdu Hehuachi Market increased from 200 to 2800 (see Table 5.3). Such high mobility is a result of their long history of peddling. Based on this tradition, Yiwu merchants have been very sensitive to changes in market conditions, and thus they constantly move around China and even overseas, in search of better marketing opportunities.[8]

After its incipient stage, some of the Yiwu merchants constructed a strong channel between Yiwu and these markets. With strong support from the Yiwu local government (see Chapter 4), a few Yiwu merchants attempted to establish branch markets in China's main cities.[9] We can observe 12 such cases in Table 5.2. Comparing Tables 5.2 and 5.3, it

Table 5.3   Yiwu merchants in various cities in China (1990)

Province	City	Sales outlet	No. of merchants or booths
Beijing	–	Tianwaitian Market	136
Tianjin	Nankai District	Longfeng Market	48
Hubei	Wuhan	Hangzhengjie Market	150
Hebei	Qinhuangdao, Beidaihe	–	147
	Shijiazhuang	–	200
Liaoning	Dalian	Dalian Apparel Transaction Market	99
Jilin	Changchun	Heishui Road Wholesale Market	400
Jiangsu	Lianyungang	Haizhou Market	16
	Yancheng	–	5
	Changshu	Zhaoshang Market	300
	Huaiyin	Huaiyin County Commodity Market	300
	Suining	Huaiyin County Huanchengxilu Market	200
	Xuzhou	Xuanwu Road Commodity Market	190
Guangxi	Liuzhou	Jiae Market	120
Sichuan	Chengdu	Hehuachi Market	200
Shanxi	Xi'an	Shengli Road Industrial Products Market, Chenghuang Temple Market	300
Xinjiang	Urumqi	Xinhua Hotel and other three hotels (all are markets)	600–700
Shandong	Tengzhou	Shanbei Road Market	117
	Weifang	Renmin Road Market	100
	Heze	–	200
	Liaocheng	Liaocheng Market	120
	Dezhou	–	700–800
	Yantai	West Street Commodity Market	40
	Qingdao	–	220

Table 5.3   (continued)

Province	City	Sales outlet	No. of merchants or booths
Henan	Zhengzhou	Yuanling Market	47
	Shanxian	Sanmenxia West Wholesale and Retail Market	76
	Shangqiu	Xizhakou Industrial Products Market	50
Zhejiang	Hangzhou	Huancheng Road Commodity Market	90
Ningxia	Yinchuan	Mingdexiang Commodity Market	150
Hunan	Changde	–	600
Guizhou	Zunyi	Goujiajin Market	300
Gansu	Lanzhou	Eastern Market	500
Yunnan	Kunming	Luoshiwan Market	200
		Panlong District Qingnian Road Industrial Products Market	200

Source: Compiled by the author based on data from YYLGEO (1992, p. 263).

is clear that all of these branch markets were established after 1990. Generally, the branch market managers invited Yiwu merchants to open booths in the market. They also told local merchants about Yiwu, helping them to access and purchase from Yiwu Market. The management style of Yiwu Market has also been applied to these markets.

Likewise, Yiwu's leading hometown factories also played an important role in strengthening this market network. As these factories grew, some of them intended to build their own sales network. However, the cost of marketing was so high that they had no choice but to make use of the existing market network. As a result, they organized Yiwu merchants, local merchants or merchants from other regions as their agents.[10] Table 5.2 suggests there are at least 13 markets (no other forms of sales outlets exist) where local merchants or merchants from other regions sell commodities as agents of Yiwu factories.

Lastly, the role of managing committees or managing companies of these main city markets is as important as the Yiwu merchants in the formation of this market network. Generally, they not only invite Yiwu merchants to open booths, but also send a group of inspectors to Yiwu to learn from the Yiwu Market management experience. Table 5.2 presents 19 such managing committees or managing companies.

We can definitely verify that the efforts of merchants from outside Yiwu, Yiwu's leading factories and the managing committees (or companies) in various markets have succeeded in stimulating a great number of non-Yiwu merchants to become buyers of Yiwu Market commodities. In 1990, at least 10,000 visitors per day came to Yiwu Market to make purchases. In the same year, the number of merchants originally from Yiwu but now working outside Yiwu was 7582 (YYLGEO 1992, pp. 262, 263). In 1998, 110,000 visitors per day came to Yiwu Market to make purchases. In that year, the total number of people originally from Yiwu but now working outside Yiwu exceeded 50,000 (Wang and Zhang 2000, pp. 34, 55). In the first half of 2007, 214,000 visitors came to Yiwu (including a few foreigners) every day.[11] The number of people originally from Yiwu working outside Yiwu in 2007 is not clear, but, since the resident population of Yiwu on 20 December 2006 was only 706,684,[12] we can infer that the majority of domestic buyers in 2007 were undoubtedly non-Yiwu merchants.[13]

5.5   DISTRIBUTION NETWORK BEYOND CHINA'S MAIN CITIES

As section 5.4 suggests, a network primarily dealing in Yiwu Market commodities has been formed between Yiwu Market and the markets located in China's main cities. After being sold to such a powerful network, where are Yiwu commodities being dispersed to? Who is engaged in the sales of Yiwu commodities? In the SMRD, the data related to this stage are not as complete as in the first stage from Yiwu to the main cities. Thus, it is necessary to narrow our focus down to some basic features (Table 5.4).

First, beyond the market network Yiwu commodities are still circulating with a comparatively wide scope. Five markets and one more sales outlet of a different form are circulating commodities beyond the city but inside their home provinces, 12 markets circulate commodities beyond the home province but inside China, and four markets circulate commodities to foreign countries and elsewhere inside China.

More importantly, there are at least 13 markets and one more sales outlet that clearly cover a number of small cities or counties and eight markets that have the possibility to cover small cities or counties. These markets and other sales outlets must have come to occupy the big gap that existed for a long time between the large low-end consumer demand in these areas and the poor distribution network. Marukawa (2004a) has provided powerful proof for this point. Based on a question- naire survey involving two local markets in Guangyuan, Sichuan, this study showed that there are strong linkages between the local markets in Guangyuan and the large markets in Chengdu (Sichuan's provincial capital).

Second, by examining who the buyers are who purchase from these markets, we discover that the majority are still small merchants. Limited information shows that they probably operate booths in local markets. On the other hand, the modern distribution organizations, such as depart- ment stores and supermarkets, can be observed in at least 12 markets. The phased market approach has always stated that the traditional distribu- tion system, such as wholesale markets, must give way to the new system (Zheng et al. 2003). The market stratification approach also asserted that these two systems never have any points of contact (Li 2003). However, as Table 5.4 suggests, the relationship between the markets on the one hand and the supermarkets or department stores on the other is not one of rivalry but is complementary.

Lastly, we try to analyze the methods for forging linkages with the markets in the main cities. At this level, the role of Yiwu merchants is limited. In three markets they tried to open shops for direct sales of Yiwu commodities, and in two markets and one more sales outlet of a different form they organized local merchants to sell Yiwu commodities. However, all these are just minor cases. Mostly, local merchants go to the market and purchase commodities themselves.

5.6   CONCLUSION

5.6.1   A Market-Based Distribution System

The analysis in sections 5.3, 5.4 and 5.5 indicates that Yiwu Market and its related markets in the cities have created a strong market-based distri- bution system, a model case of the specialized market system, in the daily necessities industry. We can generally divide this system into three stages (Figure 5.2).

The first stage is from the clusters to the Yiwu Market. As section 5.3 suggests, not only those in Yiwu, but also small producers in other parts of Zhejiang Province are making use of this market as one of their major dis- tribution channels. In fact, there are also a large number of SME clusters in others provinces of China that have strong linkages with Yiwu Market.

Table 5.4 The distribution network beyond the main cities

Province	City	Sales outlets	Sweep of the markets in the main cities*	Links with smaller cities or counties**	Buyers	Methods of forming linkages with the markets in the main city***
Beijing	–	Beijing Yiwu Commodity Wholesale Market	–	–	Wholesale merchants, companies, schools, citizens	3
	–	Beijing Tianyi Market	C	Δ	Merchants from other markets, departments, supermarkets	3
Shanghai	–	Chenghuang Temple Market	C	–	Merchants from other markets in Shanghai	–
Chongqing	–	Chaotianmen General Wholesale Market	B	Yes	Wholesale merchants in local county	2
Inner Mongolia	Hohhot	Tongda Market	B	Yes	Wholesale merchants in local city	3
		Various places in the city	B	Yes	Wholesale merchants in local city	2
Liaoning	Shenyang	Wuai Market	C, D	Δ	Wholesale merchants in local city, supermarkets	3
Jilin	Changchun	Heishui Road Market	C	Yes	Wholesale merchants in big city and local city, departments	2 or 3
Zhejiang	Ningbo	Yiwu Commodity Direct Sales Center	–	–	Consumers, local governments, schools	3

Table 5.4 (continued)

Province	City	Sales outlets	Sweep of the markets in the main cities*	Links with smaller cities or counties**	Buyers	Methods of forming linkages with the markets in the main city***
Jiangsu	Xuzhou	Xuanwu Market	C	Δ	–	2 or 3
	Suzhou	Suzhou Yiwu Commodity Direct Sale Supermarket	A	–	Consumers	3
Anhui	Hefei	70–80 wholesale markets in Hefei	B	–	Departments, supermarkets	–
Shandong	Jimo	Jimo Commodity City	C, D	Δ	–	–
	Heze	Huadu Market	C	Yes	–	–
Henan	Zhengzhou	Clustering of several markets	C	Yes	–	–
	Luoyang	Guanlin Market	B	Yes	Merchants from other markets, departments, supermarkets	1
Hubei	Wuhan	Hanzhengjie Market	C, D	Δ	Wholesale merchants, schools, restaurants	3
	Yichang	Changjiang General Wholesale Market	C	Yes	Supermarkets, departments	1
Hunan	Changsha	Gaoqiao Market	C	Yes	–	–
	Zhuzhou	Clustering of more than 40 apparel markets	C	Yes	–	–
Sichuan	Chengdu	Hehuachi Market	C	Δ	Merchants, departments, supermarkets	1,3

Yunnan	Dali	Ziyun Market	A	Δ	Departments, supermarkets	3
	Kunming	Luoshiwan Daily Necessities Wholesale Market	C	Δ	Companies, departments, supermarkets	3
Tibet	Lhasa	Bakuo Street	–	–	Tourists	3
		Chongsaikang General Wholesale Market	B, D	Yes	Merchants from other markets, departments	3
Shanxi	Xi'an	Kangfu Road Market	C	Δ	Departments, supermarkets (shirts)	4
Qinghai	Xining	Yiwu Commodity City	A	Yes	Consumers	4
Xinjiang	Urumqi	Changzheng Wholesale Market	B, D	Yes	Merchants from other markets	3
		Markets Cluster around South Station	B	Yes	Departments, supermarkets	1,2

Notes:

* Sweep of the markets in the city.
  A: Inside the city; B: Beyond the city but inside the province; C: Beyond the province but inside China; D: Foreign countries.

** Links with smaller cities or counties.
   Δ: No description about whether or not the commodities are sold to smaller cities and rural areas, but from the context the possibility is large.

*** Methods of forming linkages with the markets in the main city.
    1: Yiwu merchants open shops directly.
    2: Yiwu merchants or makers organize local merchants to sell Yiwu commodities.
    3: Buyers come to the main city market for purchasing.
    4: Other ways.

**** –: No description.

***** Some information is derived from a few individual cases.

Source: Compiled by the author based on data from SMRD.

It was estimated by the Yiwu government that the shares of the commodities of Yiwu, other parts of Zhejiang Province and other provinces China in Yiwu Market are 40 percent, 30 percent and 30 percent respectively.[14]

The second stage is from Yiwu Market to the markets in China's main cities. Unlike the specialized market, the main booth-keepers in these markets are purely merchants. Section 5.4 indicates that, as the core of this distribution system, most of the Yiwu Market commodities command an absolute majority in these markets.

In the third stage, we observed that Yiwu commodities are not only spreading across a wide area, but are also trickling down to some smaller cities or counties.

A noteworthy fact is that this market-based distribution system is constantly in the process of evolution. We found products from leading firms in the Zhejiang clusters in the first stage, and products of leading firms

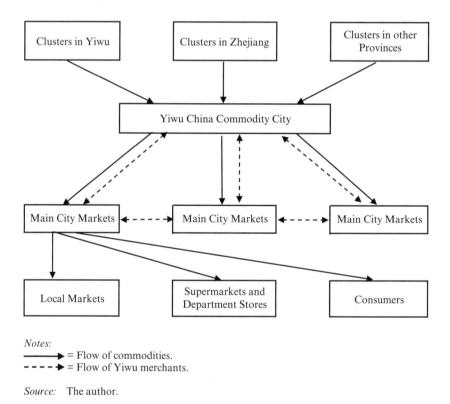

Notes:
——▶ = Flow of commodities.
- - - -▶ = Flow of Yiwu merchants.

Source: The author.

Figure 5.2   The specialized market system in the daily necessities industry: an observation from Yiwu Market

in Yiwu clusters in the second stage. Correspondingly, in the third stage, supermarkets and department stores, nodal points in modern distribution systems, have appeared. This trend illustrates that the upgrading of China's specialized-market-based industrial clusters is not stimulated by the development of any single company, but by the evolution of the whole of the specialized market system.

5.6.2   The Role of the Yiwu Merchants

The above distribution system is a typical market-platform-based system. In order to establish such a system, it is necessary to have these platforms exhibit sufficient indirect network effects and thus attract an increasing number of buyers and sellers. In the real world, the mobility of the buyers and sellers from different regions differs quite considerably. Only those merchant groups that were sensitive to market information and were happy to move around between various distant markets in search of opportunities were able to play a key role in the formation of this system. The Yiwu merchants are one such an example. Their role in the formation of the market-based distribution system can be summarized as follows (see Figure 5.2).

In the initial stage, usually as first movers, Yiwu merchants moved around various clusters and marketplaces over the whole country and broadly disseminated information on Yiwu Market. As a result, an increasing number of non-Yiwu SMEs came to establish linkages with Yiwu.

In this process, the Yiwu merchants gradually began to formalize the network between the Yiwu Market and the markets in the main cities. They established branch markets where on the one hand large numbers of Yiwu merchants were invited to operate booths, and on the other hand the non-Yiwu merchants were supported in traveling to Yiwu. The leading factories in Yiwu also organized both the merchants now outside Yiwu and non-Yiwu merchants as their sales agents. As a result, a powerful network has been formed between Yiwu Market and the main city markets.

It must be emphasized that although the formation of the specialized market system in the daily necessities industry has been greatly promoted by the Yiwu merchants, it has indeed transcended their Landsmann network (the network based on merchants of the same geographical origin).[15] Currently, the large numbers of non-Yiwu merchants have become by far the major actors supporting this system. This results from the following two reasons. The first is the outstanding platform governance in Yiwu Market, which has enabled buyers and sellers from different regions to develop mutual trust quickly (see Chapter 4). The second reason is the efforts of the Yiwu merchants themselves. Whether in the initial stage or mature stage, they have provided opportunities to travel to Yiwu for purchasing to a large number of non-local merchants. Both of these reasons are the very preconditions for Yiwu Market to overcome the limitation of the Landsmann network and exhibit a smoothly increasing and strong indirect network effect.[16]

NOTES

1. This chapter is a revised version of the article: "Distribution System of China's Industrial Cluster: Case Study of Yiwu China Commodity City" in *Asian Industrial Clusters, Global Competitiveness and New Policy Initiatives*, by Ding Ke and edited by Bernard Ganne and Yveline Lecler, Copyright © 2009, World Scientific Publishing Co.

2. http://www.ywnews.cn/gzywscjj/index.htm (accessed 2 October 2006). In this chapter, we use the acronym SMRD to refer to both SMRD and the Yiwu News Network materials for brevity.

3. We define a leading firm as one that is clearly described in the reference material as being in the top level of an industrial cluster.

4. Mainland China (except for Hong Kong and Macau) has a total of 31 provinces or provincial level regions.

5. There are often dozens of submarkets in a marketplace in China. For details, see Chapter 4, subsection 4.4.1.

6. In 1990, the number of merchants originally from Yiwu but now working outside Yiwu was 7582, and the (largest) number of Yiwu merchants in Table 5.3 was 7321 (YYLGEO 1992, pp. 262, 263). Therefore, information on most of the Yiwu merchants working outside Yiwu is covered in this table.

7. An exception is southeast China, including Guangdong Province and Fujian Province. As shown in Table 5.3, there were no Yiwu merchants in these two provinces. This is because in the 1980s, the Yiwu merchants primarily purchased from this region. For them, Guangdong and Fujian were a production base and not a distribution base.

8. From SMRD, we also found that there were many merchants from other locations in Zhejiang Province in the main city markets. Because of a similar local tradition of peddling or itinerant craftsmen, their mobility is as high as the Yiwu merchants. It is easy to imagine that the competition between markets in the clusters and in the main cities to attract and hold on to these merchants will be extremely fierce. We will further discuss this point in the case of Changshu Zhaoshang City (see Chapters 8 and 9).

9. In most of the cases, the Yiwu government helped Yiwu merchants to negotiate with local government officials in main cities. The National Industrial Products Wholesale Markets Association introduced in Chapter 4 also contributed to the formation of strong relationships between Yiwu Market and the main city markets.

10. It should be noted that after several tradings early on, most factories in Yiwu Market usually send their commodities off to main city markets directly without using Yiwu Market. However, Yiwu Market is still necessary for them to find new buyers.

11. CWPIP 12 July 2007, accessed 10 February 2009.

12. enorth.com.cn 28 February 2007, accessed 10 February 2009.

13. The SMRD did not show clear data for non-Yiwu buyers in every case, but by calculating the sum of the branch markets, the markets with agents from leading Yiwu firms and the markets that had formed links with Yiwu (stimulated by managing committees or managing companies), we can confirm that there are at least 31 markets from which non-Yiwu merchants visit Yiwu Market for purchasing.

14. Interviews with a number of the staff of the Yiwu government (September 2007). It is

natural that in addition to Yiwu, the firms in these clusters also have other marketing channels in the domestic market. Most of them have long made use of local or other regional specialized markets. Some have even constructed their own sales network. Even after becoming connected to Yiwu, they may be still very hesitant to completely abandon these existing channels. The trend that Yiwu Market is transforming into an increasingly important *hub market* in China's daily necessities industry distribution system, however, is crystal clear. It is noteworthy that, however, Yiwu is not the sole distribution center for daily necessities in China. The other important hub is Guangzhou and its neighboring areas.

15. According to Ho (1966, p. 1), the nearest Western equivalent to the Chinese term "Tongxiang" is the German word Landsmann.

16. On the other hand, we should not overstate the role of Yiwu merchants. In linking the Zhejiang clusters and the Yiwu Market their role was not as obvious as it was in the linking of the Yiwu Market and the main cities markets. This is because most of these clusters also have a similar tradition of commerce. The role of Yiwu merchants in distributing commodities from the markets in the main cities to the local markets was also limited. Each main city already had its existing distribution system. To be precise, therefore, the role of the Yiwu merchants was simply to have succeeded in connecting Yiwu Market and the markets in China's main cities.

6. Overseas linkages of specialized markets

Source: The author.

Figure 6.1   A foreign resident office in Yiwu

6.1 INTRODUCTION

In recent years, the specialized markets have rapidly begun to establish business linkages with overseas markets. On the one hand, specialized markets have attracted a number of foreigners to China for purchasing. On the other hand, a large number of merchants from Zhejiang and other locations have started up businesses in developing countries. Thus, a new type of globalized distribution system has been emerging in the developing world.

The Global Value Chain (GVC) approach is a well-known approach for analyzing international trade. According to Schmitz (2006a, Section 4), the basic structure of the GVC is that "there are lead firms . . . which set and enforce the parameters, under which other firms in the chain operate." Compared to the GVC, however, the emerging specialized market system has completely different features.

First, the commodities in the specialized market system are mainly circulated to the low-end market in developing countries. In contrast, the ultimate destination of commodities in GVCs is the developed country market, in which the middle class forms the majority.

Second, the main actors in the specialized market system are numerous SMEs, especially those people who have historically engaged in long-distance trade. Physical marketplaces have played a crucial role in organizing them. In contrast, GVCs are organized by the "lead firms," which usually have strong organizational capabilities.

Third, the many supporting institutions (Landsmann networks, purchasing agents, etc.) in the specialized market system ensure that even small businesses are readily able to take part in international trade. In contrast, because of the lead firm's strict standards, the entry barrier for SMEs is much higher in GVCs.

The current state of statistical information in developing countries does not yet allow us to show the above features with decisive macro data. It is also difficult to clarify in depth the institutional factors present in other developing countries (besides China) that have caused the above structural changes. This chapter thus simply attempts to describe the situation through case studies. Regarding foreign buyers, we choose the case of Yiwu Market, as it has the largest number of foreign buyers in China. As for overseas Chinese merchants, the case of Africa will be discussed.

6.2 FOREIGN BUYERS IN YIWU MARKET

6.2.1 Foreign Resident Offices in Yiwu

As a result of the strategy of building an international trade city, exports from Yiwu Market rapidly increased. In 2007, the share of exports accounted for 60 percent of the total transaction volume of Yiwu Market. Foreigners played an increasingly important role in the export business. In 2007, a total of 260,000 foreigners visited Yiwu. Some foreign buyers tended to reside permanently in Yiwu and many resident offices were established. In just 2006 and 2007 alone, the number of foreign resident offices increased from 939 to 1340. This number accounts for one-third of the total number of foreign resident offices in Zhejiang Province.[1]

This subsection will analyze the features of foreign buyers by focusing on these foreign resident offices. The Yiwu Foreign-concerning Service Center (YFSC) has published an annual yearbook entitled *Yiwu Foreign Countries and Hong Kong, Macao, Taiwan Resident Offices Yearbook* since 2006. These yearbooks contain information on the nationality of the resident office, name of the representative, date of establishment, and business scope of each office. In the 2006 version, the nationality of each representative was also published. These materials will help us gain a deeper understanding of the features of the foreign buyers.

We first confirm from the data that most of the foreign resident offices in Yiwu are mainly serving small variety shops in their home countries. According to the 2007 yearbook, among the 790 offices on which information is available, only 23 specialized in some specific commodity (or a small number of commodities). All the remaining offices are dealing in all-round, general commodities (YFSC 2007).

In general, in order to respond to small customer orders in the home country,[2] the staff of these offices had to go to Yiwu Market almost every day. In order to buy just one type of small commodity, they need to visit many booths to find the cheapest items, just as a housewife will do when out shopping. A resident office may have relationships with several hundred suppliers in Yiwu, but these relationships are generally fluid.

Concerning the geographical distribution of these foreign resident offices, a characteristic feature is that most of them represent developing countries. As Table 6.1 shows, among these offices, the greatest number represent Asian countries and regions. The top ten countries or regions having foreign resident offices in Yiwu in 2006 were (1) Pakistan 233, (2) Hong Kong 100, (3) UAE 57, (4) Iraq 43, (5) South Korea 40, (6) Afghanistan 24, (7) Yemen 16, (8) India 16, (9) Russia 15, (10) Mauritania 14 (YFSC 2007). Except for Hong Kong, South Korea, Russia and Mauritania, all the remaining offices in this group represent developing Asian countries or regions. Table 6.1 also suggests that Asian countries and regions were the earliest to set up offices in Yiwu.

The number of European resident offices is second to Asia. However, more than half of them are from Eastern Europe. Of a total of 62 offices in 2006, the number of Russian offices amounted to 15; Ukraine had seven and Bulgaria had six. In contrast, the total number of offices representing Western European countries was a mere 19. Moreover, careful examination of the representatives' names and nationalities reveals that many of the representatives of Western Europe resident offices were originally from developing countries.

Table 6.1   *Number of foreign and Hong Kong, Macao and Taiwan*
             resident offices in Yiwu

Year	Number of countries and regions						Total number
	Asia	Europe	North America	South America	Africa	Oceania	
1997	2						2
1998	1						1
1999	5						5
2000	12	2	1				15
2001	11	2	1		1		15
2002	31	2	1	1	3	1	39
2003	57	5	1		3	1	67
2004	131	7	2		11	2	153
2005	150	15	4		17	3	189
2006	244	29	5	2	23	1	304
Total	644	62	15	3	58	8	790

Source: Compiled by the author based on data from YFSC (2007).

Africa also deserves attention. As Table 6.1 shows, despite the great distance, 58 offices representing this continent were established in Yiwu. Notably, the number of African merchants exhibited a sudden increase in the three-year period 2004 to 2006.

Commodity trades in developed countries are primarily controlled by a small number of big retailers such as Wal-Mart or Carrefour. Thus the number of resident offices representing developed countries in Yiwu is much smaller. However, their number is also increasing. The most important reason for this is the rapid growth of e-commerce business, especially C2C (Consumers to Consumers) business, which has a large demand for cheap and small-batch commodities. Yiwu Market responds well to such special demands.[3]

Lastly, we discuss the features of the representatives of Yiwu's foreign resident offices. As mentioned above, in the 2006 version of the foreign offices' yearbook, the nationality of each representative was also published. It is interesting that there is sometimes an inconsistency between the nationality of the office and the nationality of the representative (Table 6.2). This fact indicates that these representatives have previously left their home countries and have been doing business in other countries for a while and are currently resident in Yiwu. In other words, just like the Yiwu merchants in China, they are always changing their business base in order to search for better market opportunities.

Table 6.2   *Inconsistency between nationality of representatives and nationality of the resident offices (top 10 countries with the most numerous resident offices)*

Nationality of foreign resident office	Nationality of representatives → Afghanistan	India	Jordan	Pakistan	Iraq
Asia	10	10	7	8	4
Europe	4	0	0	0	3
America	0	0	1	0	0
Oceania	1	1	0	0	0
Africa	0	2	0	0	0
Total	15	13	8	8	7

Nationality of foreign resident office	Nationality of representatives → Iran	China	Syria	Chinese Taiwan	Somalia
Asia	6	2	1	3	1
Europe	0	2	2	0	0
America	0	2	0	0	0
Oceania	0	0	0	0	0
Africa	0	0	0	0	1
Total	6	6	3	3	2

Source: Calculated based on YFSC (2006).

By analyzing Table 6.2, a further three interesting points can be discovered. The first is that the top ten countries or regions whose merchants prefer to engage in business in foreign countries are Afghanistan, India, Jordan, Pakistan, Iraq, Iran, Mainland China, Syria, Chinese Taiwan, and Somalia. The cases of Afghanistan, Iraq and Somalia may be because of war. The remainder clearly result from a long tradition of long-distance trading.

The second point is that the Afghan, Indian and Chinese merchants are scattered the most widely around the world. They have moved from three continents to Yiwu for trade. Following these are Jordanian, Iraqi, and Syrian merchants, who have traveled from two continents to Yiwu for trade. Following these are merchants from Pakistan, Iran, Chinese Taiwan, and Somalia, who have traveled from one continent to Yiwu for trade.[4]

The third point is that the world's commodity trade center is gradually shifting from the UAE and Hong Kong to Yiwu. The UAE and Hong Kong have previously been world centers for commodity trade. Currently, among the foreign resident offices in Yiwu, the UAE and Hong Kong have the largest number of representatives of different nationality. In concrete terms, there are 36 foreign resident offices representing the UAE, but of these, 24 of the representatives are non-UAE citizens. There are 54 foreign resident offices representing Hong Kong, but of these, 21 of the representatives are non-Hong Kong citizens (YFSC 2006). This suggests that a number of these representatives have previously resided in the UAE or Hong Kong, but have currently transferred their business base to Yiwu.

6.2.2   Purchasing Agents in Yiwu Market

Besides foreign resident offices, there are a large number of foreign buyers who visit Yiwu Market irregularly. Generally, the cost of engaging in international trade is very high for these small merchants. In Yiwu, however, they have been responsible for the smooth export of a great variety of commodities. A key to the understanding of this phenomenon is the presence of a large number of purchasing agents around Yiwu Market. It is still difficult to describe the whole situation surrounding these agents, and thus, for the present, this subsection will introduce a typical case concerning purchasing agents.[5]

As a typical purchasing agent, Company A's basic service flowchart is as follows:

> Reception → Agency with Company A → Customer places order → Customer pays deposit to Company A → Company A purchases goods for customer → Production follow up → QC → Customer settles balance of payment with Company A → Collect goods → Warehouse storage → Draw up shipping documents → Load container → Inland and ocean transportation arrangements → Customs declaration

In this flowchart, the most interest point is that Company A provides optional services in response to various kinds of requests from foreign customers. For example, three types of service are provided for quality control.

1. Simple QC: Only for normal items that can be checked visually or manually without the use of any equipment or professional knowledge; the checking sample is around 5–10 percent of the total quantity of each item.

2. Fixed quantity QC: Checking of 50 percent of the total quantity for each order. Company A charges 8–10 percent of the total value for this service.
3. Complete QC: Every piece of every item is checked. Company A charges 8–10 percent of the total value for this service.

Their processing service also has multiple options.[6] In concrete terms:

1. Partial product processing: Labor cost + accessory cost + commission 3%. In this case, Company A can offer a combination processing service for both the product and its accessory.
2. Complete processing: Labor cost + material cost + commission 8–12%. In this case, Company A can arrange complete production for a customer's special requirements.
3. OEM processing: Consulting cost + sharing 15%. In this case, if a market opportunity with local producers is created, Company A can share in the profits with its partners.

The case of Company A clearly reveals the features of market demands in developing countries. Within these countries, quality standards are not strict and processing methods can be flexibly adjusted in terms of the customers' requirements. Within a market such as this, no single firm can carry out efficient control of the production and distribution process. Only the various SME support institutions, such as purchasing agents, are qualified to fulfill such a role in this situation.

6.3   CHINESE MERCHANTS IN AFRICA[7]

6.3.1   Fast-Growing Exports from China to Africa

In the second half of this chapter, the viewpoint is shifted to analyze Chinese merchants in African marketplaces. Their significant existence in Africa has resulted in a great increase in commodity trade between China and Africa.

During the period from 1999 to 2005, exports from China to Africa increased from 4.11 billion dollars to 18.68 billion dollars (JETRO 2000, pp. 4–5; 2005, pp. 19–20). Of China's total trade, the share of trade with Africa increased from 2.1 percent (1999) to 2.5 percent (2005). Africa is still not a very important export market for China, but the share of Chinese goods in Africa's total imports increased from 3.2 percent to 6.9 percent during the period 1999 to 2004.[8] From the perspective of Africa, China has become an increasingly important exporting country.

Among China's exports to Africa, mechanical and electrical products, textiles, clothing, and shoes accounted for 45, 15, 7.9 and 3.4 percent respectively (Song and Han 2006). The large share of mechanical and electrical exports is because of big Chinese manufacturers such as Huawei Technologies, Zhongxing Telecommunication Equipment (ZTE) and Hisence, which have invested directly in Africa in recent years. Textiles, clothing and shoes have also shown a remarkable presence, in spite of cheap prices. This has resulted primarily from the overseas development of specialized market systems. On the one hand, a number of African merchants travel to China's specialized markets for purchases (see the case of Yiwu). On the other hand, a large number of Chinese merchants have moved into various markets in Africa.

6.3.2 Chinese Merchants in Africa's Markets

We first explain the overall situation of Chinese merchants in Africa. The data in Table 6.3 have mainly been collected from the websites that encourage Chinese merchants or enterprises to invest in Africa.[9] From this table, we can derive four features concerning Chinese merchants in Africa.

The first feature is that the Chinese merchants or enterprises are broadly distributed over the whole of Africa. Arabian merchants established their own distribution system in North Africa long ago. Indian and Pakistani merchants established similar distribution systems in East Africa. As a result, the presence of Chinese merchants in these two regions is comparatively small. In other regions, we can find a large number of Chinese merchants doing business in almost every important country.

The second feature is that the Chinese merchants in Africa come primarily from the coastal regions of China. The presence of merchants from Zhejiang, Guangdong and Fujian is particularly conspicuous. There are many specialized markets in these three areas. It is easy to imagine that a powerful business network based on geographic origin should exist between these markets in China and Africa.

The third feature is that in most cases Chinese merchants are geographically located in the capital or economic center of a country. As most African countries cover a vast territory but have a sparse population density, this location is efficient for selling commodities to local small buyers.

The fourth feature is that most of the Chinese merchants are operating booths in various marketplaces in Africa. The market is obviously the

Table 6.3 Chinese merchants in Africa

Region	Country	Year	Number of merchants or enterprises	Hometown of the merchants	Business scope
North Africa	Egypt	2002	67 enterprises	–	Textile, foods, manufacturing sector, oil, building materials, infrastructure
West Africa	Ghana	2006	2000 enterprises (of which, 200 are big enterprises)	Zhejiang (70% of the total number, the majority, are from Wenzhou), Shanghai, Jiangsu (Suzhou), etc.	To sell Chinese shoes, apparel, eyewear and woolen blankets in marketplaces opened by Chinese
	Nigeria	2006	5000 enterprises		
East Africa	Kenya	2006	5000 persons	Zhejiang, Northeast China, Fujian, etc.	Aid projects, to sell daily necessities, restaurants, traditional Chinese medicine clinic, sewing factories, etc. The majority are in Nairobi
Central Africa	Congo (K)	2005	500 small merchants	Zhejiang (Wenzhou), Beijing, Shanghai, Chongqing	To sell shoes, hats, suitcases, apparel, bath towels in the downtown of Kinshasa
	Cameroon	2006	2000 merchants	Zhejiang (more than 1/4 of total)	Some of them operate booths in Wenzhou city (marketplace)

Region	Country	Year	Number	Origin	Business
Southern Africa	South Africa	2004	100,000–150,000 persons	Guangdong, Shanghai, Beijing, Fujian, Northeast China, Sichuan, Zhejiang	Trade, restaurants, tourism, etc. A number of merchants operate booths in the markets of Johannesburg
	Angola	Before 2000	Below 200 persons	—	About 50 Chinese engage in the wholesale business of daily necessities in the Sao Paulo market in Luanda. Some of them have turned to the hotel or construction businesses
	Zambia	2006	2000 persons	—	Some operate booths in the Kamuwara (transliteration) market
	Malawi	2004	100–200 persons	—	To sell apparel, shoes, hats and hardware in the shopping mall
	Namibia	2006	More than 2000 persons	—	To sell Chinese goods in markets such as China City

Source: Mainly cited and organized from various reports on Africa Investment Net. Some information is taken from other Africa-related websites.

Table 6.4   African markets opened by Chinese merchants

Region	Country	City	Market	Hometown of the owners
West Africa	Ghana	Accra	Ghana China Friendship Commodity City	Fujian
			China Commodity City	Yiwu
	Nigeria	Lagos	Zhonghua Gate Commercial Center	Yiwu
	Guinea	Conakry	China Wenzhou Commodity City	Wenzhou
Central Africa	Cameroon	–	Wenzhou Commodity City	Wenzhou
South Africa	South Africa	Johannesburg	China Wenzhou Commodity City	Wenzhou and Hong Kong
			Zhonghua Gate Commercial Center	Yiwu
			Hong Kong City	Hong Kong
	Namibia	Windhoek	China City	–

Source: Mainly cited and organized from various reports on Africa Investment Net. Some information is taken from other Africa-related websites.

most important channel through which they can establish business relationships with Africa's small merchants.

Chinese merchants not only operate booths in existing markets, but have also started to establish their own markets in Africa. From Table 6.4, we can note that most of these markets have been established in West Africa, Central Africa and Southern Africa. Their owners are mainly from Wenzhou and Yiwu in Zhejiang Province. This is consistent with the facts revealed in Table 6.3.

Why are these small merchants willing to come to Africa, a continent so far away from their homeland? We lastly attempt to analyze the motivation of these Chinese merchants. As Table 6.5 shows, undoubtedly the biggest factor is the high profits to be made in trade between China and Africa. This table clearly indicates that commodity prices in Africa are much higher than in China. Except for woolen blankets, men's shirts and washing machines, the price differentials of most commodities amounted to more than ten times.[10]

Table 6.5   Commodity prices in Africa and China

Commodity (unit)	Price in China (yuan)	Price in Africa	Country
Lamps and lanterns	50*	700–800 yuan	South Africa
Woolen blankets	30	90 rand	
Combs	3–4**	35–40 yuan	
Slippers	4–5**	40 yuan	
Men's shirts	20***	165.2 yuan	Guinea
Red bricks	0.15	1.8 yuan	Mozambique
Low-end shirts	More than 10	More than 100 yuan	Zambia
Suits	200	1000–2000 yuan	
Chinese cabbages (each weighing about two kilos)	Below 2	More than 13 dollars	Angola
Mosquito coils (box)	3	5 dollars	
Iron nails (piece)	0.5	1 dollar	
Fully automatic washing machines	1300	More than 1000 dollars	
Handkerchiefs	0.5****	2–3 dollars	Nigeria, Ghana

Notes:
* Retail price in China; ** wholesale price in Yiwu; *** factory price; **** production cost in Shanghai. For other commodities, it is unclear what type of prices they are.
1 US dollar = 7.7788 yuan (21 January 2007); 1 rand = 1.04383 yuan (18 October 2006)

Source: Mainly cited and organized from various reports on Africa Investment Net. Some information is taken from other Africa-related websites.

6.3.3   Zhejiang Merchants in South Africa's Markets

The largest number of Chinese merchants in Africa have gathered in South Africa. It is said that the total number of Chinese merchants in South Africa amounts to between 150,000 and 200,000. They are primarily engaged in trade, tourism and the restaurant business.[11] By analysis of the case of South Africa, we can gain a deeper understanding of the business model of Chinese merchants.

South Africa's Chinese merchants are mainly from Guangdong, Shanghai, Beijing, Fujian, Northeast China, Sichuan and Zhejiang. The Zhejiang merchants are the latest group to come to this country, but they have played the most crucial role in promoting trade between China and South Africa. According to an estimate by the president of the South Africa Zhejiang Chamber of Commerce, the total sales volume of 400

Zhejiang merchants in South Africa amounted to 1.5 billion yuan in 2004.[12]

Among South Africa's Zhejiang merchants, the number from Wenzhou is the largest. Most Wenzhou merchants began to travel to South Africa from the end of the 1990s. In 2004, there were 100 Wenzhou merchants in South Africa. After two years, this number had increased to 200. They are mainly living in Johannesburg.[13] According to a 2005 report, in the markets where Chinese merchants are a majority, one-third of the booths are owned or operated by Wenzhou merchants.

On the other hand, there were more than 40 Yiwu merchants in South Africa in 2005. They were mainly engaged in the wholesale business of daily necessities, such as buttons, keys, toothpicks, socks, scarves and toys (Chen 2005).

Table 6.6 presents the cases of four Wenzhou merchants and four Yiwu merchants. We can derive four important features concerning their business model from this table.

The first feature is that these Zhejiang merchants have had considerable experience before moving to South Africa. Some of them have opened factories in their hometowns; some were previously booth-keepers in China's marketplaces. Thus, even as a latecomer in South Africa, they were soon able to gain an advantage over their competitors.

The second feature is that most merchants have kept booths in a market, or even established a market themselves, in Johannesburg. This clearly shows that the specialized markets in China have succeeded in forming linkages with Africa's markets.[14]

The third feature is that the Zhejiang merchants are very sensitive to market conditions. Before moving to South Africa, some of them visited the country to survey the market. They started their businesses from commodity trade, but with changes in market demand they soon diversified into mines, newspapers, trade in precious metals, and so on.

The fourth feature is that the Zhejiang merchants are supported to a large extent by the Landsmann network. Some of them were invited to South Africa by their Landsmann. The Zhejiang Chamber of Commerce has also been established, to support Zhejiang merchants in their life and business.

6.3.4   Three Types of Distribution System in Sub-Saharan Africa

Lastly, we analyze the role of the specialized market system in exploiting the market in African countries by comparing several types of distribution system in Sub-Saharan Africa.

According to Yoshida (2007, especially pp. 20–21) and my discussion

Table 6.6 Zhejiang merchants in South Africa

Number	Hometown	Sex	Previous business	Business in South Africa	Business relationships with other Chinese
1	Wenzhou	Male	Operated booth in lamps and lanterns market in Wenzhou	Visited South Africa in 1999, then started importing Chinese commodities to South Africa. Established China Wenzhou Commodity City in 2004	The first visit to South Africa was on invitation by a Chinese market owner in Johannesburg. Established "Southern Africa Zhejiang Chamber of Commerce" in 2003
2	Wenzhou	Male	–	Started importing Chinese apparel from 1999. Bought out one booth in each of three marketplaces in Johannesburg	All the three booths were opened by Chinese
3	Wenzhou	Male	–	Came to South Africa in 2001. Spent four months surveying the local market, and then started importing Chinese apparel to South Africa. Newly entered the mine business and real estate business in 2003. Started a newspaper in 2005	Newspaper is for Chinese throughout Africa
4	Wenzhou	Female	Operated booths in the apparel market in Hangzhou	First visited South Africa in 1998. Bought out several booths in markets in Johannesburg in 2000	Both daughter and son-in-law are doing business together in South Africa

Table 6.6 (continued)

Number	Hometown	Sex	Previous business	Business in South Africa	Business relationships with other Chinese
5	Yiwu	Male	Established generating equipment factory in Yiwu	Visited South Africa twice in 1998, and then opened Zhonghua Gate Commercial Center later that year	Jointly opened the Zhonghua Gate Market with a Hong Kong merchant
6	Yiwu	Female	–	Imported Chinese commodities at first. Gradually diversified the trade into precious metals, machinery, automobiles, and so on	She is Secretary-General of the Zhejiang Chamber of Commerce
7	Yiwu	Female	Opened wig factory	Came to South Africa in 2003. Selling wigs (made in her own factory) and other commodities	Her husband is doing business together with her in Johannesburg. They employ one Chinese staff
8	Yiwu	Female	Opened perfume factory in Yiwu	Visited South Africa in 2003. Currently selling perfume made in her own factory	Supported by the Zhejiang Chamber of Commerce in daily life

Source: Mainly cited and organized from various reports on Africa Investment Net. Some information is taken from other Africa-related websites.

with him, there are three types of commodity distribution systems in Sub-Saharan Africa. The first type was established by South Asian merchants in East Africa during the colonial period. Within this system, South Asian merchants purchased commodities from South Asia and the Middle East region and sold them to East Africa's commercial outlets. Generally, these outlets were small-scale supermarkets located in downtown districts. Their main buyers were the citizens and sales price were in the middle range. South Asian merchants completely controlled the whole distribution system from wholesale to retail.

The second type was established by South African enterprises. After the South African government abolished apartheid in 1994, South African enterprises began large-scale investment in the African continent. These enterprises have constructed a modern integrated distribution system in order to compete with the traditional South Asian merchants' network. They purchase commodities from South Africa and sell them through their huge retail chains. These chain stores are middle-class oriented and their prices are the most expensive.

Compared to these two types, China's specialized market system is an extension of the Chinese distribution system to Africa. The node points of this system are various marketplaces, including the specialized markets in China, and the various marketplaces in Africa's capitals or economic centers. It thus is low-end-market oriented and charges the cheapest prices. Zhejiang merchants, with their rich experience in the domestic market, facilitated the formation of this system in a short time.

Because of the emergence of the specialized market system, large numbers of African poor were, for the first time, able to become consumers of modern industrial products. At the same time, the specialized market system has also brought about abundant opportunities for African people to start their own businesses. According to the observations by my colleagues Takahiro Fukunishi and Koichiro Kimura in Johannesburg in 2010, a large number of local African merchants were operating booths within the markets opened by Chinese merchants. As the supporting institutions for international trade advanced, just like other Chinese merchants, it became much easier for them to travel to China for purchasing.

As the analysis in Chapter 7 will show, a well-maintained and rapidly growing marketplace such as Yiwu Market is likely to drive merchants to take part in the manufacturing sector and thus trigger local industrialization. Can a similar structural change occur in African marketplaces, especially those opened by Chinese merchants? Does this provide a new opportunity for African economic development? In order to provide answers to these questions, a long-term and patient study based on fieldwork is indispensable.

NOTES

1. Yiwu Fair Website, http://www.yiwufair.com/cn/Wizard/Overview.htm, accessed 11 January 2009.
2. The smallest order might be only sufficient to fill one cardboard box.
3. Author interview with a Japanese representative in November 2007.
4. Pakistan has the largest number of foreign resident offices representing one country. However, most of the Pakistanis are engaged in trade in their own country or in Middle Eastern countries.
5. The following information is cited from the brochure of Company A.
6. We will scrutinize the processing business in Chapter 7.
7. Section 3 is a highly abridged version of Ding (2007a). The following websites (all in Chinese) are the main data sources on Chinese merchants in Africa: Feizhou Touzi Wang (Africa Investment Net, http://www.invest.net.cn); Feizhou Maoyi Wang (Africa Trade Net, http://www.ca-trade519.net); Feizhou Jingshang Wang (Africa Business Net, http://www.africa-biz.net); Feizhou Jingji Wang (Africa Economy Net, http://www.africa-economy.net); Feizhou Shangwu Wang (Africa Business Affair Net, http://www.africa.gov.cn); Zhongfei Hezuo Wang (China Africa Net, http://www.chinaafrica.com). The author accessed the above websites during the period from December 2006 to January 2007.

   In many reports on these websites, information regarding a similar theme on one website usually overlaps with reports on others, but they are also complementary. In order to collect as complete information as possible, the author has cited information from these websites according to the following principles: (1) only the name of the website is cited when citing multiple reports from the same website; (2) only the name of the main website is cited when citing multiple reports from multiple websites; (3) when citing only one report from a singe website the information is cited in as much detail as possible.
8. Data on African imports are cited from UNCTAD (2005, p. 5). Other data are cited from JETRO (2000, pp. 4–5; 2005, pp. 19–20).
9. It should be noted that all these data are collected from second-hand sources. Thus, it is difficult to provide exact numbers for these merchants or enterprises in the same year.
10. The price data were collected from the websites that encourage Chinese merchants to invest in Africa and are thus probably a little bit exaggerated.
11. The information on Chinese merchants in South Africa is mainly cited and organized from various reports on Africa Investment Net. Some of the information is taken from other Africa-related websites.
12. Before Zhejiang merchants came to South Africa, most of the Chinese were engaged in retailing. See Africa Business Affair Net (http://www.africa.gov.cn/ArticleView/2006-1-23/Article_View_1835.htm, accessed 15 December 2006).
13. The information on Wenzhou merchants in South Africa is mainly cited and organized from various reports on Africa Investment Net. Some of the information is taken from other Africa-related websites.
14. According to Matsumoto (2006), there are at least eight markets in Johannesburg in which Chinese merchants are the main booth-keepers. The total number of booths in these markets amounts to 2000.

7. Producer–distributor relationships in Yiwu Market

Source: The author.

Figure 7.1 Processors of threaded beads in Jindong, Jinhua

7.1 INTRODUCTION

As stated in Chapter 1, beneath the shell of the market platform, the producer–distributor relationships in a wholesale market in most developing countries are merchant mode. Traditional wholesale merchants dominate the booths in the markets, and the producers are required to sell products through the intermediation of these merchants (Figure 7.2).

Compared to these markets, Yiwu Market started as a merchant mode market, but is increasingly transforming into a pure market platform.

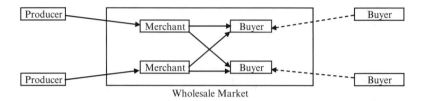

Notes:
⟶ = Flow of transactions.
- - - -▶ = Flow of purchasing.

Source: The author.

Figure 7.2   Producer–distributor relationships in wholesale markets in developing countries

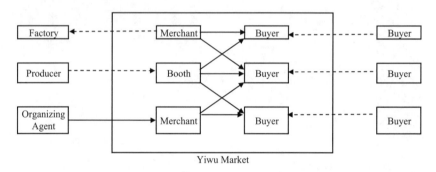

Notes:
⟶ = Flow of transactions.
- - - -▶ = Flow of factory operation, booth operation or purchasing.

Source: The author.

Figure 7.3   Producer–distributor relationships in Yiwu Market

Within Yiwu Market, the boundary between producers and merchants is becoming ambiguous. Merchants actively take part in the production process and producers are able to develop their own marketing means (Figure 7.3). An examination of the factors that cause changes in producer–distributor relationships in Yiwu Market will be extremely helpful in understanding the mechanism through which the market platform mode and the merchant mode inter-transform in developing countries.

There are three types of industrial clusters linked with Yiwu Market in terms of the initial conditions. The first is clusters that have only a tradition of long-distance trade. The second type is clusters that have a tradition of both long-distance trade and production. The third is clusters that have no tradition of long-distance trade or production.[1] We will carefully investigate the transformation process of the producer–distributor relationships in each type of cluster and clarify the factors that bring about these dynamics.

7.2   PRODUCER–DISTRIBUTOR RELATIONSHIPS IN THE YIWU DAILY NECESSITIES CLUSTER

7.2.1   Industrial Cluster Formation in Yiwu

The first type of industrial cluster linked with Yiwu Market is one that has a tradition of only long-distance trade. The daily necessities cluster located in Yiwu is a typical case of just such a cluster. As mentioned in Chapter 4, after Yiwu Market was established in 1982, a number of Yiwu merchants became booth-keepers in the market. Initially, they traveled to various clusters for commodity purchasing. Some of them gradually took part in the manufacturing process. During the period 1982 to 1990, 180 specialized handcraft villages, namely "One Village, One Product" villages, appeared in Yiwu (Zhang et al. 1993, pp. 47–8). Since the mid-1990s, influenced by the government policy of "Yinshang Zhuangong" [Exhorting merchants to shift from commerce to manufacturing], Yiwu merchants began to build modern mass-production factories (see Chapter 4, section 4.3.2). It is reported that no fewer than eight major industries had made their appearance in Yiwu by 2000, namely, socks, shirts, woolen products, jewelry,[2] zippers, toys, key blanks and printing (Wang and Zhang 2000).

However, the low-end market is characterized by low barriers to entry and exit. After only seven years, the major industrial products in Yiwu have become the following eight: socks, jewelry, seamless underwear, suitcases and leather commodities, zippers, crafts, stationery, and other daily necessities. Among the former industries of 2000, except for zippers, jewelry and socks, all have been replaced by new industries. Although the industries are rapidly changing, however, the entrepreneurs in the new sectors were generally those who had simply transferred from the former sectors.[3] We can treat all these Yiwu Market-related industries within Yiwu City as a huge daily necessities industrial cluster. The changes in the industrial structure of Yiwu City bear out this surprising formation of an industrial cluster. As Figure 7.4 indicates, after the rapid expansion of the tertiary sector, Yiwu's

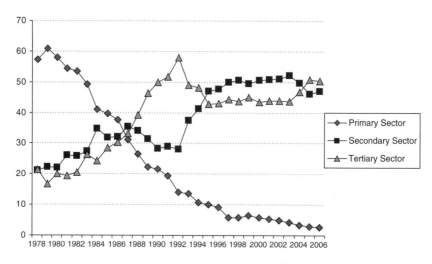

Source: Compiled by the author based on data from ZUESRG (2008, p. 12).

*Figure 7.4   Changes in the industrial structure of Yiwu (1978–2006)
(% of production value)*

secondary sector sustained remarkable growth from the 1990s onwards. This changing pattern in the industrial structure is in stark opposition to the well-known Petty-Clark's Law.

7.2.2   Why Did Merchants Become Producers?

Why did so many Yiwu merchants decide to take part in the production process? As mentioned above, this phenomenon is very rare in marketplaces in other developing countries. In addition to the policy of "Yinshang Zhuangong", were there other factors that stimulated merchants to make such important decisions? Here we use mainly the book entitled *Meiyou Weiqiang de Chengshi* [The Unwalled City] to analyze this unique phenomenon. In 1999, reporters from the "Zhongguo Qinggong Bao" [China Light Industry Newspaper] interviewed many Yiwu Market-related enterprises, all the reports being compiled into this book. Among these, the business experiences of 11 merchants, especially the reasons why they had been determined to enter the manufacturing sector, were reported in detail. As samples are limited, we will verify the qualitative conclusions derived from these cases through a certain amount of macro data concerning Yiwu Market.

The reasons for which these 11 merchants entered the manufacturing sector can be classified into three patterns.

The first is that the merchants decided to take on the risks of production because of the favorable expectations concerning market expansion. Of the 11 merchants, four merchants belong to this pattern. Their cases are as follows.

1. A woolen products maker who began to sell woolen products in Yiwu Market from 1982. He gradually realized that the potential demand in both the domestic rural regions and developing countries was very large, and so opened a factory in 1995.
2. A sock maker who sold cosmetics and daily necessities in Yiwu Market until the end of the 1980s, he then noticed that the sock market was about to undergo a great expansion. As soon as the industrial park was established in Yiwu, he opened a sock factory.
3. A ballpoint pen manufacturer who had for a long time peddled in the mountain areas of Jiangxi and Hainan Provinces, after thoroughly researching the potential market demand, opened a ballpoint pen factory in Yiwu in 1990.
4. A packing manufacturer who operated booths in Yiwu Market from 1986, he discovered a large potential demand for shirt packing in Yiwu, and opened his own packing factory in 1989.

Of the above cases, the merchants No. 1 to No. 3 discovered a large potential demand for finished goods. Merchant No. 4 noticed a large potential demand for raw materials. As explained in Chapter 5, the number of Yiwu Market buyers has thus far continuously increased. The information flow concerning Yiwu Market has also been greatly improved (see Chapter 4). Both of these two major changes in Yiwu Market enabled Yiwu merchants to obtain information on market demand in a timely manner that made such important decisions possible.

The second pattern concerns small merchants entering the manufacturing sector as a result of the decline of profit margins. The related cases are as follows.

5. A zipper manufacturer who had begun to peddle from the age of 18, purchased garment accessories from Guangdong and Fujian Provinces to sell in the periodic market in Yiwu from 1979. With a friend, he jointly opened a zipper processing workshop in 1983. Because of intense competition and declining margins, the two men opened a modern zipper factory in 1996.

6. A drinking straw manufacturer who, after experiencing peddling and business in the agricultural sector, began to operate a booth in Yiwu Market in early 1980s. He eventually discovered that all the straws in the Yiwu Market were purchased from Guangdong Province. Because of the high logistics costs, the margin was very low, so in 1994 he decided to produce the straws himself.
7. A cleaning ball manufacturer who resigned from a village-owned enterprise and started to operate a booth in Yiwu Market in 1981, for a long time purchased hats, buttons, raincoats, belts and waist pouches from Guangdong Province (Guangzhou and Swatow). He started purchasing cleaning balls from Guangzhou and Swatow from the beginning of the 1990s, but gradually realized that logistics costs were high and profit margins small. He then bought four machines from Guangdong Province and opened his own factory.

As the above cases indicate, there are two factors that caused a decline in margins. The first factor was the increasingly fierce competition in Yiwu Market. From the early 1990s, a large number of non-local merchants moved to Yiwu Market. In 1992, of 16,000 booth-keepers, local peasants accounted for 84.4 percent. In contrast, the share of non-local people was 12.5 percent, and state-owned and collective companies 3.1 percent (Zhang et al. 1993, pp. 54–9). Only five years later, however, the total number of booth-keepers had increased to 24,227, of which the share of local booth-keepers had declined to 71.4 percent, and non-local booth-keepers had increased to 28.6 percent (ZSCMC 1997, p. 23).[4] These new-comers were well educated (see Table 4.4). They also generally had their own factories[5] or had good relationships with factories in their hometown. Their purchasing costs were much cheaper. Thus, those Yiwu merchants who purchased goods from remote regions such as Guangdong or Fujian would have experienced a great decline in competitiveness if they did not own a factory.

The second factor was high logistics costs. In general, China's new factories producing daily necessities first appeared in Guangdong or Fujian Provinces, where a large number of Hong Kong- and Taiwan-funded daily necessities companies established factories. Many Yiwu merchants started their businesses by purchasing from these two areas. In the early period, the quantity of each purchase was very small. The booth-keeper could carry the commodities on trains or buses. From the early 1990s, however, purchased quantities gradually increased along with business expansion. However, the logistics system had not been well maintained up to the mid-1990s (Lu and Bai 2000), and thus the logistics costs continued to increase during that period.

The third pattern was that the merchants entered the manufacturing sector after creating a stable relationship with a comparatively powerful manufacturer.

8. A sock manufacturer who began to peddle in 1980, and who operated a booth in Yiwu Market for the sales of socks from 1983, became the general agent for a leading Taiwan shoe manufacturer in 1989. She discontinued this relationship with the manufacturer in 1993, and then opened her own sock factory.
9. A sock manufacturer who sold socks in Yiwu Market during the period 1986 to 1996, at the time subcontracted to small processors in neighboring areas. She later became the sales agent for the brand-name goods of one domestic and one Japanese manufacturer in 1997. She established her own factory with her own brand in 1999.
10. A toy manufacturer who sold toys in Yiwu Market on a consignment basis for an engineer, who not only made the toys, but also made the molds and machines himself, from 1993, jointly opened a toy factory with the engineer in 1997.
11. A leather bag manufacturer who began to sell leather bags as an agent from 1993, established her own bag factory and registered her own brand in Guangzhou in the second half of the 1990s. At the same time, she continued to sell other leather products produced by other manufacturers as a sales agent.

In the above four cases, before entering the manufacturing sector, the merchants were engaged as sales agents for a comparatively powerful maker for some time. As section 7.5 will indicate, this is also a major change in Yiwu Market since the beginning of the 1990s. In general, as the producers grew and developed their own brand-name goods, they exclusively engaged one booth-keeper in Yiwu Market for the sales of their products. They instructed the booth-keeper on quality control and the production system. At the same time, the booth-keepers themselves were required to know much more about the production processes of products in order to maintain long-term relationships with the producers. Therefore, through being engaged as sales agents, booth-keepers obtained sufficient information and skills to manage a factory.[6]

The above three patterns highlight the different factors that affect merchants when entering the manufacturing sector. In most cases, all of these factors may work together. In other words, there must be some more fundamental factors that determine the activities of merchants. We will discuss this point further in the final section.

7.3   PRODUCER–DISTRIBUTOR RELATIONSHIPS IN THE LONGWAN WRITING INSTRUMENT CLUSTER[7]

The second type of industrial cluster linked with Yiwu Market is that in which a tradition of itinerant craftsmen are found. On the one hand, SMEs in the cluster are traditionally accustomed to production, and on the other hand, most of them have experience of long-distance trade, and thus are very keen to explore new markets. A typical region with this tradition is Wenzhou (Marukawa 2001, 2004b). Chapter 5 has shown that the enterprises of at least nine Wenzhou clusters directly operated booths in Yiwu Market (Table 5.1). Here, we focus on the case of the Longwan writing instrument cluster to discuss the features of this distributor–producer relationship (see Figure 7.3).

The Longwan District of Wenzhou is one of the largest writing instrument industrial clusters in China. In 2001, there were about 200 makers of finished products in this region. Longwan's share of domestically produced writing instruments accounted for 95 percent of markers, 30 percent of propelling pencils and 30 percent of ballpoint pens. The value of the total production volume of these writing instruments reached 1.6 billion yuan, accounting for one-third of the production value of the whole of China.[8]

Longwan began to make writing instruments in the early 1980s. At that time, a small local workshop (Company A) engaged in the production of ballpoint pen bodies as a subcontractor to a collective company (Jiti Qiye). Shortly thereafter, this workshop attempted to manufacture the finished goods itself. The owner took the ballpoint pens to sell at Yiwu Market and promptly sold out. This workshop therefore employed many villagers and soon enlarged its production scale. After learning the necessary technologies from this workshop, these villagers all established their own workshops as well.

Table 7.1 contains details on four typical producers in the Longwan cluster. As this table shows, companies A, B and D had previously engaged in plastics-related business. As pen body production requires plastics processing technology, these companies were able to switch smoothly from other products to writing instruments.[9]

Initially, Yiwu Market provided a powerful marketing channel for these companies. As Table 7.1 illustrates, not only company A, but also companies C and D engaged Yiwu merchants for the sales of their products. Company C thereafter engaged merchants in other markets for the sales of its products. Company B was the last to start in the writing instrument business, but it directly operated a booth in Yiwu from the beginning. In a similar way to these companies, most of the local villagers have also

Table 7.1 Four writing instrument producers in Longwan, Wenzhou industrial cluster

Name	Products	Year of founding	No. of employees	Previous occupation	Relationship with specialized markets	Other marketing channels	Share of exports
A	Markers, ballpoint pens, propelling pencils	1985	2000	Opened a workshop for plastic production during the period 1979 to 1985.	1985–92, sold products to Yiwu booth-keepers on consignment. Currently has a direct sales outlet in Yiwu.	Participated in the Guangdong Fair in 1993. Then began to export. Has participated in international fairs in USA, Brazil, Japan and Germany since 1995.	70–80%
B	Markers	1991	300	Worked in a ceramics factory as a skilled worker. Then engaged in the button business in Qiaotou (market) for two to three years.	Directly operated a booth at Yiwu Market from 1991. Concentrated on domestic sales for some time.	Began to export to USA, Europe and Japan through participation in the international fair in Frankfurt. The local business association provided the information.	Over 90%
C	Markers, ballpoint, pens	1992	40	Worked in a mold workshop as an apprentice before taking over management of the factory in place of his father.	Sold to more than ten markets (including Yiwu) on consignment.	Introduced by the local business association, received orders from non-local merchants in the mid-1990s. Received export orders by participating in various fairs in China.	10%
D	Ballpoint pens	1989	8	Engaged in button business	100% of products sold to one booth in Yiwu Market. Yiwu merchant provided nibs.	No other marketing channels	0%

Source: Fieldwork by the author in October 2002.

established their own writing instrument factory by selling products to Yiwu Market.

Generally, villagers sold products to unspecific Yiwu Market merchants on a consignment basis (Daixiao), which is a special kind of sales agent. They had to not only collect payment after the sales, but also retrieve all the unsold goods. Furthermore, because of weak control over the manufacturing process by the merchants, the villagers had to organize the whole production process themselves, including the purchase of raw materials, ordering molds from the mold makers and so on.

This early experience affected the future upgrading pattern of Longwan companies. Being very familiar with the whole production process, these companies were very keen to increase value added in as many production stages as possible. Company A began to self-manufacture molds for pen bodies in 1998. Company B self-manufactured similar molds in 2000. Company A then succeeded in self-manufacturing pen nibs at a price below 0.5 yuan.

As an itinerant craftsmen cluster, the factories of Longwan are very keen to develop new marketing channels. Table 7.1 shows that company A participated in the Guangdong Fair (the largest international fair in China) on its own initiative and received its first export order there. Most local firms began exporting by collectively participating in international fairs, which were supported by the local trade association, established in 1996. This association also introduced new buyers to its member companies. As a result, exports from Longwan cluster rapidly increased. Exports accounted for half of the total production volume in 2001.

However, the relationship of the Longwan cluster with Yiwu Market or with other markets has not been much weakened. On the one hand, the number of small businesses in Longwan that depend on specialized markets (such as company C or company D) remains around 170. On the other hand, as exports from Yiwu Market began to expand rapidly from 2002, Longwan's leading firms tended to open booths in Yiwu Market again. According to the SMRD report (see Chapter 5), in 2004, almost all the firms with a production volume of over 5 million yuan have operated booths in Yiwu Market.

7.4 PRODUCER–DISTRIBUTOR RELATIONSHIPS IN PROCESSING CLUSTERS

7.4.1 Basic System of the Processing Business[10]

The third type of industrial cluster linked with the Yiwu Market is the underdeveloped region without any tradition of production or long-distance trade. The SMEs in these regions not only lack awareness of how to access markets, but also do not have the necessary production technologies or skills. In recent years, by engaging in the processing business for Yiwu Market, even these regions have fostered a few processing clusters.

The general flow of the processing business is as follows (see Figure 7.3). So-called organizing agents (Jingji Ren)[11] first receive an order from a booth-keeper in Yiwu Market. The agent then makes a sample himself. After confirmation from the booth-keeper, the agent receives raw materials from the booth-keeper and distributes them to the small processors. He collects the finished products himself. After a partial check of the quality of the finished goods, the agent sends the products to Yiwu Market. In general, a processor can earn more than 30 yuan per day. The annual income of an agent is from 40,000 yuan to over 100,000 yuan.

An organizing agent usually organizes no fewer than several dozen processors. The largest number may reach 5000, but because of the high organizing and monitoring costs, it is impossible for an agent to contact all the processors himself. Generally, he only manages the processors in his hometown himself. The management of processors in neighboring towns will be subcontracted to second-tier agents. At maximum, this subcontracting system extends to the fourth tier.

Table 7.2 consists of data from typical processing clusters in the neighboring regions of Yiwu. As this table shows, products from processing clusters are concentrated in the sectors where mechanization is difficult. The majority of the processors are women. As for organizing agents, the data are limited. We know only about Wucheng, where the share of women accounted for 80 percent. On the other hand, all the government officials in Jindong, Wucheng and Quzhou emphasized that because most of the local elite work in the public sector, the organizing agents are simply ordinary peasants. The features of these agents leave us with an important question: Why are those ordinary peasants able to organize large numbers of women to engage in such a large-scale processing business?

Table 7.2 also shows that the processing clusters are upgrading. As for Jindong, Wucheng and Quzhou, there are data from two points in time. By comparing these data, it is clear that the number of agents and processors greatly declined in a short time, while the total processing charges, which are net profits, increased greatly. This means that a number of agents were able to expand their business scale, while other agents and processors were eliminated through competition.

Table 7.3 shows fives cases of organizing agents. From this table, we can understand that the most important factor for organizing agents

Table 7.2 *General situation in the processing clusters surrounding Yiwu Market*

City	County	Products	Year	Number of processors	Number of organizing agents	Annual processing charges (10,000 yuan)
Jinhua	Jindong	Chinese knots, threaded beads and other daily necessities	2005	35,000 (30,000 are women)	More than 1000	12,000
			2006	39,000 (31,000 households)	More than 640	19,000
	Wucheng	Jewelry, Chinese knots, toys, greeting cards, various daily necessities	2005	50,000 (80% are women)	800	22,000
			2006	40,000	603	29,123
	Lanxi	20 types, including bedclothes, hair accessories, knitted goods, threaded beads, and so on	2003	46,305 (42,145 are women peasants; 4160 are laid-off urban women workers)	420	9218
	Panan	20 types, including hair accessories, ribbons, knitted goods, threaded beads, and so on	2004	25,830	397	616
Quzhou	Various locations	Seven types, including lanterns, knitted goods, bolt assemblies, umbrellas, threaded beads, and so on	2003	–	More than 5000	More than 20,000
			2005	280,840 (180,765 households)	2243	More than 30,000–40,000

Source: Data for Jindong and Wucheng, 2006; data for Quzhou, 2005; based on fieldwork by the author in July 2007. Other data are cited from SMRD.

Table 7.3 Organizing agents in the processing clusters surrounding Yiwu Market

No.	Sex	City	County	Products	No. of processors	Annual processing charges (10,000 yuan)	No. of Yiwu booth-keeper buyers	Other buyers	Relationship with booth-keepers**	Relationship with trading companies**
1	Female	Jinhua	Wucheng	Hair accessories	100–200 households	80	1	No other buyers	1	–
2	Male	Quzhou	Jiangshan	Threaded beads	1500	138	8, 9	No other buyers	1	–
3	Male	Jinhua	Jindong	Threaded beads	300 households or more	281	More than 10	2–3 trading companies	1 (beads), 2 (needles)	–
4	Male	Jinhua	Jindong	Stone setting	500–600 households	–	Several buyers	Several trading companies	1	2
5	Male	Quzhou	Jiangshan	Accessories	5000 households before opening a factory	200*/month when he was an agent	–	Two trading companies	–	2

Notes:
*   Maximum charge.
** Relationships with booth-keepers and trading companies.
1 = Booth-keeper provides raw materials; 2 = raw materials purchased by organizing agent.

Source: The author's fieldwork in July, 2007.

when upgrading is that they have the ability to access multiple marketing channels.

In concrete terms, the first type of marketing channel is Yiwu Market booth-keepers. As this table shows, the higher the processing charges or the number of processors, the more booth-keepers (namely the more marketing channels) the agents had contact with.

The second type of channel is trading companies. In 2005, there were 700 local and non-local trading companies clustering around Yiwu Market. Of these, 500 were from other regions. These non-local trading companies alone purchased three billion yuan's worth of goods in Yiwu Market in 2007.[12]

Trading companies sometimes purchase directly from organizing agents. When dealing with trading companies, thereby skipping over the booth-keepers, organizing agents are able to purchase raw materials from Yiwu Market themselves. Thus, they can earn higher profits. As Table 7.3 shows, among five agents, three succeeded in receiving orders directly from trading companies. Agent No. 5 eventually opened his own factory.[13]

It is clear that Yiwu Market, as an open distribution system with high accessibility, enabled the organizing agents to multiply their marketing channels. Yiwu Market also enabled them to purchase raw materials themselves. However, since these agents lack awareness of how to access the market, why are they so keen to multiply their marketing channels? How did they gain the trust of the booth-keepers?

7.4.2   The Role of Local Government in Processing Cluster Formation[14]

A critical factor in answering the above questions is the local government. As mentioned in Chapter 4, the Yiwu government formulated a policy named "Shichang Dai Baicun, Baicun Lian Wanhu" [The market links with hundreds of villages, villages link with thousands of households] to help SMEs in underdeveloped regions form links with Yiwu. Simultaneously, the local governments of each processing cluster also took measures to stimulate the processing business. In this subsection, we examine the role of local governments in processing clusters, using the case of Wucheng District, where processing charges are the highest. The Wucheng government took several measures to facilitate the processing business.

First, in order to stimulate local peasants to engage in the processing business, all processing agents and processors were permitted to omit registration as an enterprise. This measure exempted them from any burden of tax or fees.

Second, the Wucheng government established a specific department office for the processing business. This office asked the Wucheng Women's Federation to help organizing agents to mobilize women peasants for engagement in the processing business.[15] It also held various training courses in each town to teach knowledge and skills concerning law and contracts, trading, PC operation and Internet use. All these courses were free and the participants were even paid participant fees. By 2005, 580 agents had participated in these training courses.

Third, the Wucheng government established a processing office in Yiwu, which helps local agents to receive processing orders. Up to 2006, this office had helped local agents receive orders from 556 booth-keepers and 42 trading companies. These trading companies were not only from Yiwu, but also from Ningbo, Shanghai and Beijing. The processing office also helped to raise the credibility of organizing agents. Before the establishment of this office, there were only 60 to 70 agents in Wucheng. Various business difficulties, such as non-payment of processing charges or non-delivery of goods occurred frequently, but since agents and booth-keepers have been able to deliver goods and settle accounts at this office, difficulties have decreased. Furthermore, the staff in this office gave various kinds of training to the agents. They taught organizing agents the importance of credibility and how to organize the processing business in a more efficient way, and as a result of these activities the number of organizing agents in Wucheng increased to 800 in 2005 (see Table 7.2).

According to the director of this office, because of her experience she was invited to Lishui, Changan, Ningbo and Lanxi in Zhejiang Province, Shangrao in Jiangxi Province, and to Anhui Province to teach processing business stimulation know-how.[16] This contributed to expanding the processing business in Yiwu Market's neighboring areas.

7.5 PRODUCER–DISTRIBUTOR RELATIONSHIPS SHIFT TOWARDS A PURE MARKET PLATFORM MODE

This section summarizes the producer–distributor relationships observed between Yiwu Market booth-keepers and the producers in industrial clusters through the use of macro data. In concrete terms, there are four major types of these relationships.

The first type is direct sales, namely, the producers directly operate a booth in the market for selling their own goods. This is undoubtedly a typical market platform mode producer–distributor relationship. As the three cases above illustrate, an increasing number of producers have come

Table 7.4   Transformation process of producer–distributor relationships in Yiwu Market

Year	No. of booth-keepers	Share of direct sales by Yiwu producers (%)	Share of direct sales by non-Yiwu producers (%)	Share of sales agents** (%)	Share of other relationships*** (%)
1992	16,000	20	0	Less than 30	More than 50
1997	24,277	18.6	7.1	53.6	20.7
2007	58,000*	46		54	

Notes:
*   Total booth number. In the specialized market, one booth may be shared by several booth-keepers or one booth-keeper may own several booths.
**   There is a further business relationship named *Jingxiao* in Yiwu Market. In this relationship, the merchants buy the products and sell them, taking the risks upon themselves. However, in Yiwu Market, the share of *Jingxiao* appears to be very small. It was reported in 1997 that it was a mere 3.3% (ZSCMC 1997, p. 23). Following that year, *Jingxiao* and sales agents are generally reported as a combined figure. This powerfully suggested the trend that Yiwu Market is transforming into a pure market platform.
***   The data for 1992 and 1997 in "Other relationships" are the share of pure buying and selling. The data for 2007 include pure buying and selling and processing relationships.

Sources: 1992: Zhang et al. (1993, pp. 54–9); 1997: ZSCMC (1997, p. 23); 2007: Author interview with a manager of the ZCCC group in November, 2008.

to directly operate booths in Yiwu Market. They are from both Yiwu and other clusters.

Table 7.4 demonstrates this point. Between 1992 and 2007, the share of direct sales in Yiwu increased from 20 percent to 46 percent. Among the new entrants into Yiwu Market, the number of producers is much larger than the number of merchants. This suggests that producers will become the majority group in Yiwu Market in the near future.

The second type is the simple buying and selling relationship. In a merchant mode producer–distributor relationship, the booth-keepers generally purchase goods from unspecific factories under the typical arm's-length relationships (Schmitz 2006a, 2006b).[17] Many Yiwu merchants created this kind of relationship with their suppliers in the 1980s.

The third type is the sales agent. In this case, the booth-keepers sell products manufactured by several specific producers, but are not required to buy the products. This can therefore be regarded as a variant of the market platform mode producer–distributor relationship. In the incipient phase, the producers generally sell products to unspecific booth-keepers on a consignment basis. As the producers grow and develop their own brand-name goods, they shift to the exclusive engagement of one sales agent for their products. In both cases, the producers take all the sales risks.

As the cases of Yiwu and Longwan illustrate, instead of simply buying and selling, relationships with sales agents that are more stable and market-platform oriented have constantly increased in Yiwu Market. Table 7.4 reveals this point. Between 1992 and 1997, the share of simple buying and selling in Yiwu Market decreased sharply from 50 percent to 20.7 percent. In its place, the share of sales agents increased from 30 percent to 53.6 percent.

These two cases, however, also indicate that this stable relationship never resulted in a clear-cut and rigid division of labor between produc-ers and merchants. Needless to say, this is because, on the one hand, the producers can obtain access to multiple marketing channels through Yiwu Market, and on the other hand, the merchants are forced to enter the manufacturing sector because of various factors inherent in the Yiwu Market system.[18]

The fourth type is the above-mentioned processing relationship. Booth-keepers provide materials to small organizing agents and buy the finished goods from them. This is a standard merchant mode producer–distributor relationship. The case study has clearly shown that even in this relation-ship, supported by the local government, the small organizing agents are able to multiply their marketing channels. Some agents eventually open their own factories.

7.6   WHY DID YIWU MARKET BECOME A MARKET PLATFORM? A MORE DEEP-ROOTED DISCUSSION

The above sections have described in detail the changes in producer–distributor relationships in Yiwu Market, and analyzed various factors that affected these changes (the development of Yiwu Market, the tradi-tion of long-distance trade, the role of local government). In this section, we further summarize these factors from a more deep-rooted perspective. In the author's opinion, it is China's unique land use system that is the most fundamental.

Studies on Bazr-e Bozorg in Iran (Iwasaki 2002) and Dongdaemun Market in South Korea (Kim and Abe 2002) have both suggested that it is difficult for the producers to have their own booths in the markets. These case studies also mentioned, either overtly or implicitly, that further devel-opment of the markets was hindered to some extent by the limited space available in large cities or the complicated system of commercial real estate use. Although each country may have its own institutional problems, a common point shared here is that land in these countries is all owned by the private sector.

In contrast, as a socialist country in which the agrarian revolution has been carried out, in China land is owned by the public sector and only usage rights are allowed to be transacted. In just this institutional environment, the Yiwu government was able to adjust flexibly the number of booths in line with the increase in the number of sellers in the market; and as the sole owner of Yiwu Market, has been capable of working out a number of measures to maintain flexibility in transactions of the usage rights of the market booths (see Chapter 4, subsection 4.4.1). The result is that, thus far, Yiwu Market has been able to exhibit a strong indirect network effect.

This is extremely important for the producer–distributor relationships. For the Yiwu merchants, simply because of the indirect network effect, a large number of new booth-keepers have been attracted to operate booths in Yiwu, which has intensified the competition between booths. In addition, because of the indirect network effect, an increasing number of buyers have tended to come to Yiwu for purchasing, which has not only brought about a better expectation for the Yiwu merchants regarding market expansion, but also attracted a large number of comparatively powerful producers to engage Yiwu Market booth-keepers for the sales of their products. As section 7.2 pointed out, all these factors have been crucial in encouraging Yiwu merchants to enter the manufacturing sector.

For the producers, the increasing number of booths multiplied their marketing channels. On the one hand, it gave them increased opportunities to make contact with more merchants. On the other hand, the increase in the number of booths gave producers more opportunities to operate market booths themselves, thus obtaining their own marketing means.

NOTES

1. It is interesting to note that, of the clusters linked to Yiwu Market, no clusters that had a tradition of production only were found to be represented. This type of cluster will be discussed in the case of Changshu apparel cluster.
2. Most of the jewelry is low-cost.
3. Information on the major industries in 2007 is based on an author interview with an official of the Yiwu Economic Development Bureau in September 2007. He emphasized that Yiwu's producers changed the content of their business frequently, in accordance with changes in market demand.
4. The majority of the new entrants were from other locations in Zhejiang Province. Of 24,227 booth-keepers, the proportion was 23.3 percent (ZSCMC 1997, p. 23).

Currently, non-Yiwu merchants command an absolute majority in Yiwu Market. In 2008, of 58,000 booths, the share of Yiwu people had decreased to a mere one-third of the total (Xinhua Net Zhejiang Channel, 9 July 2008, accessed 14 January 2009).

5. Between 1992 and 1997, more than 1700 non-Yiwu factories began to sell products directly in Yiwu Market (calculated based on data from ZSCMC 1997, p. 23).

6. Merchant No. 11 opened her factories in Guangzhou. This is because Guangzhou is the largest leather bag cluster in China. There are also various daily necessities industrial clusters around Guangzhou. After the logistics system was improved from the second half of the 1990s, products manufactured in Guangzhou for sale in Yiwu have become a common phenomenon for Yiwu merchants (author interview with an official of the Yiwu government in November 2008).

7. This section is a revised version of Ding (2008b, section 3).

8. Basic information on the Longwan cluster in this section is based on the author's fieldwork in October 2002.

9. This is a characteristic feature of itinerant craftsmen. They are very sensitive to market conditions, while being familiar with production activities as well. Thus, itinerant craftsmen clusters can easily switch or diversify business. Marukawa (2001, 2004b) gives an interesting analysis of this point.

10. This subsection is based on the author's fieldwork in July 2007.

11. A completely different type of organizing agent has obviously been observed in Japan's industrialization. See Takeuchi (1991).

12. CAWA (23 January 2007, accessed 10 February 2007).

13. Another possible channel is to directly open a booth in Yiwu Market. Agent No. 3 said he was going to buy half a booth at Yiwu Market in the second half of 2007.

14. This subsection is a revised version of Ding (2007b, section 3). Information concerning Wucheng Processing Business is mainly based on an author interview with the director of this office in September, 2006.

15. Information concerning the Women's Federation is partially based on an author interview with an official of this organization in July 2007.

16. This is an interesting facet of modern China's administration system. While interregional competition is very intense, regional communications are also very often stimulated by this system.

17. In the incipient stage, the merchant mode producer–distributors are generally unspecified (see the case of the apparel cluster in Ho Chi Minh City). After entering the upgraded stage, however, most of the producer–distributor relationships within the merchant mode will become specified (see the case of Dongdaemun Market in Seoul, South Korea).

18. Knorringa (1999), Tewari (1999), Bazan and Navas-Aleman (2004), and Schmitz (2006b, especially section 3.3) also emphasize that multiple marketing channels are important for upgrading SMEs. The difference between these studies and mine is that I have focused more on the *possibilities* of having multiple channels. This is to say, even if no transaction occurred, the possibilities of having multiple channels would affect the growth path of the small producers.

8. Local government and inter-platform competition

Source: The author.

Figure 8.1   Zhaoshang Market in Changshu apparel cluster

8.1   INTRODUCTION[1]

Chapters 8, 9 and 10 clarify the competition mechanism and the logic of upgrading in a market platform mode cluster by presenting a case study of China Changshu Zhaoshang City (Zhaoshang City). Changshu is one of the largest domestic-market-oriented apparel clusters and Zhaoshang City is the largest specialized apparel market in China. Zhaoshang City has grown in a mere 30 years from a street market into a huge specialized apparel market with 28,000 booths and a transaction volume of 30.6

billion yuan. Accompanying this expansion, the number of sewing factories in Changshu increased from 160 to more than 5000. Some national level brands have made their appearance from among these factories. Careful investigation of such a market will be extremely suggestive to a study of the experiences of specialized market.

Chapter 8 first focuses on the situation in inter-cluster competition. As has been shown in Chapter 2, in the market platform mode, inter-cluster competition is essentially competition between various platforms (marketplaces). As platform managers, the efforts of local governments to a large extent determine the result of the competition. This chapter thus makes an intensive and detailed study of the role of the Changshu government.

8.2 THE UNIQUE INDUSTRIAL CLUSTER FORMATION IN CHANGSHU

Changshu is a county-level city under the administration of Suzhou, Jiangsu Province, with a population of about 1.84 million. In 2007, Changshu's GDP amounted to 21.851 billion yuan. Although it is located in the South Jiangsu Area, Changshu's industrial development has shown quite different features from the well-known South Jiangsu model, which is a typical rural industrialization model in China from the 1980s, characterized by a large presence of township and village enterprises (TVEs) and strong support from local governments (Fei and Luo 1988).

First, industrialization in Changshu has been largely characterized by cluster formation in which numerous private SMEs are the main actors. The self-employed enterprises had already become a large presence in Changshu by the mid-1990s (Table 8.1). Thereafter, while self-employed enterprises continued to increase, the number of private enterprises (which are of a larger business scale) increased at a more rapid pace.[2] The average registered capital of these two types of enterprises showed a great increase between 1996 and 2002, while the average scale of employment showed almost no change (Table 8.1). This suggests that private small businesses not only quantitatively expanded, but also qualitatively upgraded.

Second, because of the poor tradition of long-distance trade, most enterprises in the South Jiangsu area started as subcontract factories to state-owned enterprises in the urban areas, engaging in the production of intermediate goods. In contrast, the apparel industry, as a daily consumer goods industry, has shown a high degree of development in Changshu. In

Table 8.1   Private enterprises and self-employed enterprises in Changshu

Year	Private enterprises			Self-employed enterprises		
	No. of enterprises	No. of employees	Registered capital (10,000 yuan)	No. of enterprises	No. of employees	Registered capital (10,000 yuan)
1996	805	8998	21,200	29,126	49,360	21,860
1997	1846	16,810	45,600	31,686	52,300	42,500
1998	2480	21,500	80,600	33,962	55,278	59,396
1999	2767	34,585	119,220	35,500	60,500	66,000
2000	3567	35,928	180,080	39,059	70,077	75,867
2001	6445	58,602	485,190	44,660	71,731	92,593
2002	7691	97,394	640,597	49,643	81,864	139,313

Note: Xu Yuanming organized the data provided by Changshu AIC and Zhaoshang City Managing Committee in Xu (2002). This is one output of Jiangsu Academy of Social Science's research project entitled "Self-employed Enterprises and Private Enterprises in Changshu."

Source: Xu (2002).

2006, its total sales increased to over 60 billion yuan and the number of enterprises passed the 5000 mark. Of these, 90 percent were engaged in the production of menswear.[3]

8.3   CHINA CHANGSHU ZHAOSHANG CITY

The above-mentioned unique, private SME-led industrial cluster dynamics resulted from the development of a huge specialized apparel market, Zhaoshang City. As Table 8.2 shows, among Changshu's self-employed enterprises, more than 10,000 are concentrated in the Zhaoshang City area, despite the fact that it had an area of only 1.1 square kilometers in 2001. From this fact alone, we can understand the large influence of Zhaoshang City on local industry. The development history of this market is as follows.[4]

Changshu peasants historically engaged in the production of blue cloth, lace making and weaving as sidelines. Commune-owned sewing factories and small sewing processors had existed even in the era of the planned economy. In 1985, there were 167 sewing factories (of these 165 were TVEs) and 6000 sewing processor households in Changshu (JEYBEC 1987, pp. 40–42, VII). Because there was no tradition of long-distance trade, the enterprises and peasants concerned had to receive processing

Table 8.2   Private enterprises and self-employed enterprises in Zhaoshang City area

Year	Private enterprises	Self-employed enterprises
1996	58	13,979
1997	68	15,000
1998	82	14,206
1999	112	13,863
2001	140	14,487

Sources: Data for 1996 and 1997 are from YTCEC (2000, p. 322); data for 1998, 1999 and 2001 are from CLCEC (1999, 2000, 2002).

orders from state-owned factories, department stores, or the supply and marketing cooperatives, and so were extremely lacking in marketing channels.

In these circumstances, a number of small merchants and small producers began to crowd around the Changshu bus terminal from 1984. At first, small merchants purchased garments from small apparel TVEs or processors and sold them in front of the terminal. Gradually, some small processors came to sell apparel themselves. The number of traders increased dramatically. A street market with a length of several hundred meters soon appeared in front of the bus terminal. This market, however, often caused traffic congestion and environmental problems (litter and market refuse) around the terminal, which caused strong dissatisfaction among the neighboring residents.

In order to respond to this situation, Changshu government sounded out the opinion of the local Qinnan Town (where the bus terminal is located) government. It agreed readily, and arranged for the town-owned "Qinnan Town Multiple Businesses Service Company" (QMSC) to take charge of this market. In anticipation of doing business in a big way, the new market was named "Zhaoshang Market." Because of a land allocation problem, QMSC and Hujing Village, where the new market was to be located, jointly established a Zhaoshang Market Managing Company (ZMMC).[5]

The construction of Zhaoshang Market started in 1985, but as ZMMC felt uneasy about the management of the market, it was designed as a small wholesale market with only 404 booths. Just as they feared, despite the passing of two months, the small merchants refused to enter the formal market and Zhaoshang Market was in a very sorry plight. In order to improve this situation, the local public sector began active intervention with a series of measures. Following this, transactions in Zhaoshang

Table 8.3   Basic data for Zhaoshang Market

Year	Number of booths	Transaction volume (10,000 yuan)	Tax revenue (10,000 yuan)
1985	400	2500	46
1986	1400	6300	215
1987	2644	9258	309
1988	4525	12,000	460
1989	4700	20,100	1022
1990	5300	25,000	1348
1991	6650	35,000	1800
1992	7010	150,000	2241
1993	8150	200,000	2500
1994	9626	350,000	3700
1995	8672	420,000	4500
1996	10,000	700,000	5000
1997	8153	800,000	–
1998	7600	750,000	–
1999	8315	787,000	–

Sources: Data for "Tax revenue" are from the preprint of YTCEC (2000), which includes some data not published in the formal YTCEC (2000); other data are from YTCEC (2000, p. 305).

Market quickly flourished, and a large number of apparel enterprises inside and outside Changshu began to take up booths. Buyers from almost all provinces of China rushed in and, as a result, Zhaoshang Market soon transformed into a large specialized market. As Table 8.3 shows, the transaction volume and taxes levied in Zhaoshang Market showed a sharp increase right from the beginning. It is interesting that intervention by the public sector could bring about such an immediate effect. The relations between market development and the intervention of local government will be thoroughly investigated in the following sections.

In 1992, the Changshu government formulated the "General Plan of Jiangsu Changshu Zhaoshang City." It was determined to develop the Zhaoshang Market and its surrounding area of 3.71 square kilometers as a commercial area with wholesale activities as its main function. This area is named "Zhaoshang City."[6] Following that, various government departments and enterprises in Changshu established a large number of submarkets in the Zhaoshang City area. After several reorganizations and integrations, the number of submarkets in Zhaoshang City amounted to 35 in 2006. Among the 31 submarkets for which data are available, 18 specialize in apparel, two in fabrics, two in apparel accessories, one in sewing machines, two in other textile products, and six in other sectors.[7] We can observe a clear apparel value chain concentrated on Zhaoshang City. Chapter 10 will indicate that this is a distinct feature of the specialized-market-based cluster as compared to other types.

Along with the increase in submarkets, the transactions of Zhaoshang City expanded by leaps and bounds with the total booth number reaching 10,000 in 1992. It quickly increased to 20,000 in 1995 and is currently around 28,000. The transaction volume of Zhaoshang City increased much more rapidly than the number of booths. Between 1992 and 2006, it increased from 1.5 billion yuan to 30.6 billion yuan, expanding over 20 times. This suggests that not only did the total transaction volume increase, but also that the average business scale of each booth greatly increased. We will explain this point with more decisive data in Chapter 9.

8.4   THE MANAGEMENT SYSTEM OF ZHAOSHANG MARKET[8]

Many things are difficult before they become easy. In the following sections, we will focus on the formation process of Zhaoshang City, namely, the development trajectory of Zhaoshang Market before 1992. In this section, we first introduce the management system of Zhaoshang Market. This consists of three levels, the first of which is the Zhaoshang Market Board of Directors (Zhaoshangchang Dongshihui). The board's establishment process was as follows. Initially, the AIC, the Tax Bureau the Police Bureau and the Traffic Bureau set up branches in Zhaoshang Market as soon as it was opened. There were also a few government departments that participated in the management of Zhaoshang Market, though they did not have branches there.[9] After the market opened, however, a few difficult problems gradually became apparent, such as the need to clamp down on booth-keepers who had not received permission to trade in the market, and the need for fund-raising to enable further construction. All these problems required cooperation between various government departments.

The vice-mayor of Changshu had taken charge of the coordination with each of these departments in order to cope with the problems. At the end of 1985, the Changshu government organized the representatives of the AIC, the Tax Bureau, the Police Bureau, Qinnan Town, Hujing Village and the peasants to establish the Zhaoshang Market Board of Directors.[10] The vice-mayor was the chair of this board. He called the board members together for a meeting every three months to discuss the operations of Zhaoshang Market.[11] However, the board did not include all the government departments related to Zhaoshang Market. Thus, when important decision-making or some other difficult problem occurred, the vice-mayor sometimes called related government departments and held temporary coordination meetings.

The second level of this system is Zhaoshang Market Managing Company (ZMMC), which was in charge of the daily management and the real estate management of the market. This is very different from Yiwu Market, where the AIC exercised a larger initiative in market management.

As a typical TVE, ZMMC had dual attributes. On the one hand, in order to generate profits in addition to those from the market management business, ZMMC engaged in various businesses such as the restaurant and hotel business, and parking. The "General Manager Responsibility System," a famous management system intended to activate state-owned enterprises in 1980s, was also introduced into this company.[12]

On the other hand, the management of ZMMC was subject to a great deal of intervention from local government. The secretary of Qinnan Town's Communist Party Committee doubled as the secretary of the Zhaoshang Market Communist Party during the period 1985 to 1992. Affected by Communist Party traditions, this secretary asked Zhaoshang Market to formulate the "Changshu Zhaoshang Market Management Provisions" in 1986. These provisions included 33 items in ten articles. Many items concerning business morality, such as quality control, tax payment, legal compliance, family planning, and so on were set out in detail in the provisions. Naturally, since the head of the town government occupied the post, the coordination with various government departments came to be smoother than previously.

The third level of this management system was the self-management network, composed of booth-keepers. ZMMC established this network in 1987 in order to obtain full implementation of its policies. In this network, ZMMC organized the booth-keepers of every business zone of Zhaoshang Market into several groups. The booth-keepers themselves served in all the posts of zone leader and group leader. In 1991, there were five business zones and 146 groups in the market. Every group leader was in charge of 15 to 20 booths. While serving as a zone leader or group leader, the booth-keeper enjoyed a concessionary discount of 50 percent of the booth rent. Moreover, the post itself lent high credibility to the booth, and thus it was attractive for booth-keepers to become leaders in this network.

8.5   CREATING SELLERS[13]

In the above management system, Zhaoshang Market overcame various difficulties and the transaction scale soon expanded. As for the role of this system in the development of Zhaoshang Market, sections 8.5, 8.6 and 8.7 will focus on (1) the creation of sellers; (2) real estate management; and (3) the reduction of transaction costs, respectively.

8.5.1 Crisis in the Initial Stage

Even after the formal Zhaoshang Market was opened, since they had been used to peddling, and since booth-keepers in the market had to pay various fees and taxes, many small merchants hesitated about entering the market. Some of the booth-keepers left the formal market and returned to street selling. Many government departments were also despondent as they were not able to levy sufficient fees and taxes. As a result, Zhaoshang Market fell into crisis after only two months had passed since its establishment.

To improve this situation, ZMMC first petitioned the Qinnan Town government, then through this government, they further petitioned the Changshu government. These governments soon dealt with this problem. The Communist Party Committee of Qinnan Town invited the chief tax officer, the financial bureau, the police and the AIC to inspect the markets in Changzhou, and Danyang in Jiangsu Province. The vice-secretary of Changshu Communist Party Committee then led the staff of Qinnan Town and 11 officials of various government departments on an inspection tour of Wenzhou, where the specialized market had first appeared. Moreover, members of the Changshu Communist Party Committee and officials of ZMMC went to Liaoning, Hebei, Sichuan, Anhui, Henan, Zhejiang, Beijing and Tianjin to inspect more than 20 markets (Xia 1992).

After the above inspection visits, a guideline for developing Zhaoshang Market was drawn up. The first part dealt with how departments related to Zhaoshang Market would begin to jointly cope with the crisis on hand. Regarding economic means, the AIC levied an approximately 1.2 yuan/day AIC fee from booth-keepers inside Zhaoshang Market and 3 yuan/day from the small merchants outside the market. The Tax Bureau levied a 3 percent tax from the booths inside the market, while collecting a much higher tax from the merchants outside.[14] ZMMC set the booth rent in Zhaoshang Market at the very low level of 0.5 yuan/day. On the other hand, ZMMC and the police went to the street market and attempted to coerce the merchants to leave several times. Under this carrot-and-stick policy, the street market disappeared at the end of 1985.

8.5.2 Inviting Non-Local Sellers

After this crisis had been overcome, as part of the above guideline, ZMMC began to invite non-local sellers. They first publicized information

Table 8.4   Changshu and non-Changshu booths in Zhaoshang Market

Year	No. of booths	No. of Changshu booths	No. of non-Changshu booths
1989	4500	3420	1080
1990	5300	3344	1956
1991	6000	2340	3660

Source: Xia (1992).

concerning Zhaoshang Market through various newspapers and the TV. The mayor of Changshu and the general manager of ZMMC personally traveled to Wenzhou, Yiwu and other cities in Zhejiang Province, where the traditions of long-distance trade were well preserved and specialized markets had appeared and developed earliest. They went directly to the markets and circulated leaflets about Zhaoshang Market to booth-keepers. These leaflets contained clear information on a range of preferential treatments concerning taxes and booth rents in Zhaoshang Market (see subsection 8.5.3).

As a result, non-local merchants began to take up booths in Zhaoshang Market from the third month after the market opened. Their number gradually increased, such that in 1991, the number of non-local booth-keepers exceeded the number of local Changshu booth-keepers, accounting for 60 percent of the total number of booth-keepers in the market (Table 8.4). The largest number of these booth-keepers were from Zhejiang Province.

However, these Zhejiang merchants have extremely high mobility. Once a new market appeared and provided better preferential treatments, they quickly relocated their booths to these rival markets. According to Xia (1992), during only the period from July to August 1991, 1600 booth-keepers moved to markets in other regions. This represented more than one-fourth of the total number of booths. Xia expressed this situation with a sigh of emotion, writing, "The self-employed enterprises were 'like babies who think that everyone who feeds them with milk is their mother (Younai Bianshi Niang).' Like the migratory birds, they are always moving around, searching for markets with higher profits."

ZMMC took various specific measures to encourage non-local merchants to take root in Changshu. For example, there were two elementary schools and one kindergarten in Qinnan Town and ZMMC asked these schools to accept the children of non-local booth-keepers. In the social background of the 1980s, when non-local children were strictly prohibited from attending local primary schools, this was almost impossible in other regions. Moreover, this company established a karaoke and game center in 1990, the first of its kind in Changshu. The purpose was to create a sound environment to avoid gambling and prostitution by non-local booth-keepers, who generally have only a low educational background (see Chapter 9). Moreover, Zhaoshang Market appointed a large number of non-local merchants as leaders of the self-management network. It was hoped that they would help efficiently manage their Landsmann booth-keepers. As shown in Chapter 9, these non-local merchants gradually entered the manufacturing sector and became leading actors in the upgrading of the Changshu apparel cluster.

8.5.3 Setting Low Taxes and Fees to Attract Non-Local Sellers

Among the various measures for attracting non-local sellers, the setting of low taxes and fees deserves particular attention. Booth-keepers in Zhaoshang Market have to pay taxes and fees to the members of the above management system. Table 8.5 contains information on these. The booth rent is paid to ZMMC since it is the owner of the market. Taxes are paid to the government. Various fees, such as the AIC fee[15] are paid to government departments.

We first discuss the methods of levying these taxes and fees. From the very beginning, there was no receipt made out for each deal in Zhaoshang Market. As a result, when transactions expanded it became extremely difficult to judge the real amounts of business taking place. Zhaoshang Market thus applied Zhejiang's experience to this situation.[16] As Table 8.5 indicates, just as in the case of Yiwu Market, taxes were levied as a lump tax. The AIC fee was also levied as a fixed amount.

Concrete information on the levying method for the lump tax has been obtained. In general, the group leader of the self-management network first estimated the transaction volume. The staff of the tax bureau then reconfirmed the figure and levied the tax.[17] Because transaction volumes changed with on-season and off-season business fluctuations, group leaders re-estimated this transaction volume every three months.

Now we turn to a discussion of the main burdens of booth-keepers in Zhaoshang Market. Data for the AIC fee, taxes and booth rents are available. As Table 8.6 illustrates, booth rents constantly increased between 1985 and 1992. As emphasized in Chapter 4, because of the *physicality* of the platform, booth rents reflected the relationship of supply and demand within Zhaoshang Market. In contrast, the real amounts of taxes and AIC fees were much smaller than the standard amount. This is because

Table 8.5   Tax and fee burden on booth-keepers in Zhaoshang Market

Type	Collector	Period	Levying method
Booth rent	Zhaoshang Market	During the period before long-term booth use rights were granted	0.5 yuan/day
		After 1986, when long-term booth use rights were granted	Annual rent determined by supply and demand
Tax	Tax Bureau	Before 1986	Business tax was 3% of transaction volume; product tax was 5% of transaction volume. The tax was levied on every deal
		After 1987	Monthly lump tax
AIC fee	AIC	Before 1986	0.5%–1.5% of total transaction volume. Levied on every deal
		After 1987	Monthly fixed sum
Other fees	25 government departments (Traffic, QTS, Police, etc.)	–	Levied according to the requirements of government departments

Sources: YTCEC (2000, p. 325) and author interviews with Gu Bangjun in August and December 2001.

Zhaoshang Market had to provide much better incentives for attracting booth-keepers from other markets as there was no tradition of long-distant trade, and local people thus lacked awareness of how to access markets.

The comparison between Yiwu Market and Zhaoshang Market more clearly reveals this point. As Table 8.7 shows, compared to the gap in per booth transaction volume between these two markets, the gap in tax levied per booth is far larger. As for the share of tax in total transaction volume, the figure for Zhaoshang Market basically amounts to a mere one-third of that of Yiwu Market. From these data, we can easily imagine how intense competition between marketplaces in China's specialized market system was during this period.

Table 8.6   Burden rate of booth-keepers in Zhaoshang Market

Year	Real AIC fee per booth (yuan)	Standard AIC fee per booth (yuan)	Burden rate (%)	Real tax per booth (yuan)	Standard tax per booth (yuan)	Burden rate (%)	Booth rent per booth (yuan)
1985	255	625	40	1150	5000	23	155
1986	371	450	83	1536	3600	43	207
1987	227	320	71	1169	2800	42	294
1988	137	214	63	1017	2120	48	384
1989	260	375	71	2174	3424	63	553
1990	364	455	77	2543	3776	67	723
1991	398	487	83	2707	4208	63	716

Note: The standard AIC fee was calculated as 1% of the transaction volume of each booth. Standard tax was calculated as 3% of transaction volume as business tax and 5% of transaction volume as product tax. Income tax data are not included as the tax rate varies with income. The burden rate is real AIC fee and real taxes divided by the standard amounts.

Source: Calculated based on data from YTCEC (2000, preprint).

Another interesting fact derived from Table 8.7 is that all the merchants and producers were welcomed by Zhaoshang Market regardless of whether their business scale was large or small. Thus, per booth transaction volume of the market rapidly declined throughout the 1980s. Since total transaction volume constantly increased, however, the ZMMC and other related government departments kept their enthusiasm regarding the development of Zhaoshang Market.

8.6   MANAGING THE REAL ESTATE OF ZHAOSHANG MARKET

8.6.1   Extending Zhaoshang Market

In order to accommodate the large numbers of local and non-local booth-keepers, Zhaoshang Market has been extended several times. As Table 8.8 shows, up until 1989, Zhaoshang Market was extended three times at a cost of 11.8 million yuan. It was financially difficult for Qinnan Town to bear these large costs from their own funds, and thus ZMMC raised funds in the following ways.[18]

First, ZMMC attempted to mobilize funds from booth-keepers. According to Xia (1992), they collected a total of 6.16 million yuan from

Table 8.7 Comparison of transaction volume and tax for Zhaoshang Market and Yiwu Market

Year	Transaction volume/booth (10,000 yuan)			Tax/booth (yuan)			Share of tax in transaction volume	
	Zhaoshang	Yiwu	Zhaoshang/ Yiwu (%)	Zhaoshang	Yiwu	Zhaoshang/ Yiwu (%)	Zhaoshang (%)	Yiwu (%)
1985	6.25	1.76	355	184	474	39	0.29	2.7
1986	4.5	1.82	247	341	515	66	0.75	2.8
1987	3.6	3.57	101	333	1036	32	0.93	2.9
1988	2.65	4.32	61	383	1608	24	1.44	3.7
1989	4.28	4.64	92	508	1770	29	1.19	3.8
1990	4.72	6.81	69	539	2413	22	1.14	3.5
1991	5.26	11.61	45	514	3371	15	0.98	2.9

Sources: Data for Zhaoshang as in Table 8.3; data for Yiwu as in Table 4.6.

Table 8.8   *Investments and profits in Zhaoshang Market, and the
government revenue of Qinnan Town*

Year	Investments for the extension of Zhaoshang Market (10,000 yuan)	Profits of Zhaoshang Market (10,000 yuan)	Government revenue of Qinnan Town (10,000 yuan)
1985	50	16.4	–
1986	0	61	114.71
1987	130	90.4	210.52
1988	450	210	174.73
1989	550	321	294.03
1990	0	345	317.52
1991	0	650	468.58
1992	1650	850	–

Sources: Investment data are from YTCEC (2000, Preprint); government revenue data are from YTCEC (2000, p. 406).

booth-keepers up to 1990. This accounted for 60 percent of the total investment of 10.48 million yuan. As 1100 booth-keepers invested in Zhaoshang Market, this accounted for 22 percent of the total number of booths.[19] In order to obtain funds from booth-keepers, ZMMC determined that the booth-keepers who invested in the extension project of the market would not only acquire booth use rights, but would also enjoy exemption from booth rent for several years. In 1986, booth-keepers who invested 500 yuan in the market obtained booth use rights and were exempted from paying booth rent for the first year. In the 1989 extension project, booth-keepers who invested 3000 yuan were exempted from paying booth rent for the following three years.[20]

On the other hand, the Changshu government made an appeal to various government departments to support the Zhaoshang Market extension project. The AIC and the Tax Bureau, as members of the Zhaoshang Market Board, invested in the market. The remaining funds were made available to ZMMC through a bank loan.

8.6.2   Determining Booth Use Rights

In Zhaoshang Market, the ownership of booths was held by ZMMC, and the use rights of the booths were held by the booth-keepers themselves. At first, while there were still a few vacant booths in the market, booth-keepers were able to obtain the use rights of a booth the same day, as long as they registered with the AIC. However, from the end of 1985, an increasing number of merchants or producers came hoping to start up business in Zhaoshang Market, and their number soon exceeded the number of booths available. Consequently, almost every day, arguments concerning booth use rights were breaking out between small merchants or producers. If this situation had been left to deteriorate, it would have made it impossible for the booth-keepers to continue stable businesses in the market. Thus, in cooperation with the AIC, ZMMC worked out a plan to determine the long-term booth use rights. According to this plan, booth-keepers were first required to register with the AIC. They then had to sign a contract with ZMMC to obtain a "certificate of booth-keeping" (permission to use a booth). After payment of one year's booth rent, they could then obtain the booth use rights.

Gradually, a large number of non-local booth-keepers began to crowd into Zhaoshang Market. Although the market was extended several times, the supply of booths was not able to meet the great demand. Consequently, non-local booth-keepers came to obtain booth use rights in various informal ways. Some made advances to the staff of ZMMC, and some subleased or transferred booth use rights privately. Booth use rights transactions became a speculative business in Zhaoshang Market. Conflicts between existing booth-keepers and newcomers, local merchants and non-local merchants intensified accordingly. However, up until 1994, when the booth use rights auctions began, ZMMC had not established an appropriate system for the allocation of booth use rights.

8.7   REDUCING TRANSACTION COSTS

Like Yiwu Market, Zhaoshang Market also took various measures to reduce endogenous and exogenous transaction costs in order to maintain the business environment and thus retain the highly mobile booth-keepers. As for the former, we discuss credibility-related issues. For the latter, we discuss issues related to information.

8.7.1   Establishing Credibility

In the case of Yiwu, merchants there simultaneously existed as both the buyers and the sellers at the initial stage. Because of their common geographical origin, they were readily able to establish trust with one another. In contrast, even at the initial stage, most of the buyers and sellers in Zhaoshang Market were non-local persons. Thus it was more difficult to establish credibility between the buyers and Zhaoshang Market booth-keepers. From the very beginning, therefore, even earlier than at Yiwu Market, ZMMC, the AIC, QTS and the self-management network worked jointly to cope with this problem.[21]

ZMMC dealt with this problem in the following ways:

1. Various training courses for teaching law, quality control, and professional ethics were provided for the booth-keepers. Each booth-keeper was required to participate in this kind of course at least once a year.
2. A radio studio was set up in the market. This broadcast programs on current events, news and the law every day.
3. Communist Party members and the leaders of business zones and groups of the self-management network were requested to show their identity clearly.
4. "Good Manners Booths" [Wenming Tanwei] Contests and Credit Booths Contests were held every six months. ZMMC awarded a red flag to each of the winning booth-keepers and asked them to display this flag on their booths.[22]

On the other hand, the Qinnan AIC inspection group dealt with this problem in the following ways:

1. AIC officials went around the market to ferret out imitation goods.
2. The AIC asked all the booths to show their license and product prices in plain view in order to clarify the responsibility of each booth.
3. The AIC established a credit card system. Once a deal was concluded, a card including information on the booth number and the name of the booth-keeper was handed to the customer.[23]

At same time, the Changshu QTS came to the market irregularly to inspect the quality of commodities. The group leader of the self-management network regularly supervised booth-keepers to ensure that they observed the AIC and ZMMC regulations.

8.7.2 Information Gathering

Thousands of small buyers, who brought with them abundant low-end market demand information, visited Zhaoshang Market every day. For the small producers who did not have sufficient ability to design, however, this information alone was not sufficient for the development of new products. To resolve this problem, one important measure taken by ZMMC was to systematically collect information on middle and high-end market fashion trends in big cities and deliver it to the producers. By copying the designs of middle and high-end goods and modifying these to suit low-end demands, small apparel producers were able to develop new apparel products.

In 1986, ZMMC set up an information group that carried out the following activities.[24]

First, from the beginning, this group established the post of information investigator. These investigators went to department stores and markets in big cities to take photographs of apparel as samples. The information collected was publicized free of charge through the digital signboard in the market. From 1988, this information was also published in the newspaper *Zhaoshang Market Information*.

Second, the information group built cooperative relationships with factories, department stores and other enterprises in big cities. ZMMC provided convenient means for these enterprises to make purchases from Zhaoshang Market, and in return the enterprises regularly provided ZMMC with fashion information.

Third, the information group transmitted the collected apparel information to the SMEs around the Changshu cluster. The majority of these SMEs were booth-keepers who owned small factories. In 1986, the information group contracted with 168 such factories for the transmission of apparel information.

Fourth, in 1988, the information group began to publish a free weekly newspaper named the *Zhaoshang Market Information*. Generally, every booth was permitted to publish information on their products in this newspaper without payment. This newspaper was regularly exchanged with other major markets in China.

In terms of one issue of *Zhaoshang Market Information* in 1992, there were 12 columns in the newspaper, describing (1) exciting new goods; (2) seasonal goods; (3) the introduction of goods; (4) market dynamics; (5) market analysis; (6) a purchasing guide; (7) marketing methods; (8) predictions concerning new goods; (9) the acquisition of foreign exchange; (10) new attractions; (11) new customs; and (12) the provision of services. This newspaper gave support to small booth-keepers in various aspects of information gathering.

Besides the above measures, Zhaoshang Market also joined the National Industrial Products Wholesale Markets Association (see Chapter 4) in February 1992. Just as Yiwu Market did, Zhaoshang Market regularly exchanged information with other markets through this information network.

8.8 CONCLUSION

As the case of Zhaoshang Market suggested, in order to compete with other clusters, it is necessary for a market platform mode cluster to attract a large number of non-local sellers, such as Zhejiang merchants, who make up the majority of booth-keepers in the specialized market system and are always on the move between various locations.

As has been clarified in this chapter, Changshu government has played a crucial role in inviting these merchants into the market and having them take root. They learned a great deal from the experiences of pioneer markets in Zhejiang Province. Forced by the high mobility of booth-keepers, Changshu government innovatively came up with various policies for improving the market's business environment.

The existence of a comparatively efficient management system has enabled the local government to continually develop Zhaoshang Market in a precise way. This system consists of three levels. The first is the Zhaoshang Market Board, which consists of various departments related to market management. The second is ZMMC, which is a town-owned management company. The third is the self-management network composed of booth-keepers. Horizontally, this system coordinated the complicated relationships between various government departments, and vertically, it efficiently coordinated the relationship between the public sector and the private sector.

NOTES

1. This chapter is a revised version of Ding (2004).
2. For the definition of the self-employed enterprise and private enterprise, see Chapter 4, subsection 4.3.2.
3. 2006 data are cited from China Changshu Zhaoshang City Website (http://www.cszsc.com.cn, accessed 16 January 2009).
4. The development history of Zhaoshang Market is based on author interviews with Mr Xia Zuxing, former Secretary of the Communist Party Committee of Qinnan Town (doubling as former Secretary of the Communist Party Committee of Zhaoshang Market) in March, August and December 2001.
5. In most literature, this managing company is known as Zhaoshang Market. In order to distinguish it from the Zhaoshang Market itself, we call it Zhaoshang Market Managing Company in this book.
6. Qinnan Town was amalgamated with Yushan Town during 1992.
7. The information concerning submarkets is cited from China Changshu Zhaoshang City Website (http://www.cszsc.com.cn/mt.asp, accessed 16 January 2009).
8. This section is mainly based on author interviews with Gu Bangjun, former general manager of Zhaoshang Market, in August and December 2001. Sources will be noted only when cited from other materials.

9.   For example, the Sanitation Office was in charge of sanitary issues, the Quality and the Technical Supervision (QTS) Department was in charge of quality control.
10. No department put up any capital to this board.
11. According to YTCEC (2000, p. 322), a coordination office (consisting of the AIC, the Tax Bureau, and the police) was established in 1985, but its role is unclear.
12. Under this system, the general manager is given absolute power and has to bear full management responsibility.
13. This section is based mainly on Xia (1992) and the author interviews with Gu Bangjun. Sources will be noted only when cited from other materials.
14. Unfortunately, the exact tax rate in the street market is unclear.
15. The AIC fee was abolished on 1 September 2008 (Caijing.com.cn, 22 August 2008, accessed 16 January 2009).
16. Gu Bangjun reported that he knew most markets in Zhejiang Province levied taxes and fees as a fixed amount. He thus appealed to the Tax Bureau and AIC to introduce this method.
17. In general, the amount estimated by the group leader was less than the actual amount.
18. Gu Bangjun reported that he was proud of extending the market several times without any budgetary support from Qinnan Town.
19. As the data sources differ, Xia's (1992) data are not completely consistent with data from YTCEC (2000).
20. The booth-keepers were provided various interesting incentives. For example, in 1989, Zhaoshang Market ran a lottery to encourage investment.
21. This section is based on Xia (1992) and author interviews with Gu Bangjun.
22. One former credit booth-keeper explained that sales suddenly increased once he obtained this title (author interview with a daily necessities booth-keeper in October 2001). For the details of this booth-keeper, see case No. 8, Table 9.6, Chapter 9.
23. Of course, this is a good way to publicize information about a booth.
24. This section is based on author interviews with Gu Bangjun.

9. The logic of quantitative expansion and qualitative upgrading in the market platform mode cluster

Source: The author.

Figure 9.1 Numerous local brands gathering in Zhaoshang City

9.1 INTRODUCTION

Concerning East Asia's industrial clusters, Sonobe and Otsuka (2004) assert that both the clusters in mainland China, which have specialized markets, and clusters in Japan and Taiwan, which do not have specialized markets, have shown a development process that moves from a "quantity expansion phase" to a "quality improvement phase." During this process, along with the appearance of leading companies, a large number of SMEs are either integrated into their supplier network, or eliminated through competition. The empirical data concerning Chinese clusters, however, did not necessarily support this viewpoint. Within the children's wear cluster of Zhili, Zhejiang, which Sonobe and Otsuka consider has entered the quality improvement phase, the number of children's wear firms increased from 5700 to 8000 during the period September 2006 to September 2008.[1] The industrial upgrading of this cluster has been clearly accompanied by quantitative expansion. A similar phenomenon can be observed in various specialized-market-based clusters in China.

In the author's opinion, the reason why Sonobe and Otsuka's study cannot exactly explain China's experience is that it failed to recognize two fundamental differences between Japan, Taiwan and mainland China. The first difference is that the Japanese and Taiwanese clusters on which their study focused are in merchant mode. China's specialized-market-based clusters treated in this study, however, are in market platform mode. The second difference concerns demand conditions. In Japan and Taiwan, the domestic market (and export markets) for the products of industrial clusters became quality-oriented soon after entering the high-growth period. In mainland China, however, because of the large income gap, the domestic market, in which both the low-end market and middle or high-end markets coexist together on a large scale, has become highly stratified. The purpose of Chapter 9 is to clarify the development logic of the market platform mode cluster in such unique demand conditions, through an in-depth analysis of the Changshu apparel cluster. In the remainder of this chapter, with particular reference to Zhaoshang City, the process of quantitative expansion and qualitative upgrading of the Changshu cluster will be thoroughly investigated.

9.2   GENERAL STRUCTURE OF THE CHANGSHU APPAREL CLUSTER[2]

9.2.1   Sellers

Producers
We first discuss the producers in the Changshu apparel cluster and their relationships with Zhaoshang City. As Figure 9.2 shows, there are three types of producers in the Changshu cluster.

The first type is the small processor. These are engaged in some specific production stage or stages of garment making, such as cutting, specialized sewing (collar sewing, sleeve sewing, pocket sewing, button sewing), hole cutting and ironing. The majority of the processors are local peasants who

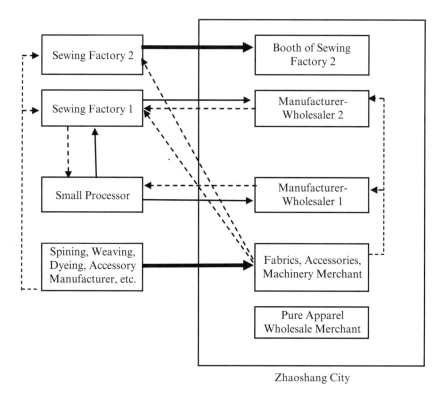

Zhaoshang City

Notes:
⟶ = Flow of finished products.
➤ = Flow of booth operation.
- - - - ➤ = Flow of intermediate products.

Source: The author.

Figure 9.2   Production flow in the Changshu apparel cluster

engage in the processing business as a sideline. They generally mobilize family members as workers and employ five or six immigrant workers only during busy periods. For example, in Mocheng Town, located close to Zhaoshang City, 2000 peasants were engaged in the processing business at the end of the 1990s. They would carry out processing work for half a year, while doing farm work in the other six months. A man could earn 5000 to 6000 yuan per year in the processing business (MTC, preprint).

After Zhaoshang Market was established, the number of small processors rose rapidly. During the period 1985 to 1996, the number increased from 6000 to 30,000 households.[3] Current data are unavailable. From the author's observation, many local peasants have opened their own sewing factories and immigrant workers have became the main actors in the processing business.

The second type of producer is the sewing factory. Sewing factories generally complete all the sewing-related stages inside a factory, subcontracting the processing stage to small processors only during busy periods. On the other hand, if the business scale expands, some large factories may integrate upstream production stages such as weaving and dyeing into the factory production system.

The total number of sewing factories has drastically increased since Zhaoshang Market was established. There were only 168 sewing factories in Changshu in 1985, increasing to 1650 in 2002, and exceeding 5000 in 2006. Some of them have become leading firms in China's apparel industry. Up to 2007, there were 35 China Noted Trademarks (for details, see Chapter 10) in Changshu. Of these, 29 are apparel-related trademarks owned by 26 apparel companies.[4] At the same time, Changshu has 22 China Top Brands (for details, see Chapter 10). Of these, eight are apparel-related brands owned by five apparel companies.[5]

The third type of producer is the supporting industry manufacturer. Some of these are engaged in the production of various raw materials, such as yarn, fabrics or apparel accessories (buttons and so on), and some are engaged in upstream textile-related businesses, such as dyeing.[6]

When the above data are combined with Table 8.1, it is clear that not only leading apparel companies but also a large number of sewing factories and small processors have grown up simultaneously in the Changshu cluster. This situation is quite different from the phased cluster development pattern assumed by Sonobe and Otsuka (2004).

A key point to the understanding of the dynamics of SMEs is Zhaoshang City, which provides multiple marketing channels for the SMEs.

In general, small processors receive orders from sewing factories or manufacturer-wholesalers (see subsection on distributors) in Zhaoshang City. As their business expands, some processors may open sewing factories and take up booths directly in Zhaoshang City.

Sewing factories generally form links with Zhaoshang City by receiving processing orders from manufacturer-wholesalers (Figure 9.2, Sewing Factory 1) or by operating booths directly in Zhaoshang City (Figure 9.2, Sewing Factory 2).[7] Currently, the latter form the majority. It is reported that among the more than 5000 sewing factories in Changshu, 90 percent are engaging in the production of menswear.[8] Of these, 70 percent are operating booths in Zhaoshang City.[9]

Manufacturers related to the supporting industries generally open booths in Zhaoshang City or sell directly to local sewing factories.

Distributors

Distributors primarily operate booths in Zhaoshang City. There are three types of distributors.

The first is the manufacturer-wholesaler (see Figure 9.2).[10] These distributors can be further classified into two types. The first is the wholesale merchant who subcontracts the whole production process to small processors (Figure 9.2: Manufacturer-Wholesaler 1). As in the traditional putting-out system, they provide fabrics or semi-finished products to processors and collect all of the finished products. In general, the relationships between merchants and processors are at arm's length (Schmitz 2006a), and the number of processors is adjusted in accordance with processing charges and market conditions.

The second type of manufacturer-wholesaler subcontracts all the production stages to sewing factories (Figure 9.2: Manufacturer-Wholesaler 2). They maintain either close or loose relationships with factories. In the case of loose relationships, the manufacturer-wholesaler contracts simultaneously with two or three factories. The sewing factories are selected only on the basis of processing charges. Sewing factories can also receive orders from several factories at one time. In the case of a close relationship, the manufacturer-wholesaler only subcontracts to one sewing factory in order to prevent leakage of business secrets, such as designs or the combinations of fabrics used. In this case, the term of a contract will be at least one year, and the sewing factory is prohibited from receiving orders from other merchants.

The second type of distributor is a pure wholesale merchant. Most of these merchants purchase apparel from other specialized markets to sell in Zhaoshang City. In recent years, influenced by the Zhaoshang City Managing Committee policy of inviting brand-name products, some wholesale merchants have become sales agents for leading apparel firms in other regions.

In 2004, the sales of Manufacturer-Wholesaler 1 accounted for 60 percent of the total sales of apparel in Zhaoshang City. The sales of Manufacturer-Wholesaler 2 and booths owned by sewing factories accounted for 20 percent of the total sales of apparel, and sales of pure wholesale merchants accounted for 20 percent of the total.[11] The data for both producers and distributors clearly reveal a crucial characteristic of the Changshu apparel cluster, namely that qualitative upgrading occurred simultaneously with quantitative expansion.

The third type of distributor is the merchant engaging in the sales of products related to supporting industries (fabrics, accessories, textile machinery, and so on) and other commodities. Comparatively old data show that of the total transaction volume of 11.6 billion yuan in 1999, the volume of apparel was 8 billion yuan. The transaction volume of goods related to supporting industries and other commodities was 3.6 billion yuan (YTCEC 2000).

As in the case of Yiwu (see Chapter 7), in accordance with the expansion of the business scale, all three of these types of distributors have the possibility of opening their own sewing factories. This is the crucial characteristic of the specialized-market-based cluster. We will present cases showing this point in detail in section 9.4.

9.3   GENERAL SITUATION OF BOOTH-KEEPERS IN ZHAOSHANG CITY

As stated above, Zhaoshang City is the key factor for exploring the mechanism through which the Changshu apparel cluster expanded and upgraded. In the following sections, we will conduct a thorough examination of the activities of Zhaoshang City's booth-keepers. Section 9.3 first discusses the general situation of these booth-keepers.

We must initially confirm that the total number and business scale of these booth-keepers have continued to grow since the establishment of Zhaoshang Market (Table 9.1).

Following that, we check the age of booth-keepers. Regarding this data, Table 9.2 consists of both data for Zhaoshang City booth-keepers in 2002 and data on the owners of private enterprises in China in 2000. By comparing these two sets of data, we can observe that the age of booth-keepers in Zhaoshang City converges on the 40s. They are comparatively younger than the owners of private enterprises who are Communist Party

Table 9.1   Basic data for firms in Zhaoshang City

Year	Transaction volume (100 million yuan)	Number of firms	Average transaction volume (10,000 yuan)
1985	0.25	400	6.25
1990	2.5	5300	4.72
1992	15	7010	21.4
1996	100	14,037	71.24
2001	132	14,627	90.24

Note: Number of firms between 1985 and 1992 is the number of booths. Up to 1992, one booth-keeper generally had only one booth, thus the number of booths is equivalent to the number of firms.

Sources: Data for 1985, 1990 and 1992 are from Xu (2002); data for 1996 are from YTCEC (2000, p. 322); data for 2001 are from CLCEC (2002).

Table 9.2   Ages of booth-keepers in Zhaoshang City and the owners of private enterprises in China

Zhaoshang City (2002) age	20–30	30–40	40–50	50–60
Share of booth-keepers (12,482) (%)	10	28	50	12
Owners of China Private Enterprise (2000) age	Under 30	30–40	40–50	Over 50
Share of owners who are party members (604) (%)	1.8	23	44.2	31.5
Share of owners who are non-party members (2449) (%)	3.4	35.9	34.3	21.4

Note: It is not clear in Xu (2002) why the number of booth-keepers is 12,482, which is inconsistent with Table 9.1. From the context, we infer that this figure is likely to have been the number of members of Zhaoshang City Self-employed Enterprise and Private Enterprise Association.

Sources: Data for Zhaoshang City are from Xu (2002); data for China Private Enterprise are from Zhang (2003, p. 87).

members, but much older than the non-party members, who are the majority of private enterprises owners in China.

Table 9.3 illustrates the educational background of Zhaoshang City booth-keepers through a comparison with data for the owners of private enterprises in China. This shows that nearly 90 percent of booth-keepers in Zhaoshang City graduated from junior school. This education level is lower than both the Communist Party member and non-party member owners of private enterprises in China. This is because the majority of these booth-keepers are self-employed enterprises (see Table 8.2).

Table 9.4 consists of data on the geographical origin of booth-keepers in Zhaoshang City. As this table shows, there are three main groups in Zhaoshang City. The first is from Changshu. As mentioned in Chapter 8, Changshu has a tradition of cottage textile industry, and thus it is inferred that most booth-keepers from this region have been engaged in apparel production. The second group is from Zhejiang Province, among which especially booth-keepers from Wenzhou, Taizhou and Jinhua command a majority. As repeatedly stated in this book, these regions are replete with the traditions of long-distance trade, and it can thus be inferred that these booth-keepers have previously been either peddlers or itinerant craftsman. The third group is from other regions, among them the majority being from areas neighboring Changshu, which have a similar tradition of the cottage textile industry.

In summary, the booth-keepers of Zhaoshang City are persons of

Table 9.3   Educational backgrounds of Zhaoshang City booth-keepers and the owners of private enterprises in China

Zhaoshang City (2002) educational background	Junior college	Secondary technical school	High school	Junior school	Primary school and below
Share of booth-keepers (12,482) (%)	0.4	0.5	8.5	85.5	5.1

Owners of China private enterprise (2000) educational background	Junior college and above	Secondary technical school or vocational high school	High school	Junior school	Primary school and below
Share of owners who are party members (608) (%)	45.6	9.9	23.5	19.2	1.8
Share of owners who are non-party members (2445) (%)	36.7	11.8	28.7	19.6	3.2

Source: As for Table 9.2.

Table 9.4   Hometowns of booth-keepers in Zhaoshang City (2002)

Province	City	County
Jiangsu: 6534	Suzhou: 6153	Changshu: 5202
		Wujiang: 375, Urban Suzhou: 222, Zhangjiagang: 156, Wuxian: 153, Taicang: 45
	Other cities: 381	Xinghua: 32, Jiangyin: 114, Other regions: 235
Zhejiang: 5438	Wenzhou	Ruian: 521, Pinyang: 278, Yueqing: 357, Urban Wenzhou: 158, Cangnan: 84
	Jinhua	Dongyang: 382, Yiwu: 594, Pujiang: 265
	Taizhou	Wenling: 778, Xianju: 665, Huangyan: 134, Tiantai: 178, Linhai: 101
	Other cities	Urban Huzhou: 214, Cixi: 62, Zhuji: 207, Other regions (including a few counties of Wenzhou, Jinhua and Taizhou): 460
Other provinces: 510		Anhui: 139, Fujian: 113, Guangdong: 10, Gansu: 4, Guizhou: 1, Hainan: 1, Hebei: 12, Henan: 98, Heilongjiang: 8, Hubei: 7, Hunan: 3, Jilin: 3, Shanghai: 111

Source: Xu (2002).

older age and lower educational background, most of whom have come from regions that have a tradition of either cottage industry or long-distance trade. It is necessary to clarify how, given this social background, Zhaoshang City booth-keepers gathered in Changshu in such large numbers and were able to realize the dynamic development.

9.4 QUANTITATIVE EXPANSION OF THE CHANGSHU CLUSTER

9.4.1 Information Derived from a Booth-Keeper List

This section discusses the mechanism of quantitative expansion in the Changshu cluster by focusing on Zhaoshang City. With regard to this issue, "The 7th Zone and Group Network Member List of Zhaoshang City Self-employed Enterprises and Private Enterprises Association (7th List)" [Zhaoshangcheng Geti Siying Jingji Xiehui Diqijie Pianzu Wangluo Zuzhi Mingdan] provides powerful clues. Zhaoshang City Self-employed Enterprises and Private Enterprises Association (ZSPA) was a social intermediary under the control of the Zhaoshang City AIC.[12] In order to effectively manage the large number of booth-keepers in Zhaoshang City, this association established a self-management network.[13] The basic information on the managers of this network was put in a members list. In the 7th List, information on 409 managers was given, namely, (1) the location of the booth (zone and submarket), (2) post in the network, (3) name, (4) sex, (5) hometown, (6) booth number, (7) business scope, and (8) telephone number. Of these, information on the booth-keepers' hometown was shown at the city level in the case of urban areas, and at the county level in the case of rural areas. This is indeed appropriate material for analyzing the regional characteristics of Zhaoshang City's booth-keepers.

In order to analyze the 7th List, we still need to explain the features of this self-management network in detail. In 2001, the association was supervised by several directors, and the management network divided blocks of booth-keepers into 13 zones (Pian). Each zone, covering several submarkets of Zhaoshang City, has one zone leader and several deputy zone leaders. There are several groups in each zone. Each group has one group leader and several subgroup leaders. One group leader or subgroup leader takes charge of 30 to 50 booth-keepers who are engaged in the same business. In order to carry out effective supervision of the regional groups, zone leaders or group leaders are generally selected from the region represented by the greatest number of booth-keepers in the zone.

Table 9.5 organizes the information (hometown, business scope,

Table 9.5 Hometowns and industries of managers of self-management network of ZSPA (2001)

Number of managers / Zones	1 person	2 persons	3 persons	4 persons	5 persons	6 or more persons
Laoqu zone	Jiangsu: 10 regions; Zhejiang: 14 regions; other: 1 region (all in apparel)	Jiangsu: Qidong; Zhejiang: Pujiang, Jiaojiang, Urban Wenzhou, Huangyan, Cangnan (all in apparel)	Zhejiang: Taizhou, Pingyang, Huzhou (all in apparel)	Jiangsu: Wuxi; Zhejiang: Xianju, Tiantai (all in apparel)	Jiangsu: Wujiang (all in apparel)	Changshu: 79 (apparel 78, knitting 1); Zhejiang: Wenling 8 (apparel 7, socks 1)
Wanli zone	Zhejiang, 2 regions (2 in daily necessities); other: 1 region (in appliances)	Zhejiang: Yueqing (suitcases 1, stationery 1), Ruian (ties 1, daily necessities 1)	0	Jiangsu: Qidong (apparel accessories 2, apparel 1, bedclothes 1)	Changshu (daily necessities 22, appliances 2, apparel accessories 1)	Zhejiang: Dongyang 18 (daily necessities 9, stationery 3, cosmetics 2, apparel accessories 2, appliances 2); Yiwu: 14 (daily necessities 6, suitcases 3, appliances 2, stationery 1, cosmetics 1, apparel accessories 1)

Xieye zone	Jiangsu: 1 region; Zhejiang: 6 regions; other: 1 region (all in shoes)	Zhejiang: Qingtian, Pingyang (all in shoes)	Changshu: (foods 2, shoes 1)	0	Zhejiang: Wenling 6 (shoes 4, agricultural products 2)
Xi zone	Jiangsu: 1 region (shoes); Zhejiang: 2 regions (apparel); other: 1 region (apparel)	Zhejiang: Taizhou (apparel 2)	0	0	Changshu: 12 (all in apparel)
Wujin zone	Changshu: (lamps); Jiangsu: 1 region (lamps); Zhejiang: 4 regions (hardware 2, appliances 2)	0	0	0	0
Bupi zone	Jiangsu: 2 regions; Zhejiang: 1 region (all in fabric)	0	0	Jiangsu: Wujiang (all in fabric)	Changshu: 23 (all in fabric)
Mianliao zone	Jiangsu: 1 region (fabric for interior decoration)	0	Changshu: (all in fabric for interior decoration)	0	0

Table 9.5 (continued)

Zones \ Number of managers	1 person	2 persons	3 persons	4 persons	5 persons	6 or more persons
Dongfang zone	Zhejiang: 4 regions (socks)	0	Zhejiang: Yiwu (apparel 2, socks 1)	0	0	Changshu: 21 (apparel 20, restaurant 1); Zhejiang: Ruian 8 (socks 7, apparel 1)
Huasheng zone	Jiangsu: 2 regions (apparel, shirts); Zhejiang: 4 regions (apparel, 3 regions, children's wear 1 region)	0	0	0	0	Changshu: 7 (apparel 4, woolen sweaters 2, children's wear 1)
Yongfeng zone	Jiangsu: 1 region (children's wear); Zhejiang: (woolen sweaters 2, shirts 1); other regions: (apparel)	0	Jiangsu: Wujiang (woolen sweaters 2, children's wear 1)	0	0	Changshu: 9 (woolen sweaters 6, children's wear 2, shirts 1)

Zone					
Xinfeng zone	Jiangsu: 3 regions (shoes); Zhejiang: 9 regions (shoes 8, apparel 1); other region: 1 (shoes)	0	Changshu: (apparel 1, shoes 1, foods 1), Zhejiang: Xianju, Pingyang (all in shoes)	0	0	Changshu: 23 (apparel 21, wool 2)
Fangjiao zone	Jiangsu: 4 regions; Zhejiang: 7 regions (all in apparel)	0	0	0	0	0
Waiwei zone	Zhejiang: 3 regions (catering, shoes, hairdressing); other regions: 2 (ceramics, catering)	0	Changshu: 4 (daily necessities 2, bicycle repairs 1, hairdressing 1)	0	0	0

Note: "Jiangsu" does not include Changshu.

Source: Compiled by the author based on data from 7th List.

163

number of Landsmann) of these *managers*. Based on the features of the self-management network, we derived two distinct features of the regional groups in Zhaoshang City.

The first is that these regional groups came to Zhaoshang City at the same time and engaged in the same business in the same zone. From Table 9.5, we can find numerous cases where two or more Landsmann managers were concentrated in the same zone and were dealing in the same commodity. By examining the booth number, we further found that in many cases, Landsmann booths were adjacent to each other. In general, these booths were constructed in the same period. From these points and the above-mentioned fact that the managers are generally selected from the regional group with the largest number of booth-keepers, we can judge that a large number of Landsmann booth-keepers moved to Zhaoshang City at same time and engaged in the same business.

The second feature is that most of the managers of the self-management network of ZSPA were dealing in the same products as the local industry of their hometowns. Concretely, most of the Changshu managers were dealing in apparel. This is natural considering the tradition of cottage textile industry in this region. Similar cases concerning apparel can be discovered among the various regional groups in Jiangsu, Zhejiang and other provinces. To analyze other textile-related commodities, such as China's largest silk and rayon cluster, Wujiang (Suzhou, Jiangsu Province), there are five Wujiang managers dealing in these fabrics. Yiwu is the largest apparel accessory cluster in China. There are thus one Yiwu manager and one Dongyang (a neighboring county to Yiwu) manager dealing in this product. In the 7th List, many apparel accessories are indeed treated as daily necessities.[14] Accordingly, six Yiwu managers and nine Dongyang managers are engaged in the sales of daily necessities. Yiwu, Zhuji and Ruian are known as the largest clusters of sock manufacture in China. We thus found one Yiwu manager, one Zhuji manager, and seven Ruian managers dealing in socks.[15] As stated below, in the initial stage the booth-keepers generally purchased from the specialized market in their home-town. We can thus confirm that various clusters in China are circulating local products through the specialized market system, which is largely based on their Landsmann network.

9.4.2   Typical Cases of Regional Groups in Zhaoshang City

In this subsection we further introduce five typical cases of regional groups in Zhaoshang City in order to verify the information derived from the 7th List.[16] The five booth-keepers interviewed are from one village in Changshu, two counties in Wenzhou, one county in Jinhua, and one county in Taizhou.[17] As Table 9.4 demonstrates, the number of booth-keepers from these five regions ranks at the top level among booth-keepers in Zhaoshang City. In addition, all of these interviewees are the leaders of their regional groups and are also managers in the self-management network. Thus, from these five cases, we can clarify the features of the Landsmann network in Zhaoshang City. In the following paragraphs, we first explain how these regional groups moved to Zhaoshang City, and then explain their connections with their hometowns. Lastly, their modes of cooperation in daily business will be clarified.

The background on how these regional groups moved to Zhaoshang City is as follows.

1. Changshu: The interviewee first operated a booth in Zhaoshang Market in 1992. In 1996, when a new submarket was established, he invited 15 persons from the same village to the submarket. Thereafter, almost all the young people in this village came to operate booths in this submarket. His wife, son and daughter-in-law also operated booths in the submarket.

2. Ruian: The interviewee and his wife first moved to Zhaoshang City in 1989. Shortly thereafter, three of his sisters and almost all his relatives on his father's side, including seven cognate cousins and their relatives, were invited to Changshu. These relatives then invited a further number of relatives. The total number of the interviewee's relatives conducting business in the market grew to something like 300 to 500 people.[18]

3. Pingyang: The interviewee and his wife first moved to Zhaoshang City in 1987. Following that, more than 10,000 people from his hometown and three neighboring towns followed him to operate booths in Zhaoshang City. However, only something over 70 households actually took root in Changshu. Of these, more than 40 households have bought their own houses there.

4. Dongyang: Villagers began to operate booths in Zhaoshang City from 1985. Invited by the villagers, the interviewee and his wife came to Changshu in 1990. Thereafter, he left Changshu and traveled around various markets. In 1997, he returned to Changshu again. In 2001, the number of Dongyang booth-keepers in Changshu amounted to 2000 (about 500 to 600 households). Of these, 55 households were from the same village as the interviewee.

5. Huangyan: The interviewee and his Landsmann group came to Changshu together in 1987. Thereafter, he left Changshu and traveled around various markets. In 1990, as an aunt was in Changshu, he and his wife returned. When a hardware submarket was established in Zhaoshang City in 1994, he switched from apparel to the hardware

business. He went to Taizhou to invite a Landsmann group to operate booths in the hardware submarket. In 2004, 150 booths in Zhaoshang City Hardware Market, and 480 booths in Xinqiao Hardware Market were owned by his Landsmann group.

As the above cases show, the booth-keepers from Changshu, Ruian and Pingyang were the first to move to Zhaoshang City in their regional groups. All of them invited Landsmann groups to this market as soon as they began to operate booths. On the other hand, the booth-keepers from Dongyang and Huangyan were invited by Landsmann booth-keepers. The Landsmann network disseminated information on Changshu and helped them to make the decision to operate booths in Zhaoshang City.[19]

The Pingyang, Dongyang and Huangyan cases also suggest the high mobility of Zhejiang merchants. As repeated throughout this book, the local government thus had no choice but to constantly improve the business environment in order to have these merchants take root, which eventually stimulated the evolution of the specialized market system.

Next, we explain the relationships between these booth-keepers and their hometowns. In concrete terms:

1. Changshu: The interviewee manufactured bamboo knitting needles himself and purchased a small number of needles from his home village from 1992. After 1996, the interviewee tended to go to Yiwu for purchasing of different products.
2. Ruian: Between 1989 and 1999, the interviewee purchased rubber shoes, scarves, cosmetics and socks from his Landsmann group in the specialized markets in Yiwu and Ruian. He opened logistics lines between Ruian and Changshu in 1994. From 1999, he subcontracted manufacturers in Ruian to process various kinds of apparel.
3. Pingyang: The interviewee helped the Changshu government to contact the Wenzhou government and enterprises when the government decided to go on an inspection tour of Wenzhou, or to invite booth-keepers from Wenzhou.
4. Dongyang: The interviewee purchased goods from Yiwu merchants in Yiwu Market on credit on the pretext that Yiwu people and Dongyang people are the same Landsmann group, since both of these two counties belong to Jinhua City. Every year, he returned to his hometown during the spring festival, and at that time met with villagers in other markets in various locations in China who had also returned for the festival. They held home parties and made a Landsmann contact list, through which they frequently exchanged information on market conditions in various locations.

5. Huangyan: The interviewee initially purchased commodities from Luqiao Market, not far from Huangyan. He gradually came to purchase goods from various locations besides Luqiao.

As the above cases indicate, all these interviewees have maintained close relationships with their hometown. The interviewees from Changshu, Ruian, Huangyan and Dongyang initially purchased commodities from their hometowns or regions nearby. Although the Pingyang booth-keeper dealt in apparel, which may be purchased from many locations, he still actively facilitated communications between the governments of his hometown and Changshu. This relationship, however, was likely to change along with growth of the markets. In the cases of Changshu and Huangyan, the purchasing channels of both interviewees have expanded.

Lastly, we explain how these Landsmann booth-keepers cooperate during daily business. The interviewees' statements are as follows:

1. Changshu: The villagers had a near monopoly on the sales of bamboo knitting needles in the submarket. They could immediately supply each other with the necessary goods when stocks ran out. They sometimes went together on purchasing trips. Information on suppliers, buyers and prices was shared generously among the villagers. In order to avoid competition with other villagers, however, the interviewee switched to the plastic dish business.
2. Ruian: The interviewee and his relatives initially sold apparel together. Gradually, they came to deal in different types of apparel. Eventually, all the relatives opened their own apparel factories. Business information was often exchanged between booth-keepers who were relatives.
3. Pingyang: When a new Pingyang merchant came to Changshu, the interviewee often helped him to borrow a house and a booth, and to negotiate with the public sector (the police and the AIC). He often looked the other way when others in his Landsmann group copied the design of his products and the selection of fabrics. He became a guarantor for Landsmann booth-keepers when they borrowed money from the bank. He also sold fabrics to others in his Landsmann group on credit. Because of the poor quality, however, he never subcontracted apparel processing to them.
4. Dongyang: Most of his Landsmann group were selling apparel accessories in the Wanli Market in Zhaoshang City. They could immediately supply each other with the necessary goods when stocks ran out. They sometimes went together on purchasing trips. The interviewee regularly organized Party members from Dongyang to learn policies or to dine together. Sometimes they petitioned the managing

committee to improve the business environment. After 2000, three Landsmann booth-keepers jointly opened an apparel accessories factory in Changshu.

5.   Huangyan: The interviewee used to supply commodities to Landsmann booth-keepers in the same submarket on credit, but gradually stopped doing this. Information on the suppliers of hardware was occasionally exchanged by Landsmann booth-keepers. In general, he and his Landsmann group were in competition with each other.

As the above cases indicate, all the Landsmann booth-keepers from these five regions were engaged in the same types of business and enjoyed close mutual cooperation in co-purchasing, information exchange and so on. The intensity of cooperative relationships, however, appeared to differ by region. In the closest relationship, the Dongyang interviewee utilized the formal Communist Party organization for mobilizing his Landsmann group. In the loosest case, Huangyan, the Landsmann booth-keepers just occasionally exchanged information.

9.4.3   Quantitative Expansion of the Changshu Cluster Observed from the Personal Experiences of Booth-Keepers

As stated above, the Landsmann network attracted a large number of small merchants, and thus caused the quantitative expansion of Zhaoshang City. This subsection will further verify that this major change eventually brought about the quantitative expansion of the whole Changshu apparel cluster. Regarding this issue, the above-mentioned cases of Ruian, Pingyang and Dongyang have indicated that booth-keepers entered the manufacturing sector.[20] We will confirm this point more systematically by presenting the personal business experiences of booth-keepers.

Table 9.6 illustrates information concerning 14 booth-keepers' previous businesses before entering Zhaoshang City, the first business after beginning to operate a booth in Zhaoshang City, and the latest known business. Among these booth-keepers, some were introduced to the author by the managing committee of Zhaoshang City during fieldwork, and some are mentioned in the publicity materials published by the managing committee. They can therefore be treated as very typical cases of booth-keepers in Zhaoshang City.

As this table illustrates, of eight booth-keepers from Changshu, five have previously been workers in the textile industry. In contrast, except for the booth-keeper from Ruian, all the Zhejiang booth-keepers have operated booths in other markets before moving to Changshu. This clearly reveals the local traditions of these two regions.

Table 9.6 *Personal business experience of booth-keepers in Zhaoshang City*

Number	Hometown	Previous occupation	Initial business when began to operate booths in Zhaoshang City (year)	Latest business (year)
1	Changshu	Worker in commune-owned glove factory	Made apparel at workshop to sell in Zhaoshang Market (1986)	Opened one sewing factory with own brand (1997)
2	Changshu	Tailor	Made apparel at workshop to sell in Zhaoshang Market (1986)	Opened one sewing factory with own brand (1997)
3	Changshu	Worker in township textile factory	Purchased apparel from township factories to sell in Zhaoshang Market (1985)	Opened several sewing factories, logistic company and hotel (1997)
4	Changshu	Director of city-owned radiotelegraphy factory	Purchased woolen sweaters from township factories to sell in Zhaoshang Market (1987)	Opened one sewing factory and one dyeing factory. Subcontracted weaving to four factories and sold the fabric at his own booth in Zhaoshang City (2004)
5	Changshu	Tailor	Manufacturer-Wholesaler 1 (1986)	Opened casual wear factories with own brand. Strategically cooperated with 16 sewing factories for processing (2005)
6	Changshu	Peddler	Sold apparel in Zhaoshang Market (1985)	Sold apparel related products in Zhaoshang City. Opened restaurant and hotel (2001)
7	Changshu	Worker in light industrial machine factory	Sold and repaired sewing machines (1988)	Opened sewing machine market in Zhaoshang City (2000)
8	Changshu	Peasant making bamboo knitting needles as sideline work	Made bamboo knitting needles to sell in Zhaoshang City (1992)	Sold ceramics at Zhaoshang City and provided gifts for a gas station (2004)

Table 9.6 (continued)

Number	Hometown	Previous occupation	Initial business when began to operate booths in Zhaoshang City (year)	Latest business (year)
9	Suzhou	Manager of a joint venture	Made apparel at own factory to sell in Zhaoshang City (1996)	Opened apparel factories with own brands (2007)
10	Yueqing	Booth-keeper in Wuhan Hanzhengjie Market	Engaged in apparel processing business (1994)	Opened apparel factories with own brand (2007)
11	Ruian	Sock maker in Ruian (products sold to Yiwu Market)	Purchased bedclothes from Hangzhou to sell in Zhaoshang Market (1989)	Opened integrated underwear factory and subcontracted suits, shirts, woolen sweaters, ties, and leather shoes to big apparel makers in other region with own brand. Leased booth in Zhaoshang City. Opened logistics company (2004)
12	Pingyang	Booth-keeper in Hangzhou Hongtaiyang Market	Sold casual wear in Zhaoshang Market (1987)	Opened casual pants factory and sold apparel and fabric in Zhaoshang City with own brands (2004)
13	Dongyang	Booth-keeper in various markets in China	Sold apparel accessories in Zhaoshang City (1997)	Sold apparel accessories in Zhaoshang City (2001)
14	Huangyan	Booth-keeper in various markets in China	Sold suits in Zhaoshang Market (1990)	Hardware sales agent (2004)

Sources: Data for Nos. 1, 2, 3 and 7 cited from CSPA (1997, 99–106; 115–21; 122–8; 55–62); data for No. 4 based on author interviews in August 2001 and February 2004; data for Nos. 5, 9, 10 cited from Xu and Xu (2005); data for No. 6 based on an author interview in August 2001; data for No. 8 based on author interviews in August 2001 and February 2004; data for Nos. 11 and 12 based on an author interview in February 2004; data for No. 13 based on a author interview in August 2001; data for No. 14 based on author interviews in August 2001 and February 2004.

After operating booths in Zhaoshang City, most of these booth-keepers then began to take part in the manufacturing sector. The major experiences of these booth-keepers can be summarized as follows.

1. Before entering Zhaoshang City, only three booth-keepers had had their own workshops or factories. This number increased to five after they began to operate booths in Zhaoshang City. At the latest known time, nine booth-keepers had come to have their own sewing factories.[21]
2. Seven booth-keepers who operated factories registered their own brands.
3. Five booth-keepers with their own factories invested in upstream or downstream businesses in the apparel industry. Of these, two booth-keepers began the production of fabrics or apparel accessories. Two opened logistics lines or hotels.
4. Two booth-keepers with their own factories simultaneously subcontracted some products to other sewing factories. Of these, one was from a distant region.
5. As for the five booth-keepers who did not own factories, three were engaged in apparel-related business. Two switched to a business unrelated to the apparel industry.

From the above facts, we can confirm that an increasingly large number of booth-keepers taking root in Zhaoshang City eventually resulted in the industrial cluster formation of Changshu cluster. We will further analyze the role of these booth-keepers in upgrading the apparel industry.

9.5   QUALITATIVE UPGRADING IN THE CHANGSHU CLUSTER

This section discusses the qualitative upgrading of the Changshu apparel cluster. As a part of the fashion industry, progress in design and brand creation became the most marked upgrading pattern in this cluster. According to Fang (1992), as early as 1992, dozens of new designs were being developed in Zhaoshang City every day. The total number of apparel designs in a year in Zhaoshang City amounted to several tens of thousands. Regarding the recent situation, it is reported that Changshu had a total of 10,000 trademarks by 2006, ranking it in the first position among all of Jiangsu's counties and county-level cities. It is also reported that more than 70 percent of the factories in Changshu were manufacturing products with their own trademarks.[22] Most of these trademarks were inferred to be owned by the apparel industry.[23]

Table 9.7   Visitors and booths in Zhaoshang City

Year	Average no. of visitors per day	No. of booths in Zhaoshang City	No. of visitors/ no. of booths	No. of logistics lines
1988	40,000–50,000	4525	8.8*	–
1991	80,000	6650	12	24
1992	100,000	10,000	10	24
1995	120,000	20,000	6	172**
2008	200,000 or more	28,000	7.1	241

Notes:
*   Calculated on the basis of 40,000 buyers.
**   Data for 1996.

Sources: Data for 1988: Xia (1988); other data: Zhaoshang Market and Zhaoshang City brochures for various years.

There are three factors that stimulated the progress in design and brand creation in the Changshu apparel cluster.

The first is that Zhaoshang City, the largest specialized apparel market in China, always puts competitive pressure on the booth-keepers. According to Xu and Xu (2005), the No. 5 booth-keeper in Table 9.6 started to design apparel goods himself with his own brand name in 1990 and the No. 10 booth-keeper began the same strategy in the mid-1990s. Although the timing was different, both of them stated that under intense price competition in Zhaoshang City, they had no choice but to differentiate their products. This naturally resulted from the increasingly large number of booth-keepers who were producing mainly undifferentiated products with low value added, and exhibited very frequent entry into and exit from Zhaoshang City. However, their total number did indeed tend to increase constantly.

It is noteworthy that, even for the companies that succeeded in creating brands, competition remained extremely intense. This is because since 2001, the managing committee of Zhaoshang City has begun to invite leading domestic and overseas apparel companies to establish sales outlets in Zhaoshang City. In 2001, 280 domestic and 50 overseas leading apparel companies established sales outlets in Zhaoshang City (*Suzhou Daily*, 26 November 2001). In 2006, the number of upper province-level brands owned by leading domestic and overseas apparel companies amounted to more than 500.[24]

The second factor is that Zhaoshang City always attracts a large number of small, low-end market buyers.[25] As Table 9.7 shows, the business scale of visitors (buyers) is much smaller than booth-keepers (sellers). The number of visitors exceeds the number of booths by a large extent.

Table 9.8   Sources of design ideas of apparel manufacturers in Changshu

	Year of founding		Present	
	Number of Firms	Share (%)	Number of Firms	Share (%)
Designed by owner	11	20.75	10	18.87
Designed by designer	13	24.53	25	47.17
Ideas drawn from other products	17	32.08	4	7.55
Assigned by customers	12	22.64	14	26.42
Total	53	100	53	100

Source: Xu and Xu (2005).

Along with the increase in market booths, the number of visitors has also increased. The acceleration in the number of visitors has slowed since the early times of the 1990s, but the basic situation where buyers far outnumber sellers has remained unchanged up to now.

These buyers are from the whole of China. Xia (1988) showed that in 1988, buyers in Zhaoshang City had come from 29 provinces (or major cities[26]), 800 counties (or districts) in China. In 2008, the geographical distribution of buyers expanded to more than 1000 cities (including county-level cities). The number of logistics lines connecting Changshu with distant markets clearly bears out this point. As Table 9.7 indicates, during the period 1991 to 2008, the number of logistics lines increased from 24 to 241, expanding more than ten times.

These small buyers had no specific requirements for high quality and sophisticated design. Thus, even goods designed by small producers without any particular design ability were accepted by the customers. On the other hand, these buyers constantly brought distant market information with them to Zhaoshang City booth-keepers. The ZMMC also simultaneously collected fashion trend information from big cities (see subsection 8.7.2). As a result, it is reported that as early as 1992, information on popular new apparel design in various cities was being transferred to Zhaoshang City in a mere three days (Fang 1992). In such a unique business environment, some producers gradually acquire a higher ability to design and create brands.

Survey data from a questionnaire on Changshu apparel manufacturers clearly bore out this point.[27] As Table 9.8 shows, of 53 available samples, in the initial stage, 20.75 percent of firm owners designed the apparel themselves, and 32.08 percent of firms drew (copied) ideas for designs from the products of other companies. The share of design carried out by a designer was a mere 24.53 percent. In accordance with business scale expansion and market segmentation upgrading, however, the ability of each firm to design greatly developed.[28] At present, the share of ideas drawn from other products has decreased to 7.55 percent, while in contrast, the share of designs carried out by designers has increased to 47.17 percent.[29] The share of designs by the owners remains at about 20 percent.

On the other hand, because of the high accessibility of market information, of 54 available samples, whether in the initial stage or at present, 66.67 percent of the apparel manufactures in Changshu were able to release new apparel products in one month. Of these, whether in the initial stage or at present, 11.1 percent of the manufacturers (six firms) were able to release new products in a mere three days (Xu and Xu 2005).

The third factor is that the majority of booth-keepers in Zhaoshang City are Zhejiang merchants. They share a powerful information exchange network with their Landsmann throughout China. Furthermore, most of the Zhejiang booth-keepers have had the experience of moving around various marketplaces in China (see Table 9.6 and the interview records of the regional group leaders). They are thus very familiar with the demand side of the specialized market. After entering the manufacturing sector, they have been able to implement smooth creation of their own brands.[30]

9.6   CONCLUSION

As described in this chapter, the total number and transaction volume of small producers and small merchants in the Changshu cluster have constantly expanded since the beginning. Among them, some have grown into leading apparel companies. This indeed suggests that qualitative upgrading and quantitative expansion did occur simultaneously.

This interesting phenomenon resulted from the completely different development logic of market platform clusters compared with the merchant mode cluster. In the merchant mode, industrial clusters and markets are separated by the merchants. The number of producers depends on the *quality* of market demand. In Japan and Taiwan, along with economic development, the low-end market disappeared and the quality requirements in the domestic market (and the export markets) became increasingly stronger. Accompanying this change in demand conditions, small producers making low value-added products were gradually eliminated through competition and some leading firms were nurtured. The development process of a cluster can thus be clearly delineated into a quantity expansion phase and a quality improvement phase.

In contrast, in the market platform mode, industrial clusters and markets are engaging in active interaction. The *number* of producers changes sensitively in accordance with the change in the number of buyers, and vice versa. In China's high-growth period, the low-end market not only did not disappear, but rather become increasingly large. The low-end market is characterized by low barriers to entry and exit, and this results in there always being sufficient numbers of potential buyers. On the other hand, since the demand for apparel goods is full of variety and undergoes rapid change, the apparel industry thus has more potential buyers. Because of the large numbers of the reserve army of buyers, the number of producers in clusters aiming at the domestic market, particularly in apparel clusters, is likely to continue to increase, even though some of the firms have begun to upgrade into the high value-added market segment.

In Changshu, regional groups of merchants, especially the Zhejiang merchants, have also played a key role in continuing to increase the number of producers. Based on the networks of these regional groups, a great number of SMEs continued to gather in Zhaoshang City. They were connected with their hometown and received mutual help in their daily business activities. As a result, many of them were likely to take root in Changshu, and consequently entered the manufacturing sector.

Various regional groups are constantly moving to Zhaoshang City, and thus have always put great competitive pressure on the booth-keepers. Two factors have further accelerated the competition. On the one hand, concentrated in a small space, the booth-keeper in Zhaoshang City can easily obtain business information and be closely involved in various competitions. On the other hand, the managing committee of Zhaoshang City is actively inviting leading apparel companies to establish sales outlets in the market. As a result, regardless of whether a company is an ordinary small business or one of the leading companies, or whether it is in the incipient stage or in the mature period, the booth-keeper in Zhaoshang City has to continue to upgrade in order to survive the competition.

Booth-keepers in Zhaoshang City primarily upgraded through the method of defining their own goods and creating brands. The majority of regional groups in Zhaoshang City are the Zhejiang merchants, who have experienced long-distance trade before and thus are very familiar with the demand side of the apparel clusters. On the other hand, the large number of regional groups attracted a larger number of small, low-end market buyers to Zhaoshang City. These buyers generally do not have specific requirements concerning quality and/or sophisticated design, but they can carry a great deal of apparel market information into the Changshu cluster. As a result, even small producers can easily define products themselves. With this unique starting point, some producers eventually acquired a higher ability to create brands, and thus enter the higher market segmentation.

NOTES

1. Zhejiang Online Jiaxing Channel, 11 September 2006, accessed 2 February 2009; Huzhou Online News Website, 6 September 2008, accessed 2 February 2009.
2. Sections 9.2, 9.3 and 9.4 are a revised version of Ding (2005). Basic information in section 9.2 is based on the author's fieldwork in March, August, October and December 2001 and February 2004. The author collected fragmentary information in 2001 and subsequently organized and confirmed the information in 2004 through an interview with a zone leader of Zhaoshang City Self-employed Enterprise and Private Enterprise Association.
3. Data for 1985 are from JEYBEC (1987, pp. 40–42, VII). Data for 1996 are from Xue (2001, p. 18).
4. Changshu Economy and Trade Net, 16 January 2008, accessed 22 January 2009.
5. Changshu Economy and Trade Net, 10 January 2008, accessed 22 January 2009.
6. Information on textile-related manufacturers has been confirmed from the Telephone Directory of Changshu (2004 version).
7. Figure 9.2 is merely an ideal type. It is natural that some sewing factories receive orders from manufacturer-wholesalers and operate booths in Zhaoshang City simultaneously. The situation concerning manufacturer-wholesalers is similar to the sewing factories.
8. China Changshu Zhaoshang City website (http://www.cszsc.com.cn, accessed 16 January 2009).
9. China Apparel News website, 24 October 2008, accessed 22 January 2009.
10. We can observe this type of manufacturer-wholesaler in almost all apparel clusters in developed countries. For the case of Capri cluster in Italy, see Ogawa (1998); for the case of the Gifu cluster in Japan, see Koike (1999); for the case of the Dongdaemun cluster in South Korea, see Kim and Abe (2002). Compared to Changshu, the division of labor between manufacturer-wholesalers and sewing factories is very clear in these clusters.
11. Information on the share of various types of booths is based on an author interview with a zone leader of Zhaoshang City Self-employed Enterprise and Private Enterprise Association in February 2004.
12. Information concerning the Self-employed Enterprise and Private Enterprise Association is based on an author interview with Gu Zhenghua, president of the association, in August 2001.
13. Chapter 8 mentioned that a self-management network was established in Zhaoshang Market in 1987. However, it is not possible to judge the relationship between these two networks from the existing literature.
14. This information is based on author fieldwork.
15. There are also some cases that are unrelated to textiles. For example, Yiwu is a large stationery cluster. We can thus find one Yiwu manager and three Dongyang managers dealing in stationery on this list. Wenzhou is a leather shoe cluster. Of the Wenzhou merchants, five Pingyang managers, three Qingtian managers, one Yueqing manager, one Ouhai manager and one Yongjia manager are engaged in the business of leather shoes. For the general situation of industrial clusters in Zhejiang, see Jin (2004).
16. The case of Dongyang is based on an author interview in February 2001; the cases of Changshu and Huangyan are based on author interviews in August 2001 and February 2004; the cases of Ruian and Pingyang are based on an author interview in February 2004.

17. Unfortunately, I was not able to make contact with Yiwu merchants in Zhaoshang City.
18. In this case, although all the interviewees were related persons connected by kinship networks, their number is large and all originated from the same location. Thus, the kinship group is also a group based on a common geographical origin.
19. We should not overestimate the role of the Landsmann network in inviting Changshu booth-keepers. Compared to Zhejiang booth-keepers, they are living in Changshu, and so it is easier for them to obtain information directly on Zhaoshang City.
20. The interviewees from Changshu, Ruian, Pingyang, Dongyang and Huangyan are respectively cases No. 8, 11, 12, 13 and 14 in Table 9.6.
21. Of these 14 cases, only booth-keeper No. 5 started as a manufacturer-wholesaler and booth-keepers No. 1 and No. 4 had previously been manufacturer-wholesalers. Since it is easy to enter the manufacturing sector, it is difficult to find cases of successful manufacturer-wholesalers in the existing literature.
22. Jiangsu SMEs Net, 22 January 2007, accessed 2 February 2009.
23. The major industrial products of Changshu consist of electricity generation, yarn, fabric, printed and dyed fabric, apparel, artificial boards, machine-produced paper and cardboard, rubber tires, steel products, household freezers, and copying machines. Of these products, only apparel and household freezers are consumer goods. Therefore, it can be judged that most of the trademarks of Changshu are owned by the apparel industry (China Changshu Government Net, 23 June 2008, accessed 25 January 2009).
24. China Changshu Zhaoshang City Website (http://www.cszsc.com.cn/mt.asp, accessed 16 January 2009).
25. Schmitz (2006b) pointed out clearly that buyers in developing countries are generally small and are design takers. The author's understanding concerning the low-end market buyers has benefited to a large extent from this study.
26. Major cities refer to municipalities directly under the jurisdiction of the central government.
27. This survey includes data for 62 apparel manufacturers and one dyeing manufacturer. The sample distribution by number of employees is as follows. 11–50: 7; 51–100: 16; 101–200: 17; 201–300: 10; 301–400: 7; 401–500: 4; 501–600: 0; over 600: 2. This survey does not include information concerning the relationships between Zhaoshang City and these manufacturers. Because of their overwhelmingly large presence, however, their business activities must to a large extent have been affected by this market.
28. A minor point concerning the improvement of design capability is the clustering of supporting industries in Zhaoshang City. This enabled apparel firms to adjust immediately to a new combination of fabrics and accessories for a new product.
29. It is interesting that the share of designs assigned by customers increased slightly between the year of founding and the present. This may be because these factories mainly receive orders from wholesale-manufacturers in Zhaoshang City.
30. Since the floor space of Zhaoshang City was a mere 2.8 square kilometers (2007), it is easy to imagine how many booth-keepers from other regions were affected by the business activities of Zhejiang merchants.

10. The typology of apparel clusters in China

Source: The author.

Figure 10.1   A trading broker negotiating with the owners of an apparel factory

10.1   INTRODUCTION[1]

This chapter will clarify the structural features of the market platform mode cluster through a comparison of the three types of apparel clusters in China. Our basic viewpoint is that the structures of industrial clusters could differ depending on the ways in which the cluster and the market are connected. From this viewpoint, we introduce the key concept of the *intermediary* for classifying and comparing the industrial clusters. The intermediary is an enterprise or an institution which connects the industrial cluster and a distant market, being positioned precisely on the boundary between production and distribution.

In terms of the different market conditions, intermediaries can be classified into various types. For example, as a consumer goods industry, China's apparel clusters generally manufacture products for three types of markets, namely the domestic low-end market, the developed country market, where the majority of consumers are middle class, and the domestic middle and high-end market.[2] Accordingly, there are three types of apparel organizers in China. The first type is a market platform mode cluster (see Figure 2.3) and the second and third types are merchant mode clusters (see Figure 2.2). In terms of the differences between these three organizers, China's apparel clusters can be classified into three types, namely the specialized-market-based cluster, the export-oriented cluster, and the big-company-dominated cluster. The first type is a market platform mode cluster, and the second and the third types are merchant mode clusters.

The first half of this chapter will show data sources, geographical distribution and a number of indices concerning China's apparel clusters. In the remainder of this chapter, we will first present a typical case of each type of organizer. The structural features derived from each case will then be verified by macro data for 65 typical apparel clusters. The influence of organizers on the structure of industrial clusters will be summarized in the final section.

10.2   DATA SOURCES

In China, an increasing quantity of textile and apparel products have come to be manufactured in industrial clusters. According to a survey by the China Apparel Association, 49 clusters manufactured 77 percent of the apparel for the whole of China in 2005 (CTIA 2006, p. 93).[3] Because of this situation, the China Textile Industry Association began to designate various cities, counties and towns as "China Textile Industry Base City (County)" or "Textile Industry Famous City (Town)" from 2002. In this process, most of the local governments went public with basic information on the clusters. Under China's statistical system, the collection, organization and analysis of this information is the sole method used to describe the general situation concerning apparel clusters.[4]

Currently, there are three major sources of comparatively complete information on the apparel clusters:

1. *2006 China Famous Textile Apparel Base Practical Business Map*, edited by China Apparel Magazine Press/China Textile Newspaper Press (CAMP/CTNP 2006).
2. The website for industrial clusters on the China Apparel Association website.
3. The website for industrial clusters on the China Textile Economy Information Net.

We collected data on 65 typical apparel clusters from the above data sources. Of these, 60 clusters were designated "China Textile Industry Base City (County)" or "Textile Industry Famous City (Town)" by the China Textile Industry Association during the period 2002 to 2005.[5] The remaining five clusters, namely, Shenzhen, Ningbo, Hangzhou, Wenzhou and Quanzhou have not been so designated. Information on these clusters is, however, given in both CAMP/CTNP (2006) and the China Apparel Association website. In view of the importance of these clusters, this chapter also takes these five cities into account.

10.3   GEOGRAPHICAL DISTRIBUTION OF APPAREL CLUSTERS

We first take an overview of the geographical distribution of these 65 apparel clusters. There are two important features (Table 10.1).

The first feature is that China's typical apparel clusters are all located in coastal areas. Of these, 58 clusters are agglomerated in four provinces, namely Guangdong, Zhejiang, Jiangsu and Fujian. This accounts for nearly 90 percent of the total number.

Table 10.1   Geographical distribution of China's industrial apparel clusters

Province	City	County	Town	Total
Zhejiang	3	7	5	15
Jiangsu	0	3	7	10
Guangdong	3	5	15	23
Fujian	1	2	7	10
Shandong	0	4	0	4
Hebei	0	2	0	2
Liaoning	0	1	0	1
Total	7	24	34	65

Source: Compiled by the author based on data from CAMP/CTNP (2006).

The second feature is that regarding the administrative areas in which apparel clusters are found, the number of town-level clusters is the largest, followed by county-level clusters and then city-level clusters. The administrative areas in which clusters are located show large differences by province. On the one hand, Shandong, Hebei and Liaoning Provinces have only county-level clusters, whereas town-level clusters are widely distributed in Zhejiang, Guangdong, Fujian and Jiangsu Provinces. Especially in the cases of the Changshu cluster in Jiangsu Province, the Hangzhou and Ningbo clusters in Zhejiang Province, the Jinjiang and Shishi clusters in Fujian Province, and the Dongguan and Kaiping clusters in Guangdong Province, not only the city or the county itself is a cluster, but various county- or town-level clusters have also appeared inside it. This suggests that the inter-regional division of labor in the apparel industry has greatly advanced in these areas.

There are three reasons that explain the high agglomeration rate of apparel production in coastal areas.

The first is that the coastal areas have a long tradition of textile production. A number of historical studies have shown that the peasants in China's coastal areas, especially Jiangnan, have engaged in spinning and weaving as cottage industries since the Ming (1368–1644) and Ching (1644–1911) Dynasties (Peng 1957; Xu 1992; Huang 2000). After China began the policy of reform and opening-up, numerous SMEs inherited these traditions and quickly formed a number of textile and apparel clusters (Jin 2004; Sonobe and Otsuka 2004).

The second reason is that a large number of immigrant workers have continued to move from inland areas to coastal areas. The apparel industry is a typical labor-intensive industry, and it is precisely because of this constant labor supply that the apparel clusters in coastal areas were able to continue to expand over several dozen years.[6]

The third reason is that from 2002, the China Textile Industry Association began to hold a range of frequent meetings or forums in the apparel clusters, which provided a wealth of communication opportunities for local government officials.[7] As a result, both inter-regional competition and inter-regional learning have become very active in China's apparel clusters, and this has strengthened the competitiveness of existing industrial clusters in the coastal areas.

10.4   INDICES FOR APPAREL CLUSTER ANALYSIS

We derived six qualitative indices from the materials concerning the above-mentioned 65 clusters.[8] The basic features of each type of apparel cluster can be clarified by analysis of these indices, which are as follows:

1.   Whether the share of exports in total production volume exceeds 50 percent or not.
2.   Whether specialized markets have been established or not.

From the above two indices, we can judge what types of intermediaries these clusters have:

3.   Whether a "big company" exists or not: We treat all the following cases as a "big company." Concretely, the company is reported as a leading company [Longtou Qiye], the company owns a national-level brand, and the production volume of a company clearly commands a majority in a cluster. We can judge whether the SMEs of a cluster are capable of growing into a big company or not by examination of this index.
4.   Whether supporting industries have been formed in the apparel cluster or not: We judge that a cluster has formed supporting industries provided the production of fabric, dyeing or other textile production stages can be confirmed. From this index, we can evaluate whether or not the effects of backward linkage have been sufficiently generated in the cluster.
5.   Whether the cluster holds a trade fair or not: A trade fair has the functions of publicizing the cluster and inviting qualified buyers and sellers. From this index, we can judge whether a cluster is likely to establish a regional brand or not, and whether local SMEs in a cluster are likely to trade with qualified buyers and sellers or not.
6.   Whether a local company in a cluster owns a national-level brand or not: In China, the State Administration for Industry and Commerce awards the title of "China Noted Trademark" [Zhongguo Chiming Shangbiao], and the State Quality and Technical Supervision Bureau awards the title of "China Top Brand" [Zhongguo Mingpai] to the brand-name products of leading companies. We judge that a cluster has national-level brands provided a company or companies in the cluster has either of these two titles or has a brand that clearly has nationwide influence. By examining this index, we can understand whether the cluster is able to foster companies with excellent ability in design and branding.

By combining indices 1 and 2, we can classify the 65 apparel clusters into the following four types:

1.   The cluster has a specialized market and the share of exports is less than 50 percent. Of the 65 clusters, there are 31 of this type.

2. The cluster has a specialized market and the share of exports is more than 50 percent.[9] There are four clusters of this type.
3. The cluster does not have a specialized market and the share of exports is more than 50 percent. There are 19 clusters of this type.
4. The cluster does not have a specialized market and the share of exports is less than 50 percent. There are 11 clusters of this type.

Among the above four cluster types, the intermediaries of both type 1 and type 2 are the specialized market. Thus we treat them as specialized-market-based apparel clusters. Type 3 is inferred as having trading companies as its intermediaries. Thus we treat it as an export-oriented apparel cluster. Type 4 is inferred as having a small number of big companies as its intermediaries. Thus we treat it as a big-company-dominated apparel cluster.

As Table 10.2 shows, indices 3 to 6 show clear differences for each type of apparel cluster. We will clarify the structural features of specialized-market-based apparel clusters and other types through an analysis of these indices.

From the materials concerning the 65 clusters, we also derived information on the number of firms and total production volume. As stated in the notes to Table 10.2, it is difficult to make precise comparisons of these two indices. In order to paint an overall picture of China's apparel clusters, however, our analysis will include these two indices while being cautiously aware of the constraints.

10.5 FEATURES OF THE SPECIALIZED-MARKET-BASED CLUSTER

The specialized-market-based cluster is the most typical type of apparel cluster in China. Of 65 apparel clusters, 35 are linked with specialized markets (Table 10.2). The features of the specialized market as an organizer have been clearly identified through the case of Zhaoshang City (Chapter 9). The indices of the specialized-market-based apparel clusters clearly reveal its features (Table 10.2).

First, the basic structure of the specialized-market-based cluster is that a number of leading "big companies" and numerous SMEs are stratified within a cluster. On the one hand, SMEs show a large presence in specialized-market-based clusters. As Table 10.2 shows, although the data are not very precise, the average number of firms in specialized-market-based clusters is much larger than in the other two types, especially the big-company-dominated clusters. In contrast, the average production volume of this type of cluster is comparatively small.

Table 10.2 Three types of industrial apparel clusters in China

Index	Type	Specialized-market-based	Export-oriented	Big-company-dominated
No. of clusters		35	19	11
Share of exports exceeds 50%		3+1	19	0
Specialized markets exist		28	0	0
Big companies fostered		28+5	16+1	11
Supporting industry formed		28+2	11	5+1
Trade fairs held		13	3	1
Local company has national-level brand		11	2+2	6
Average production volume (100 million yuan)		60.73	85.37	51.49
Average number of firms		1434.34	1255.5	523

Notes:

1. Basic information is primarily cited from CAMP/CTNP (2006). Incomplete information was supplemented by other sources, in turn: (1) the website for industrial clusters on the China Apparel Association website; (2) the website for industrial clusters on the China Textile Economy Information Net; (3) other internet sources. More recent data were given priority.

2. Qualitative indices are basically data for 2005. In some materials, however, the years of some indices were not clearly stated (although it can be judged that all the data are post-2002). In these cases, the author attempted to search for the 2005 data on the Internet as far as possible. These qualitative indices illustrate the basic structure of a cluster. Thus, they are unlikely to change over a period of two or three years.

3. Average production volume and average number of firms are cited from CAMP/CTNP (2006). Although most of the data are for 2005, this material also mentioned that some data are for 2003. Which data are from which year is not clearly stated. Since China's apparel industry continues to expand, the real values for 2005 are inferred to be much larger than the values in the table.

4. In CAMP/CTNP (2006), some data for apparel clusters are not production volume but are total sales, regional industrial production (including both the apparel industry and other industries) or GDP. Total sales are not so different from production volume, and thus were directly cited without revision. In the case of regional industrial production or GDP, we attempted as far as possible to search for the production volume data for 2005 on the Internet.

5. Regarding the average production volume and average number of firms, the statements are sometimes given as "more than . . . yuan" or "less than . . . firms." In these cases, only the value is cited.

6. When calculating the average production volume and average number of firms in the case where a city, county or town overlapped, we excluded the data of the upper level county or city. Concretely, the data for Hangzhou, Wenzhou and Ningbo in Zhejiang Province; Quanzhou, Shishi, and Jinjiang in Fujian Province; Dongguan and Kaiping in Guangdong Province; and Changshu in Jiangsu Province were excluded. However data from these clusters were not excluded when compiling the six qualitative indices. This is because the cluster in the upper administrative level and the cluster in the lower administrative level may show some qualitative difference.

7. It is stated on the website of industrial clusters on the China Apparel Association website (www.cnga.org.cn/news/text/123.doc, data inferred to be for 2002) that there are specialized markets in some export-oriented clusters (Shenzhen, Ningbo and Xiangshan) and in some big-company-dominated clusters (Wenzhou, Leqing, Rongcheng and Jinjiang). However these markets are not confirmed from other publicity materials on this website or from any other materials for 2005. This suggests that the specialized markets have drastically declined or that they are not so important for those clusters. We thus judged that these clusters do not have specialized markets.

8. Figures after "+" indicate the number of unverified but possible clusters.

Sources: Compiled by the author based on data from CAMP/CTNP (2006), the website for industrial clusters on the China Apparel Association website, the website for industrial clusters on the China Textile Economy Information Net (http://www.ctei.gov.cn/chanyejidi/) and other internet sources.

On the other hand, a number of big companies have developed. Of 35 clusters, big companies can be observed in 28. Including the unverified but possible cases, big companies can be observed in 33 clusters. This clearly shows that the specialized market has a powerful big company incubating function.

Second, the share of supporting industry formation in specialized-market-based clusters is the largest. As explained in Chapter 2, in a market platform mode cluster, distant market buyers are constantly attracted to the cluster. Although the orders placed by each buyer may be very small, the total quantity of orders is sufficiently large. As a result, merchants as booth-keepers are likely to take on the risks of entering the manufacturing sector and producers downstream in the industry will take on the risks of investing in the upstream capital-intensive and technology-intensive sectors.

Third, specialized-market-based clusters are obviously more keen to hold trade fairs than the other two types. Most of the trade fairs are organized by the local government. For example, in the Changshu cluster, the "Changshu Apparel Festival" is held by the Changshu government and co-organized by Zhaoshang City managing committee in the autumn of each year. Compared to the specialized market, a trade fair gathers more qualified buyers and sellers. The market demands surrounding the cluster can thus be upgraded.

Fourth, the leading firms fostered in a specialized-market-based cluster are likely to have strong capabilities in design and branding. As Table 10.2 indicates, companies that have national-level brands have appeared in nearly one-third of the specialized-market-based clusters. This runs counter to common sense. Scholars usually consider that the overwhelming preference is for price and that a brand strategy will never be formulated in specialized markets, since they are low-end market oriented. This notion is incorrect. Even in the low-end market, there is still a large demand for brand-name products. As analyzed in detail in Chapter 9, on the one hand, the buyers in the low-end market are small merchants who are design-takers. On the other hand, these small merchants go to the clusters themselves for purchasing, and have brought with them into the clusters a great deal of distant market information. Therefore, the makers in the clusters have adequate opportunities to formulate their own brand strategy. Initially, they were only able to create brand-name products with low value added, which is almost the same as being undifferentiated. However, some companies will survive the intense competition and create a national-level brand. In this sense, specialized markets have not hindered, but indeed have accelerated the formulation of brand strategies.

10.6   EXPORT-ORIENTED CLUSTERS

10.6.1   The Rise of Local Trading Companies

Export-oriented clusters are engaged in OEM (original equipment manufacturer) production for developed country markets. In China, the import and export business requires a license. For many years, only a few local trading companies and leading factories (local or foreign-capital enterprises) were able to obtain this license. Under this protectionist policy, a number of local trading companies grew into strong intermediaries for export-oriented clusters.[10] This subsection will examine the role of these companies, using primarily the case of Company X, which is the largest apparel trading company in Jiangsu Province.[11]

The business flow of Company X is as follows. This company seeks new customers by participating widely in various trade fairs, such as China's Guangzhou Fair or East China Fair, or the overseas fairs held in Paris, Düsseldorf, and so on. They then receive orders. When negotiating with buyers, in order to strengthen their bargaining power, Company X usually suggests to the buyers what kinds of fabrics are to be used. This company also purchases the fabrics itself. A number of textile clusters are located in Jiangsu and Zhejiang Provinces, and 90 percent of the fabrics required by Company X are thus purchased from these areas. Company X also provides apparel accessories to the sewing factories. Many accessories companies opened by Zhejiang merchants are located in the same city as Company X. Thus, it is very easy for them to purchase the accessories.

After receiving an order, Company X subcontracts the processing of the apparel to the sewing factories in various apparel clusters. In the case of the person interviewed, he places orders with the factories in Jintan, a "China Export Apparel Production Famous City." He generally charters five to eight production lines from one factory and attempts as far as possible to have the lines run full-time, but he never charters all the lines in one factory. This is because the factory manager will have a stronger incentive if he can receive orders from multiple companies. Company X has established a team that has skilled workers who previously worked in sewing factories as core members. This team is often sent to sewing factories to monitor and improve quality.

Company X has previously attempted to sell apparel with its own brand in the domestic market, but failed. According to the interviewee, design and marketing are quite different problems from production. Company X is not alone; other leading trade companies in China also have the same weak point.[12]

In export-oriented clusters, another intermediary that deserves attention is the trading broker, spun off from leading trading companies.[13] The business scale of the broker is very small. In the extreme case, they may start business with only one or two employees, in a one-room office, with one PC and a facsimile machine. Brokers do not have an import/export license. In order to export products smoothly, they are formally subordinate to a large trading company and pay a procedural fee to the company every year. Compared to big companies, brokers usually trade with previous customers. They also never charter production lines, nor do they provide fabrics and accessories. Of course, they never establish a quality control team. Instead, the broker himself goes to the factory frequently and maintains close communications with the owners and workers. Despite the poor organizing capability, however, the number of brokers is extremely large. In Jiangsu Province, including other sectors, their number has reached more than 10,000.

10.6.2   Features of the Export-Oriented Cluster

Because of the growth of local trading companies, the export-oriented industrial clusters show the following features (see Table 10.2).

The first feature is that both big companies and SMEs are likely to be fostered in this type of cluster. The share of clusters that fostered big companies in the export-oriented clusters is as large as in the specialized-market-based clusters. However, the big sewing factories have a tendency to integrate all the necessary stages within their own factories. They only place orders with other small sewing factories when an order exceeds their production capacity. In this sense, their role as intermediaries is limited.[14]

On the other hand, the average number of firms in export-oriented clusters is more than 1000. Although these data are not so precise, we can also confirm that SMEs have shown a large presence in this type of cluster. This has resulted from the large number of brokers. As it is easy to receive orders and get guidance from brokers, SMEs thus have many opportunities to start up.

The second feature is that the supporting industries are not as developed as in specialized-market-based clusters. The number of cases of the formation of supporting industries is only 11 in a total of 19 export-oriented clusters. This number clearly falls far behind the specialized-market-based clusters. This is because big trading companies are capable of purchasing fabrics and accessories from the most appropriate locations. Moreover, trading companies are not always located inside the clusters.

The third feature is that there are cases of export-oriented clusters where extremely few trade fairs are held. As sewing factories in clusters can access developed country market by receiving orders from trading companies, they do not have a very strong incentive to hold trade fairs to attract qualified buyers or create local brands.

The fourth feature is that it is very difficult for the sewing factories to create their own brands in an export-oriented cluster. The number of clusters where local companies have national-level brands is the smallest of all three types in export-oriented clusters. This is because the sewing factories in this type specialize in OEM production. They have had to take the designs of buyers from developed countries and have no marketing risk. This point is in stark contrast to the specialized-market-based clusters that aim at the domestic low-end market.

For reference, we examined average production volume per cluster. For this index, the value of export-oriented clusters is particularly large. This is because sewing factories can receive large-volume orders when engaging in OEM production. However, it is pointed out that the average margin of China's textile and apparel export products is a mere 3 percent.[15] In export-oriented clusters, large quantity simply compensates for the low margin.

10.7   BIG-COMPANY-DOMINATED CLUSTERS

The third type of apparel cluster is dominated by big companies, and aims at the domestic middle and high-end market. Big companies could be located either or outside the cluster. Whatever the case may be, the big company organizes the production and distribution itself and never relies on the specialized market.

10.7.1   An Integrated Big Apparel Company

In terms of the relationships with subcontractors, big companies can be classified into two types. The first is the integrated big business, such as China's largest apparel company, Youngor Group.[16]

Youngor was established in 1979. In 2005, the total sales and profit of this company reached 16.7 billion yuan and 1.018 billion yuan, respectively. Up to 2005, the production volume of Youngor's suits and shirts had held the top position in China's domestic market for seven and 12 years, respectively.

Regarding sewing, Youngor's head office in Ningbo has merged with and acquired a small number of factories sewing shirts, suits and fashion wear since the 1980s. In 2005, this company established two new factories in Chongqing in order to explore the inland market. Youngor manufactures most of its apparel inside the company, only a few products being subcontracted.

With regard to fabrics, this company established a wool factory in 1985. It then gradually integrated the spinning, weaving, dyeing and after-finishing stages. In 2003, Youngor established an integrated production base named Youngor Textile City with a one-billion yuan investment. This production base engages in the R&D and production of dyed yarn, fabrics printing, and knitted products, in cooperation with a Japanese company.

As for marketing, Youngor has consistently made efforts to explore the domestic market. During the period 1995 to 2005, this company established more than 2000 domestic stores. Of these, 300 are direct management stores.

Youngor also attempted to carry out its own R&D. It established a center for the R&D of apparel design, high-grade fabrics, lining and the retail chain system. The company invested 1.7 billion yuan for R&D on the retail chain system alone. Youngor also has a plan to establish a three-dimensional human body database.

Since the apparel sector needs to turn a profit on design and marketing, highly integrated businesses such as Youngor are somewhat extreme cases. In China, it is also debated whether this strategy is appropriate or not. Whatever the case might be, because of the large presence of integrated companies, in some big-company-dominated clusters, the growth of SMEs has been greatly constrained.

10.7.2   Branded Marketer

Compared with integrated companies, the so-called "branded marketer" has also appeared in China.[17] As the case of Nike indicates, the feature of the branded marketer is that it concentrates all its business resources into design and marketing, and places all the production stages under the charge of subcontractors. Thus, a key point for branded marketers is whether or not a powerful sales network can be established. In China, many examples of this type of company have appeared in Wenzhou. As is repeated in this book, the Wenzhou business network has spread across the whole of China. Utilization of this network has enabled Wenzhou companies to succeed in constructing their own sales networks in short timeframes.

Taking the case of the Ruian menswear cluster in Wenzhou, there are 300 apparel companies agglomerated within it. These companies had opened nearly 10,000 stores in China's domestic market up to 2005.[18] We explain the features of Wenzhou's branded marketers by analyzing the case of Company L in Ruian.

Company L is a representative Ruian casualwear company.[19] Although it is a newcomer, starting business in 2001, Company L's production output reached 6 million pieces in 2005, amounting to 80 million yuan in sales.

With regard to design, this company established a design company in Zhongshan, Guangdong Province and established a branch company in Shanghai. It invested several million yuan per year to develop new products. By 2006 this company had developed more than 1000 types of casual wear.

Regarding production, Company L widely subcontracts the production stages to swing factories in various apparel clusters in Shanghai, Guangzhou and Zhongshan. Different factories manufacture different types of products, the design of each product being determined by the head office in Ruian. Fabrics and accessories are also provided by the head office. Company L occasionally sends quality control staff to sewing factories to conduct surveys.

Company L maintains stable relationships with 70 percent of the swing factories. The share of production volume of these factories accounted for 80 to 90 percent of the total sales. On the other hand, Company L adjusted its relations with the remaining 30 percent of the sewing factories each year, based on technological capability, state of the machinery, and the quality of the employees, and discontinued the subcontracting relationship with factories it judges to be substandard.

Company L's products are mainly sold to middle-class residents of domestic medium-size and small cities and county-level cities. This company has established more than 400 chain stores to cover this broad geographical scope. The stores are primarily located in Shanghai (50 to 60 stores), Zhejiang (110 stores), Jiangsu (just under 100 stores), and the three provinces of Northeast China (100 stores). Most of the stores are run by sales agents. Some 60 to 70 percent of Company L's agents are from Wenzhou, and were recruited for the company through the intermediation of the Wenzhou Chamber of Commerce in various cities in China.

The head office of Company L in Ruian has only 120 employees. An information center was established in the company for intensive management of the information on design, production and sales. More than ten employees are engaged in the maintenance of the information system. In order to manage the collection and shipment of the apparel, a large warehouse has also been established at the head office. Furthermore, various brand promotion events and sales agents' meetings are held at the head office.

As stated above, the business style of Company L is in strong contrast to the Youngor Group. Most big apparel companies are probably in a middle position between these two cases. With their comparatively high organizational capabilities, big companies can utilize business resources both inside and outside the industrial clusters. The barrier to entry of a big-company-dominated cluster is also higher than for other types of cluster. As a result, the presence of SMEs in big-company-dominated clusters has increasingly declined. This point can be confirmed from the above-mentioned indices.

10.7.3   Features of the Big-Company-Dominated Cluster

Here we return to Table 10.2 and analyze the basic features of big-company-dominated clusters.

First, big companies show an overwhelmingly large presence in all the clusters of this type. By examining the average production volume and the average number of enterprises, we can estimate the production scale of each company. Although the data are not very precise, we may note that the per company production scale of the big-company-dominated cluster is the largest of the three types.

On the other hand, compared to the other two types, SMEs have an extremely small presence in big-company-dominated clusters. As Table 10.2 shows, except for the overlapping cases (see notes to Table 10.2), the average number of firms in these clusters is a mere 500.

Second, because of the overbearing presence of big companies, supporting industries in this type of cluster are the most underdeveloped. As Table 10.2 shows, supporting industry formation has occurred in less than half of the big-company-dominated clusters. This is because the big company can absorb the necessary business resources both from the local clusters and from other regions.

Third, except for one cluster, the clusters in this type do not hold trade fairs. This has also resulted from the features of big companies. They have their own brands and usually construct the sales network themselves. Thus it is unnecessary in clusters dominated by big companies to hold trade fairs to upgrade the regional brand.

Fourth, in order to explore the domestic middle and high-end market, big companies are very active in formulating brand strategy. As a result, the share of clusters where a local company owns a national-level brand is the largest of the three types of cluster.

10.8   CONCLUSION

Previous studies on the typology of industrial clusters focus primarily on the producers' side. Industrial clusters have been classified in various ways, depending on whether the leading actors of a cluster are big companies or small firms, or are local firms or firms from other regions (Markusen 1996).[20] However, the two-sided market theory has inspired us to note that industrial clusters could differ depending on the ways in which the cluster and the market are connected.[21] The typology of China's apparel clusters clearly revealed this point.

The first type of apparel clusters in China is the specialized-market-based cluster. As an intermediary, the specialized market is a low-end market-oriented platform, which deals primarily in undifferentiated products with low value added. As the entry barrier into the low-end market is low and the accessibility of the specialized market is high, a large number of producers and small merchants thus have the potential to enter the market. When the specialized market exhibits an indirect network effect, an increasing number of buyers and sellers can gather in the cluster. Therefore, the largest number of SMEs is found in the specialized-market-based apparel clusters. The supporting industries and the trade fairs are also the most developed.

The features of buyers also had a large effect on the structure of the specialized-market-based cluster. Generally, the buyers in the specialized market are much smaller than the producers, who are thus design-takers for the small producers. On the other hand, these small buyers always bring to the clusters a great deal of demand information from distant markets. Hence, right from the start, the producers in the specialized-market-based cluster are potentially capable of defining and designing their own products.

The second and third types is of apparel clusters are the export-oriented and the big-company-dominated cluster. Compared to the specialized market, trading companies and big companies are the typical merchant mode intermediaries involved in the overseas and domestic middle-end market. In order to provide differentiated apparel products with high value added, it is necessary for them to set higher quality standards, which thus raises the barriers to entry. As a result, it is not as easy for the number of small producers in these two types of clusters to increase as in the case of the specialized-market-based cluster.[22] Accordingly, the supporting industries and the trade fairs are not as developed as in the case of the specialized-market-based cluster.

On the other hand, in the export-oriented clusters and the big-company-dominated clusters, producers are generally separated from the market. It is precisely for this reason that producers with a high ability to design and brand their own products are rarely fostered in exported-oriented clusters. In big-company-dominated clusters, only the big company itself has such an ability.

NOTES

1. This chapter is a revised version of Ding (2008a).
2. Developed country markets command an absolute majority in China's apparel exports. In 2005, of the top ten countries to which China exported, nine were developed and only Russia was an emerging market country.
3. As for China's textile industry, nearly one-third of the products are manufactured in industrial clusters (Meng and Niu 2006).
4. Under China's statistical system, only data for enterprises with at least five million yuan sales per year can be obtained.
5. The list of the above-mentioned 49 clusters has not been publicized. However, it is clear that of these 49 clusters, 39 were designated as "China Textile Industry Base City (County)" or "Textile Industry Famous City (Town)" in 2005. Thus, we can infer that the 65 clusters treated in this chapter cover most of the apparel clusters in China.
6. In China, the average wage of apparel workers has not risen significantly for a long time. On the one hand, this became an important premise for sustaining the price competitiveness of China's apparel industry. This low wage structure also resulted in the formation of China's huge low-end market. We must pay particular attention to the causality between low wages and industrial upgrading in order to understand economic growth in contemporary China.
7. Author interview with the vice-president of the China Textile Industry Association, Chen Shujin in August 2007.
8. All of these six indices reflect the development level of an apparel cluster. Moreover, the data sources for these indices are government publicity materials. Because of these two reasons, if the phenomenon related to the index can be clearly observed in a cluster, the related information is clearly noted in the material, and if not, the statement concerning the index will either be ambiguous or avoided. The author has paid particular attention to this facet of publicity materials when judging each index.
9. Three cases of the second type of cluster are the Jun'an cluster in Guangdong Province, the Shenhu cluster in Fujian Province, and the Gaoyou cluster in Jiangsu Province. One further cluster, where the share of exports likely exceeds 50 percent, is the Humen cluster in Guangdong Province.
10. After China was affiliated to the WTO, it became much easier to apply for an import/export license. However, application procedures are still complicated. Moreover, trading requires different abilities. Thus, even nowadays, most of the small sewing factories still depend on trading companies.
11. Author interview with a trader of Company X in July 2006.
12. The most powerful apparel trading company in the world is the Hong Kong Li & Fung Group. The Li & Fung Research Center (2003, p. 6) gave the following interesting case. In order to accomplish an order of 10,000 pieces from Europe, Li & Fung purchased yarn from South Korea. This yarn was weaved and dyed in Taiwan. The zippers were bought from YKK, a Japanese manufacturer operating factories in mainland China. Lastly, because of the constraints of quotas and employment conditions, the company arranged for five sewing factories in Thailand to finish the sewing stage. It took only five weeks from receiving the order to shipment, despite the fact that the value chain was scattered over the whole of East Asia. From this case, we can note there is still a considerable gap in organizational capability between Li & Fung and mainland China's trading companies.
13. This section is based on an author interview with Jiang Shaojun, a broker in Nanjing, in July 2007.
14. Author interview with a general manager of a top level textile and apparel trading company in Nanjing, Jiangsu Province, in July 2006. This point was also confirmed by the author's fieldwork in the export-oriented clusters of Pinghu in Zhejiang Province, and in Zhutang, Changan and Donggang in Wuxi City, Jiangsu Province. Of these,

both Pinghu and Zhutang have been designated by the China Textile Industry Association as a "China Apparel Export Famous City (Town)."

15. Author interview with a general manager of a top level textile and apparel trading company in Nanjing, Jiangsu Province, in July 2006.

16. The major part of the information on the Youngor Group is based on an author interview with a staff member of the PR department of the Youngor Group in July 2006. Some information is cited from a Youngor brochure.

17. For branded marketers in the US market, see Gereffi (1999).

18. Ruian Net, http://www.66ruian.com/Html/ramp, accessed 7 February 2007.

19. Information on Company L is based on an author interview in the head office of Company L in October 2006.

20. Seki (2001) noticed that the structure of Japanese clusters is related to market conditions. This idea, however, has not been further developed.

21. This means that even if there were no difference in firm size or firm number between particular clusters, simply because of the differences in the mode of market linkages, the industrial clusters may have entirely different structures.

22. It is noteworthy that the average number of SMEs in export-oriented clusters is clearly much larger than the average number in big-company-dominated clusters. An explanation is that there are countless numbers of brokers who have the potential to start up businesses more easily, and their number can change more flexibly along with changes in the number of producers in the cluster. Some indirect network effects may arise between them.

APPENDIX

Table 10A.1 Specialized-market-based industrial apparel clusters in China (2006)

Province	City	County (city, district)	Town (sub-district)	Title
Guangdong	Dongguan	–	Humen	China Ladies' Wear Famous Town
Guangdong	Dongguan	–	Dalang	China Woolen Sweater Famous Town
Guangdong	Guangzhou	Zengcheng	Xintang	China Jeans Famous Town
Guangdong	Foshan	Chancheng	Huanshi	China Children's Wear Famous Town
Guangdong	Foshan	Nanhai	Yanbu	China Underwear Famous Town
Guangdong	Foshan	Shunde	Jun'an	China Jeans Famous Town
Guangdong	Foshan	Shunde	Zhangcha	China Knitwear Famous Town
Guangdong	Jieyang	Puning	–	China Textile Industry Base City (County)
Guangdong	Swatow	Chaonan	Chendian	China Underwear Famous Town
Guangdong	Swatow	Chaonan	Liangying	China Knitwear Famous Town
Guangdong	Zhongshan	–	Shaxi	China Casual Wear Famous Town
Jiangsu	Suzhou	Changshu	–	China Casual Wear Famous City
Jiangsu	Suzhou	Changshu	Guli	China Down Jacket Famous Town
Jiangsu	Suzhou	Changshu	Haiyu	China Casual Wear Famous Town
Jiangsu	Suzhou	Changshu	Shajiabang	China Casual Wear Famous Town
Jiangsu	Suzhou	Changshu	Xingang	China Sweater Famous Town
Jiangsu	Suzhou	Changshu	Xinzhuang	China Knitwear Famous Town
Jiangsu	Suzhou	Wujiang	Hengshan	China Sweater Famous Town
Jiangsu	Yangzhou	Gaoyou	–	China Down Jacket Manufacturing Famous City

Province	City	County/City	Town	Designation
Zhejiang	Hangzhou	–	–	China Famous Textile and Silk City
Zhejiang	Huzhou	Wuxing	Zhili	China Children's Wear Famous Town
Zhejiang	Jiaxing	Tongxiang	Puyuan	China Woolen Sweater Famous Town
Zhejiang	Jinhua	Yiwu	–	China Socks Famous City
Zhejiang	Jinhua	Yiwu	–	China Seamless Knitwear Famous City
Zhejiang	Shaoxing	Zhuji	Datang	China Socks Famous Town
Zhejiang	Shaoxing	Shengzhou	–	China Necktie Famous City
Fujian	Quanzhou	Jinjiang	Shenhu	China Underwear Famous Town
Fujian	Quanzhou	Shishi	–	China Casual Wear Famous City
Fujian	Quanzhou	Shishi	Lingxiu	China Sports Casual Wear Famous Town
Fujian	Quanzhou	Shishi	Hanjiang	China Trousers Famous Town
Fujian	Quanzhou	Shishi	Baogai	China Apparel Accessories Famous Town
Shandong	Linyi	Tancheng	–	China Menswear Processing Famous City
Shandong	Qingdao	Jimo	–	China Knitwear Famous City
Hebei	Handan	Cixian	–	China Children's Wear Processing Famous City
Liaoning	Anshan	Haicheng	–	China Textile Industry Base City (County)

Source: As for Table 10.1.

Table 10.A.2 Export-oriented industrial apparel clusters in China (2006)

Province	City	County (city, district)	Town (sub-district)	Title
Guangdong	Chaozhou	–	–	China Wedding Dress Famous City
Guangdong	Dongguan	–	–	China Textile Industry Base City (County)
Guangdong	Foshan	Nanhai	Lishui	China Socks Famous Town
Guangdong	Huizhou	Huicheng	–	China Menswear Famous City
Guangdong	Jiangmen	Kaiping	–	China Textile Industry Base City (County)
Guangdong	Jiangmen	Kaiping	Sanbu	China Jeans Famous Town
Guangdong	Maoming	Gaozhou	–	China Gloves Famous City
Guangdong	Shenzhen	–	–	China Famous Apparel City
Guangdong	Swatow	Chaoyang	Gurao	China Knitted Underwear Famous Town
Guangdong	Swatow	Chenghai	–	China Artistic Sweater Famous City
Zhejiang	Hangzhou	Tonglu	Hengcun	China Knitwear Famous Town
Zhejiang	Jiaxing	Pinghu	–	China Export Apparel Manufacturing Famous City
Zhejiang	Ningbo	–	–	China Famous Apparel City
Zhejiang	Ningbo	Xiangshan	–	China Knitwear Famous City
Fujian	Quanzhou	Jinjiang	Yinglin	China Casual Wear Famous Town
Fujian	Quanzhou	Jinjiang	Xintang	China Sportswear Famous Town
Fujian	Quanzhou	Shishi	Fengli	China Children's Wear Famous Town
Jiangsu	Changzhou	Jintan	–	China Export Apparel Manufacturing Famous City
Shandong	Yantai	Haiyang	–	China Sweater Famous City

Source: As for Table 10.1.

198

Table 10A.3 Big-company-dominated industrial apparel clusters in China (2006)

Province	City	County (city, district)	Town (sub-district)	Title
Zhejiang	Shaoxing	Zhuji	Fengqiao	China Shirts Famous Town
Zhejiang	Wenzhou	–	–	China Famous Apparel City
Zhejiang	Wenzhou	Ruian	–	China Menswear Famous City
Zhejiang	Wenzhou	Yueqing	–	China Casual Wear Famous City
Fujian	Quanzhou	–	–	China Famous Apparel City
Fujian	Quanzhou	Jinjiang	–	China Textile Industry Base City (County)
Guangdong	Swatow	Chaonan	Xiashan	China Home Wear Famous Town
Guangdong	Zhongshan	–	Dayong	China Jeans Famous Town
Hebei	Baoding	Rongcheng	–	China Menswear Famous City
Jiangsu	Suzhou	Zhangjiagang	Tangqiao	China Cotton Sweater Famous Town
Shandong	Weifang	Zhucheng	–	China Menswear Famous City

Source: As for Table 10.1.

199

11. Conclusion

*Figure 11.1   A marketplace opened by Chinese merchants in
Johannesburg, South Africa*

11.1 FUNDAMENTAL DIFFERENCES BETWEEN SPECIALIZED MARKETS AND TRADITIONAL MARKETPLACES

As long as transaction activities occur there must be marketplaces. An extremely complicated market-based trading system was formed in traditional China (Skinner 1964, 1965a, 1965b, 1977). In the early age of European industrialization, marketplaces had spread to Paris, London and all the big cities (Braudel 1992). Even in modern times, marketplaces still survive indomitably in most developing countries (Geertz et al. 1979; Goto 2005; Iwasaki 2002). Previous studies have treated specialized markets as a mere *modern piracy* of these traditional marketplaces. The "phased market approach" considers that the specialized market system must be replaced by a more modern distribution system. The "market stratification approach" merely noted that the specialized market system will survive for a long period because China has a huge low-end market. However, all these studies have failed to forecast the situation in which the traditional market system itself is modernized. The case we have made throughout this book is that revolutionary changes have occurred in the specialized market, changes that have profoundly improved the means of market access, enriched the driving forces of value chains, and eventually changed the business environment of small businesses.

11.1.1 Traders

The changes in traders in the specialized markets clearly revealed the differences between specialized markets and traditional marketplaces. We first discuss the changes in the sellers, namely, the booth-keepers in the specialized market.

The first change is that the share of producers among the specialized market booth-keepers has constantly risen. As the case of Yiwu suggests, although the share of wholesale merchants (including manufacturer-wholesalers) still accounts for more than half of the total booths, the share of producers increased faster than any other type of booth-keeper. Furthermore, within the remaining booths, a number of booth-keepers are sales agents who do not have ownership of the commodities. In this sense, the specialized market is shifting towards a pure market platform.[1]

The second change is that the geographical distribution of sellers in specialized markets has become increasingly broader. In the early stage, the majority of sellers were generally local traditional traders (peddlers or small producers). Gradually, based on the Landsmann network, and sometimes invited by the local government, non-local booth-keepers began to move into the markets to become the majority of booth-keepers.

The third change is that leading firms such as brand-name owning companies have shown an increasingly larger presence in the specialized market. The cases of both Yiwu and Changshu indicate that, on the one hand, many local SMEs have grown into the leading firms, and on the other hand, local governments have played an important role in inviting leading firms into other locations.

The changes in buyers in the specialized markets have also been significant. The first change is that the geographical distribution of buyers in specialized markets has also become increasingly broader. As the case of Yiwu indicates, in the initial stage buyers in specialized markets were primarily local merchants scattered in distant markets. Gradually, stimulated by these merchants, a large number of non-local merchants began to make purchases in specialized markets. Along with advances in logistics and communications technology, buyers in developing countries, whose market conditions are similar to China's domestic market, also began to come to the specialized market for purchasing.

The second change is that linkages between buyers and specialized market booth-keepers have become increasingly formalized. In the initial stage, these buyers and sellers were generally linked through the informal merchants' network. Gradually, various government departments began to intentionally form links with the buyers and sellers by opening branch markets or by establishing the National Industrial Products Wholesale Markets Association. As a result, a powerful specialized market system has been formed. Currently, even markets in developing countries have begun to make an appearance in this system.

The third change is that qualified buyers have made an appearance in the specialized markets. On the one hand, supermarkets and department stores have appeared as final retail outlets for the specialized market system. On the other hand, large numbers of trade fairs for attracting more qualified buyers came to be held from the 1990s onwards.

11.1.2   Transaction Platforms

The specialized market not only cultivated a large number of new types of buyers and sellers, but also built an efficient platform for supporting their transactions. This platform succeeded in circumventing the possibility of the market developing as an informal transaction space, which is often observed in developing countries, and facilitated the upgrading of industrial clusters.

First, the specialized market has continuously provided the necessary infrastructure to support transactions. Along with the expansion of the scale of transactions, the specialized markets accordingly expanded the areas available for market transaction buildings, thus increasing the booth numbers. They also worked out various measures to stimulate flexible transactions of the usage rights of booths and to maintain taxes, booth rents and other fees at an appropriate level. The result was that the accessibility of specialized markets became much higher than for markets in other developing countries. This high market accessibility provided small producers with a *Chinese dream*. As long as one has a market booth, one can have one's own marketing channels and thus grow rapidly. This proved to be a great boost for SME entrepreneurship.[2]

The second point is that the specialized market manager has provided an efficient transaction environment that reduces various transaction costs. Regarding exogenous transaction costs, various measures such as the classification of commodities by industry and location, have been carried out in specialized markets. As for endogenous transaction costs, various credibility management systems have also been designed by the local governments.

Third, the specialized market has established an efficient management system, which generally consists of three levels. The first level is the managing committee, composed of all the specialized-market-related government departments. This committee is under the control of the top-tier officials of the county and primarily takes charge of the important decision-making concerning specialized market development. The second level is the AIC, other concerned government departments and a market managing company, which take charge of the daily management of the specialized market. The third level is the self-management network, which coordinates the relationship between the public and the private sectors, and is generally under the control of the AIC. Horizontally, this system coordinates the complicated relationships between various government departments, and vertically, it efficiently manages a large number of highly mobile small businesses. As a result, the local government has become able to manage specialized markets in a precise way.

11.2 WHY DID THE SPECIALIZED MARKET SYSTEM EMERGE IN CHINA?

11.2.1 The Domestic Market

Throughout this book the case has been made that the specialized market system is nothing but a unique product of China's transitional economy. There are five factors that have affected the formation of the specialized market system, the first being China's domestic market. Four features concerning this market were crucial for the specialized market system.

The first feature is that China has potentially had massive domestic demand for consumer goods from the beginning of the reform and opening-up policy. China implemented a strategy of priority for heavy industry development during the planned economy period, greatly restraining domestic consumer production and demand for many years. The appearance of the specialized market system is simply an institutional response to such a restriction. During the time when the specialized market system was formed, 1978 to 2009, the "total retail sales of social consumer goods" increased by more than 90 times (NBSC 1979–2010).

The second feature is that this huge domestic market is highly stratified and the majority of demand is actually in the low-end market. China's Gini Coefficient increased from 0.382 to 0.454 between 1988 and 2002, which means that China's income gap became increasingly larger during the 1990s (Zhao, Li and Riskin 1999; Li and Yue 2004). Furthermore, this income gap will probably continue in the future. According to Huang (2009), the population engaged in China's informal economy, which suffers from low income and poor welfare, increased explosively from 15,000 to 168,200,000 during the period from 1978 to 2006. At the same time, the population engaged in the formal economy rose only from 95 million to 115 million. Unlike the experience of developed countries, a social structure within which the majority are either informal economy employees or part of the agricultural population (300 million in 2006) is likely to continue in China for a considerable period of time.

For the specialized market system, the significance of the low-end market is not only the *size* of the demand, but also the *number* of traders. The low-end market is characterized by price competition, small batch demand and low barriers to entry and exit. A large number of small merchants and small producers thus appear in such a market, and it is the existence of these large numbers of small merchants and producers that has generated the institutional demand for the specialized market system.[3]

The stratification of the Chinese market has also brought about great upgrading opportunities for the specialized market system and its users. Because of the considerable scale of middle and high-end demand in the Chinese market, various modern distribution systems were thus able to make their appearance and establish linkages with the specialized market system. On the other hand, since the market is stratified, firms making use of the specialized market system were thus able to avoid being involved in a situation where "bad money drives out good money." In contrast to firms in a homogeneous market, specialized market users have the option of formulating different upgrading strategies and thus entering a different market segmentation.

The third feature is that the expansion of China's huge domestic demand has been accompanied by the collapse of the existing distribution system. During the planned economy period, China's distribution system was extremely rigid.[4] The commodity wholesale system was highly fragmented and segmentary, and within the system almost all the wholesale enterprises were state-owned companies. All purchasing and selling activities in this system were required to be under the control of the economic plans. From the 1980s, this system became increasingly inefficient and was soon paralyzed (Chen 1999, pp. 297–9). In these circumstances, the newly emerging small businesses encountered no huge and powerful actors during their period of growth.

Conversely, the formation of the specialized market system has also greatly stimulated market integration in China, at least in its low-end segmentation. Before the emergence of this system, whether in the periods of traditional society or of the planned economy, China's domestic market was to some extent fragmented. As the specialized market system developed, however, these isolated markets became gradually interconnected, and China did indeed become a huge and integrated market. Currently, the markets of some developing countries have also been integrated into this market.

11.2.2 Regional Groups of Merchants

The second factor that affected the formation of the specialized market system is the regional groups, who were historically engaged in long-distance trade. As the duration of China's planned economy was not as long as that of the Soviet Union, the traditions of long-distance trade were well preserved in some regions such as Zhejiang (Nakagane 2002). The regional groups of merchants can be further classified into two types.

The first type is the peddler who traveled around various locations in China selling agricultural products or daily necessities, but had no skills regarding production. A typical case discussed in this book is the Qiaotang Bang of Yiwu. The second type is the itinerant craftsmen, who traveled around distant markets selling or repairing self-manufactured products. Wenzhou is just such a typical case.[5]

Mainstream economics consider that as the scale of transactions expand, personalized transactions must give way to impersonal transactions (North 1990; Greif 2006). The cases of the regional groups of merchants in the specialized market system, however, tell us that the relationships in these types of transactions consist not of rivalry but of complementarity.[6] The roles of these regional groups of merchants in the development of the specialized market system are as follows.

First, the peddlers and itinerant craftsmen existed as both the buyers and the sellers in large numbers in the specialized market system. This fact is important in the following two senses. On the one hand, because they were of the same geographical origin, they were readily able to establish business relationships with each other. In the initial stage, this enabled some markets to easily exceed the critical mass, and thus cause the indirect network effects to arise. On the other hand, these regional groups, especially the itinerant craftsmen, are easily able to move freely around between the production side and the distribution side of the specialized markets. As producers, they are familiar with market demand information. As distributors, they mastered the knowledge on production. Therefore, the information flow within the specialized market system became increasingly smooth, and thus increasingly more active interactions occurred between producers and distributors.

Second, the Landsmann network of these peddlers and itinerant craftsmen enabled large numbers of them to travel around the whole of China. As a result, when they moved to marketplaces in the cities, they disseminated information on the specialized markets in their hometowns. When they moved to industrial clusters outside hometowns, they ensured the constant increase of sellers and thus facilitated the formation of a new specialized market. A specialized market system based on the networks of regional groups thus appeared. As the cases of both Yiwu and Changshu indicate, however, because of the outstanding platform governance and the efforts by merchants themselves, this system has indeed transcended the traditional Landsmann network. Currently, the large numbers of small producers and small merchants, who come from regions without the tradition of long-distance trade, have become by far the major actors supporting the specialized market system.

Third, the high mobility of these peddlers and itinerant craftsmen stimulated competition between the marketplaces in the specialized market system. As Xia (1992) appropriately pointed out, these people are simply like migratory birds, always traveling from one region to another in search of new market opportunities. This high mobility exerted great pressure on local governments. The business environment of the marketplaces in the specialized market system thus has required ceaseless improvement in order to retain these customers.

Fourth, it is necessary to emphasize the unique entrepreneurship of these peddlers and itinerant craftsmen, although this point has not been sufficiently discussed in the case studies. Their entrepreneurship is characterized by acute sensitivity to market conditions, which has greatly stimulated the thorough exploration of the low-end market. This is eloquently demonstrated by the statement of Zhou Xiaoguang, a former booth-keeper in Yiwu Market, who is currently the president of China's largest jewelry company (Xinguang).

> From my own practical experience, I think although most of Yiwu's firms are at a very low level and appear to be backward, they are greatly suited to China's conditions, cultural background and development stage. They are able to grasp

immediately the most suitable goods for the current stage and what kind of organization is right for the current situation. Once the environment changes, they will go upward as well. (*Zhejiang Daily*, 13 January 2005)

11.2.3 Local Government

The third factor that affected the formation of the specialized market system is local government. As previous studies have generally shown in their analysis, under contemporary China's decentralized fiscal system, the local public sector was strongly motivated to intervene in regional development, and was thus very keen to encourage the establishment of and support the management of specialized markets (Chen 1999, pp. 315–16, 336–45; Zheng et al. 2003, p. 50; Zhu 2003, pp. 105–106). After a thorough examination of local government activities in specialized markets, we find that two points concerning local government involvement still need to be emphasized.

First, since China carried out the agrarian revolution, local government has become almost the sole landowner in the country. As a result, the land use problem, the largest institutional bottleneck for the reconstruction of a distribution system, has been smoothly overcome. For most of the successful specialized markets, local governments have constantly provided necessary land along with the development of the markets.

Second, in the market platform mode, both buyers and sellers are targets for competition. Therefore, as a platform manager, the local government is generally under greater competition pressure in a specialized market than in other platforms such as an industrial park. Two factors have further intensified this platform competition.

On the one hand, as main actors in the specialized market, the regional groups of merchants are sensitive to market conditions and always wish to search out better market opportunities. In order to retain these merchants, the local government thus has had to constantly work out innovative management methods for the specialized market.

On the other hand, the active mutual learning between local governments has also stimulated competition among markets in the specialized market system. As has been clarified in Chapter 3, in China the central government and provincial government often intentionally publicize the experiences of successful regions and the lessons of unsuccessful regions to all other related regions. They also encourage local governments to make inspection tours to learn from their rivals. The result is that all the information concerning specialized market management is evenly shared between local governments. This has caused sufficiently intense inter-regional marketplace competition to take place.

11.2.4   Other Factors

A further two factors still need to be emphasized here. These exist in most countries, and thus are not China-specific but, for the formation of the specialized market system, they are indispensable.

The first factor is the tradition of rural cottage industry. As cases in this book have indicated, the solid foundation of rural cottage industry in Zhejiang and Jiangsu has been an important premise for specialized market development in these areas. The existence of the rural cottage industry has provided large reserve armies of specialized market booth-keepers. It has also enabled the continued increase in the share of producers (among booth-keepers) in the specialized markets.

The second factor is that the technological constraints on producing low-end market oriented commodities are diminishing. A typical case is numerical control (NC) technology. With NC technology, as long as machine tools and data are provided, and high machine accuracy is not required, it has become increasingly easier to manufacture molds.[7]

11.3   SIGNIFICANCE OF THE SPECIALIZED MARKET FOR DEVELOPING COUNTRIES

There are a great many marketplaces in developing countries. An important purpose of studying the experience of the specialized market is precisely to explore the possibility that these marketplaces can be improved and thus become an institution that contributes to poverty reduction and economic development. Although the specialized market was a unique product of China's transitional economy, its experience is significant for developing countries in at least the following two fields.

11.3.1   An Efficient Distribution System for the Exploration of Emerging Markets

Although emerging markets are growing rapidly, the majority of consumers in these markets are still in the low-income class. Firms aiming at emerging markets thus inevitably encounter various difficulties. As Karnani (2007, pp. 91–2) has pointed out:

> The poor are often geographically dispersed (except for the urban poor concentrated into slums) and culturally heterogeneous. This dispersion of the rural poor increases distribution and marketing costs and makes it difficult to exploit economies of scale. Weak infrastructure (transportation, communication,

media, and legal) further increases the cost of doing business. Another factor leading to high costs is the small size of each transaction.

Karnani (2007, p. 91) thus argues that the cost of serving the markets at "the bottom of the pyramid" can be very high, and it is unlikely to be very profitable for a large company such as a multinational to sell to the poor.

The specialized market, however, can easily deal with the above marketing difficulties. As described in the cases of Yiwu and Changshu, the main actors taking charge of production and distribution in emerging markets are the numerous small producers and small merchants. It can be said that the difficulty of distribution and marketing in the emerging markets is precisely how to effectively organize transactions between such large numbers of small businesses. With regard to this point, the indirect network effect arising in the specialized market plays a crucial role. As a result of just this effect, the large numbers of small buyers who brought about both the scattered small orders and heterogeneous demand information, can be attracted to the specialized market. Simply by trading with these buyers, small producers making use of the specialized market can easily enter a new market without constructing their own sales networks and exploiting the economies of scale. Furthermore, simply by communicating with these buyers and watching the salability of products in the market, producers can obtain timely heterogeneous demand information from any location in the emerging markets. Consequently, the "fortune at the bottom of pyramid," the huge potential demands in the developing world, can for the first time be exploited to the fullest.

11.3.2 A New Model of Industrialization

In many developing countries, industrial structural changes have not shown the pattern that the Petty-Clark Law has forecast. Despite the fact that the tertiary sector is thriving immensely, the secondary sector remains less developed. Common problems for these countries are that, on the one hand, the domestic market is fragmented into various local markets, and on the other hand, traditional merchants firmly control the distribution channels and never enter the manufacturing sector themselves. Many previous studies thus consider that it is difficult to realize takeoff merely by the exploitation of the domestic market in developing countries. The only method of stimulating economic development is regarded to be trade with developed countries.

Because of the existence of the specialized market, however, the situation in China is completely different. As indicated by what has occurred in Yiwu and Changshu, in the initial stage a large number of merchants flowed into the specialized market, and the tertiary sector indeed thrived before the expansion of the secondary sector. Thereafter, however, one merchant after another began to take on an extensive role in the manufacturing sector. Both the number of producers and the share of the secondary sector in GDP have shown a constant increase.

Nothing but the specialized market pushed forward such a decisive structural change. Along with the progresses in platform governance, and as the linkages between specialized markets and other marketplaces became increasingly close, a large number of buyers were attracted to the markets. In these circumstances, the risks for merchants entering the manufacturing sector became increasingly lower. On the other hand, as competition continued to intensify, the profit margins of each merchant became smaller and smaller. In order to survive the competition, they had no choice but to manufacture the products themselves. In this way, the experience of the specialized markets has inspired us to believe that developing countries are likely to promote industrialization by improving the domestic distribution system first.

11.3.3   Premise for Learning the Experience of the Specialized Markets

Can other developing countries learn from the experience of the specialized markets that emerged under the unique socio-economic conditions of China's transitional economy? In the author's opinion, this depends on whether or not a country has the following three basic factors.

The first factor is whether there are sufficient potential traders in the market. Generally, a large potential demand for low-end commodities broadly exists in a developing country that has a huge population. The problem is whether the potential traders in this market will be allowed to enter the marketplace or not. If the government cannot recognize the importance of small businesses, using a similar strict standard to collect taxes or implement quality control with small firms as with big firms, the institutional barriers to entry for these potential traders will become extremely high. On the other hand, if the number of booths of a specialized market is limited and potential sellers are not able to operate their own booths, the marketing channels will be dominated by a small number of existing merchants.

The second factor concerns the tradition of long-distance trade. As Chapter 6 indicates, merchant groups engaging in long-distance trade broadly exist in the developing countries. However, there are two crucial problems. First, as distant market buyers, can they actively disseminate market information to other buyers and not monopolize it? Second, can the merchants obtain enough support in the aspects of technology, infrastructure and human resources when they are provided with incentives (or are under pressure) to enter the manufacturing sector?

The third factor is the platform manager. Powerful local governments are undoubtedly a source of China's economic development. It is difficult to expect that other countries would also have such a strong economic actor. We must note, however, that the essence of the local government for specialized market development is nothing but a platform manager. For other countries, such a manager is not necessarily a government. The platform manager could be an enterprise, or some other form of organization. The key factor is whether the platform manager can benefit from the marketplace development and whether there is sufficient competition between the marketplaces or not.

11.4 THE FUTURE OF SPECIALIZED MARKETS

Specialized markets are being challenged by various seemingly more modern distribution systems, such as the department store, the supermarket, and e-commerce platforms. Is it therefore possible that specialized markets will continue to exist for a long time in the future? In the author's opinion, there are three factors that are aiding the specialized markets to survive and thrive in the future.

The first factor is the increasingly lower costs of long-distance trade. Each market has a great number of potential buyers. When transportation and communication technologies were less developed, the logistics system was not advanced, and only a limited number of trading companies were able to engage in long-distance trade. In contrast to traditional society, in the era of globalization the means of transportation, communication and logistics have been greatly improved, and various trade support institutions (such as purchasing agents introduced in Chapter 6) for SMEs have made their appearance. The result is that the costs of trade for small firms have decreased drastically, and this has made it possible for increasing numbers of buyers to continue to appear in the market. Since these new buyers require a platform on which to establish business relationships with producers, their large presence thus forms a solid foundation that ensures the long-term prosperity of specialized markets.

The second factor is the increasingly smaller optimal scale of production of final products. A trend of current technological innovation is the platformization of core components. As the case of the Intel platform in the PC industry, and the MTK platform in the cell phone industry suggest, platforms have greatly reduced the optimal scale of production, enabling small firms with only a few dozen employees to engage in the production of final products (Tatsumoto, Ogawa and Fujimoto 2009; Ding and Pan 2011). Since these small producers need a shared platform to help them exploit new markets, as in the case of buyers, their large presence thus also forms a foundation that ensures the long-term development of specialized markets.

The third factor that helps the specialized markets survive and thrive is tacit knowledge. The market platform consists of both a physical marketplace and a virtual e-commerce platform. However, as most of the goods are not completely standardized, a great deal of the knowledge and information that is exchanged between buyers and sellers is thus tacit knowledge. For traders, face to face communication is necessary for obtaining such kinds of knowledge and information. This provides a large demand for the specialized market and ensures that it is not replaced by e-commerce platforms in the future.

NOTES

1. However, if constraints of land and the commercial real estate use system (especially in urban areas) become apparent, the number of booths will not be adjusted flexibly to accommodate the change in the number of buyers. In this situation, the share of merchants is likely to increase.
2. Market accessibility has a great influence on the business model in a society. The case of Japan stands in contrast to China. In Japan, as it was the merchants who traditionally dominated the distribution system, innumerable small businesses were forced to specialize in a narrow production sector. The division of labor between small producers has thus greatly advanced in Japanese industry (Takeuchi 1991).
3. A good counter-example is the USA. The purchasing power of the US market is much larger than that of China. However, the majority of people in the US market are middle class and have a strong requirement for high quality products. Thus, up until the emergence of e-commerce, distribution in the USA had been controlled by a limited number of big distributors.
4. Concretely, in the planned economy period, China's distribution system was divided into four subsystems, namely, the consumer goods distribution system controlled by the Ministry of Commerce, the means of production distribution system controlled by the Ministry of Procurement, the agricultural distribution system controlled by the Supply and Marketing Cooperative, and traded goods controlled by the stated-owned trading companies (Wang and Qian 2003, pp. 62–3). All these subsystems were completely separate.
5. Itinerant craftsmen can also be observed in the early period of industrialization in Japan. However, the purpose of itineration in these two countries was very different. In the Chinese case, the itinerant craftsmen simply wanted to earn a living, whereas in the Japanese case, the craftsmen wished to further improve their production skills.
6. In my opinion, personalized and impersonal transactions are also likely to coexist at different levels of a market economy. In January 2008, the author visited two markets opened by Wenzhou merchants, one in Lanzhou, Gansu Province, and the other in Urumqi, Xinjiang Autonomous Region. I found that when a new market is being established, the Landsmann network still matters in a number of important particulars.

   Three steps are apparent when Wenzhou merchants establish a new market. The first step is fund-raising. It was reported that most of the necessary funds are gathered from Wenzhou. The second step is known as Da Zhaoshang (big invitation). Market managers usually travel to Wenzhou to persuade local firms or citizens to take up the ownership of the new market's booths. The third step is Xiao Zhaoshang (small invitation). This refers to the market managers inviting small merchants to operate booths in the new market. In this step, both the Wenzhou merchants and the non-Wenzhou merchants have been invited.

7. This point was made by Professor Yukio Watanabe of Keio University, Japan.

Bibliography

ENGLISH PUBLICATIONS

Armstrong, Mark (2006), "Competition in Two-Sided Markets," *Rand Journal of Economics*, **37**: 668–91.

Armstrong, Mark and Julian Wright (2008), "Two-sided Markets," in Steven N. Durlauf and Lawrence E. Blume (eds), *The New Palgrave Dictionary of Economics*, Second Edition, New York: Palgrave Macmillan.

Bazan, Luiza and Lizbeth Navas-Aleman (2004), "The Underground Revolution in the Sinos Valley: A Comparison of Upgrading in Global and National Value-chains," in Hubert Schmitz (ed.), *Local Enterprises in the Global Economy: Issues of Governance and Upgrading*, Cheltenham, UK and Northampton, MA, USA: Edward Elgar.

Biglaiser, Gary (1993), "Middlemen as Experts," *Rand Journal of Economics*, **24**: 212–23.

Boudreau, Kevin J. and Andrei Hagiu (2009), "Platform Rules: Multi-sided Platforms as Regulators," in Annabelle Gawer (ed.), *Platforms, Markets and Innovation*, Cheltenham, UK and Northampton, MA, USA: Edward Elgar.

Braudel, Fernand (1992), *The Wheels of Commerce (Civilization and Capitalism: 15th–18th Century, Volume 2)*, Berkeley: University of California Press.

Caillaud, Bernard and Bruno Jullien (2003), "Chicken and Egg: Competition Among Intermediation Service Providers," *Rand Journal of Economics*, **34**: 309–28.

Ding, Ke (2009), "Distribution System of China's Industrial Clusters: Case Study of Yiwu China Commodity City," in Bernard Ganne and Yveline Lecler (eds), *Asian Industrial Clusters, Global Competitiveness and New Policy Initiatives*, Singapore: World Scientific.

Ding, Ke (2010), "The Role of the Specialized Markets in Upgrading Industrial Clusters in China," in Akifumi Kuchiki and Masatsugu Tsuji (eds), *From Agglomeration to Innovation: Upgrading Industrial Clusters in Emerging Economies*, London: Palgrave Macmillan.

Ding, Ke and Jiutang Pan (2011), "Platforms, Network Effects and Small Business Dynamics in China: Case Study of the Shanzhai Cell Phone Industry," IDE Discussion Papers 302.

Economides, Nicholas (1996), "The Economics of Networks," *International Journal of Industrial Organization*, **14**: 673–99.

Economides, Nicholas and Charles Himmelberg (1995), "Critical Mass and Network Evolution in Telecommunications," in Gerard Brock (ed.), *Toward a Competitive Telecommunications Industry: Selected Papers from the 1994 Telecommunications Policy Research Conference*, Philadelphia: Lawrence Erlbaum Associates, Inc.

Evans, David S. (2003), "The Antitrust Economics of Multi-Sided Platform Markets," *Yale Journal on Regulation*, **20**: 325–82.

Evans, David S. (2009), "How Catalysts Ignite: The Economics of Platform-based Start-ups," in Annabelle Gawer (ed.), *Platforms, Markets and Innovation*, Cheltenham, UK and Northampton, MA, USA: Edward Elgar.

Fah, Daniel (2008), "Markets, Value Chains and Upgrading in Developing Industrial Clusters: A Case Study of the Narrow Fabric Industry in Yiwu, Zhejiang Province, P.R. China," Zurich: Diploma Thesis Submitted to the Faculty of Science Department of Geography, University of Zurich, Switzerland.

Fujita, Masahisa, Paul Krugman and Anthony J. Venables (1999), *The Spatial Economy: Cities, Regions, and International Trade*, Cambridge, MA: MIT Press.

Geertz, Clifford, Hildred Geertz and Lawrence Rosen (1979), *Meaning and Order in Moroccan Society: Three Essays in Culture Analysis*, Cambridge: Cambridge University Press.

Gereffi, Gary (1999), "International Trade and Industrial Upgrading in the Apparel Commodity Chain," *Journal of International Economics*, **48**: 37–70.

Global Value Chain Initiative Website, http://www.globalvaluechains.org, accessed 1 October 2006.

Greif, Avner (2006), *Institutions and the Path to the Modern Economy: Lessons from Medieval Trade*, New York: Cambridge University Press.

Hagiu, Andrei (2006a), "Pricing and Commitment by Two-Sided Platforms," *Rand Journal of Economics*, **37**: 720–37.

Hagiu, Andrei (2006b), "Two-Sided Platforms: Pricing, Product Variety and Social Efficiency," mimeo, Harvard Business School.

Hagiu, Andrei (2007), "Merchant or Two-Sided Platform?," *Review of Network Economics*, **6**: 115–33.

Hirschman, Albert O. (1957), *The Strategy of Economic Development*, New Heaven, CT: Yale University Press.

Humphrey, John and Hubert Schmitz (2000), "Governance and Upgrading: Linking Industrial Cluster and Global Value Chain Research," IDS Working Paper 120.

International Labor Organization (ILO) (1972), *Employment, Income and Equality: A Strategy for Increasing Productive Employment in Kenya*, Geneva: ILO.

Karnani, Aneel (2007), "The Mirage of Marketing to the Bottom of the Pyramid: How the Private Sector Can Help Alleviate Poverty," *California Management Review*, **49**: 90–111.

Knorringa, Peter (1999), "Agra: An Old Cluster Facing the New Competition," *World Development*, **27**: 1587–604.

Krugman, Paul (1991), *Geography and Trade*, Leuven, Belgium and Cambridge, MA, USA: Leuven University Press and MIT Press.

Kuchiki, Akifumi and Masatsugu Tsuji (eds) (2005), *Industrial Clusters in Asia: Analyses of their Competition and Cooperation*, New York: Palgrave Macmillan.

Kuchiki, Akifumi and Masatsugu Tsuji (eds) (2008), *Flowchart Approach to Industrial Cluster Policy*, New York: Palgrave Macmillan.

Markusen, Ann (1996), "Sticky Places in Slippery Space: A Typology of Industrial Districts," *Economic Geography*, **72**: 293–313.

Marshall, Alfred (1920), *Principles of Economics*, Eighth Edition, London: Macmillan.

Marukawa, Tomoo (2004a), "Marketing and Social Network in Inland China," Paper Presented at the Kobe University – Sichuan Academy of Social Science Conference on the Development of Inland China.

McMillan, John (2002), *Reinventing the Bazaar*, New York: W.W. Norton & Company.

Mills, C. Wright (1951), *White Collar: The American Middle Classes*, New York: Oxford University Press.

Nishiguchi, Toshihiro (1994), *Strategic Industrial Sourcing: The Japanese Advantage*, New York: Oxford University Press.

North, Douglass (1990), *Institutions, Institutional Change and Economic Performance*, New York: Cambridge University Press.

North, Douglass (1991), "Institutions," *The Journal of Economic Perspectives*, **5**(1): 97–112.

O'Hara, Maureen (1995), *Market Microstructure Theory*, Hoboken, NJ: John Wiley & Sons.

Otsuka, Keijiro and Tetsushi, Sonobe (2011), "A Cluster-Based Industrial Development Policy for Low-Income Countries," Policy Research Working Paper 5703, World Bank.

Piore, Michel J. and Charles F. Sabel (1984), *The Second Industrial Divide: Possibilities for Prosperity*, New York: Basic Books.

Qian, Yingyi and Barry R. Weingast (1997), "Federalism as a Commitment to Preserving Market Incentives," *The Journal of Economic Perspectives*, **11**: 83–92.

Rochet, Jean-Charles and Jean Tirole (2003), "Platform Competition in Two-Sided Markets," *Journal of the European Economic Association*, **1**: 990–1029.

Rochet, Jean-Charles and Jean Tirole (2006), "Two-Sided Markets: A Progress Report," *Rand Journal of Economics*, **37**: 645–67.

Rubinstein, Ariel and Asher Wolinsky (1987), "Middlemen," *Quarterly Journal of Economics*, **102**: 581–93.

Rust, John and George Hall (2003), "Middlemen vs. Market Makers: A Theory of Competitive Exchange," *Journal of Political Economy*, **111**: 353–403.

Schmalensee, Richard (2002), "Payment Systems and Interchange Fees," *Journal of Industrial Economics*, **50**: 103–22.

Schmitz, Hubert (1995), "Collective Efficiency: Growth Path for Small-scale Industry," *The Journal of Development Studies*, **31**: 529–66.

Schmitz, Hubert (2006a), "Regional Systems and Global Chains," in *Keynote Papers and Session-Papers' Abstracts*. Beijing: The Fifth International Conference on Industrial Clustering and Regional Development 2006.

Schmitz, Hubert (2006b), "Learning and Earning in Global Garment and Footwear Chains," *European Journal of Development Research*, **18**: 546–71.

Schmitz, Hubert and Khalid Nadavi (1999), "Clustering and Industrialization: Introduction," *World Development*, **27**: 1503–14.

Sengenberger, Werner and Frank Pyke (1991), "Small Firm Industrial Districts and Local Economic Regeneration: Research and Policy Issues," *Labour and Society*, **16**: 1–24.

Skinner, G. William (1964), "Marketing and Social Structure in Rural China, Part I," *The Journal of Asian Studies*, **24**: 3–42.

Skinner, G. William (1965a), "Marketing and Social Structure in Rural China, Part II," *The Journal of Asian Studies*, **24**: 195–228.

Skinner, G. William (1965b), "Marketing and Social Structure in Rural China, Part III," *The Journal of Asian Studies*, **24**: 363–99.

Skinner, G. William (ed.) (1977), *The City in Late Imperial China*, Stanford, CA: Stanford University Press.

Sonobe, Tetsushi and Keijiro Otsuka (2006), *Cluster-based Industrial Development: An East Asian Model*, New York: Palgrave Macmillan.

Spulber, Daniel F. (1996a), "Market Making by Price-Setting Firms," *Review of Economic Studies*, **63**: 559–80.

Spulber, Daniel F. (1996b), "Market Microstructure and Intermediation," *Journal of Economic Perspectives*, **10**: 135–52.

Stahl, Dale O. (1988), "Bertrand Competition for Inputs and Walrasian Outcomes," *The American Economic Review*, **78**: 189–201.

Takeuchi, Johzen (1991), *The Role of Labour-Intensive Sectors in Japanese Industrialization: Technology Transfer, Transformation, and Development*, Tokyo: United Nations University Press.

Tatsumoto, Hirofumi, Koichi Ogawa and Takahiro Fujimoto (2009), "The Effect of Technological Platforms on the International Division of Labor: A Case Study of Intel's Platform Business in the PC Industry," in Annabelle Gawer (ed.), *Platforms, Markets and Innovation*, Cheltenham, UK and Northampton, MA, USA: Edward Elgar.

Tewari, Meenu (1999), "Successful Adjustment in Indian Industry: The Case of Ludhiana's Woolen Knitwear Cluster," *World Development*, **27**: 1651–72.

United Nations Conference on Trade and Development (UNCTAD) (2005), *UNCTAD – Handbook of Statistics 2004*, New York/Geneva: United Nations.

United Nations Industrial Development Organization (UNIDO) (2007), *International Yearbook of Industrial Statistics 2007*, New York/Geneva: United Nations.

Wright, Julian (2004), "Determinants of Optimal Interchange Fees in Payment Systems," *Journal of Industrial Economics*, **52**: 1–26.

CHINESE PUBLICATIONS

Africa Business Affairs Net, http://www.africa.gov.cn, accessed 15 December 2006.

Africa Business Affairs Net, "Zhongguo Shangren Zai Nanfei" [Chinese Merchants in South Africa], http://www.africa.gov.cn/ArticleView/2006-1-23/Article_View_1835.htm, accessed 15 December 2006.

Africa Business Net, http://www.africa-biz.net, accessed 15 December 2006.

Africa Economy Net, http://www.africa-economy.net, accessed 15 December 2006.

Africa Investment Net, http://www.invest.net.cn, accessed 15 December 2006.

Africa Trade Net, http://www.ca-trade519.net, accessed 15 December 2006.

Business Daily (2007), "Yiwu Shichang: Quanguo Zhishi Chanquan Gonzuo De Xianweijing" [Yiwu Market: A Microscope of China's Protection of Intellectual Property Rights], 28 April 2007.

Caijing.Com.Cn (22 August 2008), "Quangguo Quxiao Geti Gongshanghu, Jimao Shichang Guanlifei" [China Abolished Market Administration Fees for Self-employed Enterprises], http://www.caijing.com.cn/2008-08-22/110007695.html, accessed 16 January 2009.

Changshu Economy and Trade Net (16 January 2008 and 10 January 2008), "Changshu Shi Huode De Zhongguo Mingpai Chanpin Mingdan (1), (2)" [A List of China Top Brands in Changshu (1), (2)], http://www.cssme.gov.cn/ChineseBrandsshow.asp?ID=454 and http://www.cssme.gov.cn/ChineseBrandsshow.asp?ID=455, accessed 22 January 2009.

Changshu Economy and Trade Net "Changshu Shi Huode De Zhongguo Chiming Shangbiao Mingdan (1),(2)" [A List of China Noted Trademarks in Changshu (1),(2)], http://www.cssme.gov.cn/FamousChineseTradeshow.asp?ID=477 and http://www.cssme.gov.cn/FamousChineseTradeshow.asp?ID=478, accessed 22 January 2009.

Changshu Local Chronicle Editing Committee (CLCEC) (1999), *1999 Changshu Nianjian* [1999 Changshu Yearbook], Beijing: China County and Town Yearbook Press.

Changshu Local Chronicle Editing Committee (2000), *2000 Changshu Nianjian* [2000 Changshu Yearbook], Beijing: Chinese Communist Party History Press.

Changshu Local Chronicle Editing Committee (2002), *2002 Changshu Nianjian* [2002 Changshu Yearbook], Beijing: Chinese Communist Party History Press.

Changshu Self-employed Enterprise and Private Enterprise Association (CSPA) (ed.) (1997), *Guangcai Shiye Guangcai Ren: Changshu Shi Geti, Siying Jingji Lveying* [Brilliant Program, Brilliant People: A Glimpse of Self-employed Enterprises and Private Enterprises in Changshu City], Internal Material.

Chen, Jianjun (1999), *Zhongguo Gaosu Chengzhang Diyu De Jingji Fazhan: Guanyu Jiangzhe Moshi De Yanjiu* [The Economic Development of the High Rapid Growth Region in China: A Study on the Development Model of the Jiangsu-Zhejiang], Shanghai: Shanghai People's Publishing House.

Chen, Ming (2005), "Yiwu Xiaoshangpin Miaozhun Nanfei Shichang" [Yiwu Commodities Aim at South African Market], Sina Net, http://chanye.finance.sina.com.cn/sm/2005-12-26/272775.shtml, accessed 15 December 2006.

China Africa Net, http://www.chinaafrica.com, accessed 15 December 2006.

China Apparel Association Website, Website for Industrial Clusters, http://www.cnga.org.cn, accessed 11 November 2006.

China Apparel Association Website, Website for Industrial Cluster List, www.cnga.org.cn/news/text/123.doc, accessed 11 November 2006.

China Apparel Magazine Press/China Textile Newspaper Press (CAMP/CTNP) (2006), *2006 Zhongguo Zhuming Fangzhi Fuzhuang Chanye Jidi Shiyong Shangwu Ditu* [2006 China Famous Textile Apparel Base Practical Business Map], Beijing: China Apparel Magazine Press/China Textile Newspaper Press.

China Apparel News Website (24 October 2008), "Zhongguo Fuzhaung Liutong Chanye Jiqun De Jueqi Lujing: Zhongguo Changshu Fuzhuangcheng Chuangxin Fazhan Jishi" [The Emerging Path of China's Apparel Distribution Industrial Cluster: Record of the Innovation and Development in China Changshu Apparel City], http://www.cfw.com.cn/zgfsb/html/2008-10/24/content_34624.htm, accessed 22 January 2009.

China Changshu Government Net (23 June 2008), "2007 Changshushi Guoming Jingji Yu Shehui Fazhan Tongji Gongbao" [2007 Changshu National Economic and Social Development Statistical Communiqué], http://www.changshu.gov.cn/content/2008/0623/000004 44592387n1086704.html, accessed 25 January 2009.

China Changshu Zhaoshang City Website, http://www.cszsc.com.cn, accessed 16 January 2009.

China Fashion Brand Net (2007), "2006 Fuzhuang Shichang 'Zhuhou Biandi, Bazhu Nanxun'" [Too Many Feudal Barons, but Little Overload in the 2006 Apparel Market], http://content.chinasspp.com/News/Detail/2007-1-5/43612-3.htm, accessed 6 November 2007.

China Industry & Commerce Association (CICA) (ed.) (2007), *Zhongguo Siyingqiye Daxing Diaocha (1993–2006)* [A Large-scale Survey on Private Enterprises in China (1993–2006)], Beijing: China Industry & Commerce Association Press.

China National Agricultural Wholesale Market Association (CAWA) (23 January 2007), "Guonei Pifa Jiaoyi Chengxian Shiwuzhong Moshi [15 Models are Arising in China's Wholesale Business], http://www.cawa.org.cn/ArticleInfo.aspx?ID=4647, accessed 10 February 2007.

China Textile Economy Information Net, Website for Industrial Clusters, http://www.ctei.gov.cn/chanyejidi, accessed 25 January 2008.

China Textile Industrial Association (CTIA) (2006), *Zhongguo Fangzhi Gongye Fazhan Baogao (2005/2006)* [China Textile Industry Development Report (2005/2006)], Beijing: China Textile Press.

China (Yiwu) Website for Protecting Intellectual Property (CWPIP) (12 July 2007), "Shanghu Yingli Tigao, Shichang Xinxin Chongzu" [The Profit of Booth-keepers Has Increased, and the Market Has

Sufficient Confidence], http://yiwu.ipr.gov.cn/ipr/yiwu/info/Article. jsp?a_no=95158&col_no=833&dir=200707, accessed 10 February 2009.

Enorth.Com.Cn (28 February 2007), "Zhejiang Yiwu Renkou Da 180 Wan, Bendiren Buzu Sicheng" [Population of Yiwu, Zhejiang amounted to 1.8 million, Local People are under 40%], http://news.enorth.com.cn/system/2007/02/28/001560539.shtml, accessed 10 February 2009.

Fang, Zhengya (1992), "Cujin Shangpin Liutong, Fanrong Chengxiang Jingji" [Stimulate the Distribution of Commodities, Enliven the Urban and Rural Economies], *Commercial Economy and Management*, **1**.

Fei, Xiaotong and Hanxian Luo (1988), *Xiangzhen Jingji Bijiao Moshi* [Comparative Model of Township Economies], Chongqing: Chongqing Press.

Fu, Yiling (1956), *Mingqing Shidai Shangren Ji Shangye Ziben* [Merchants and Commercial Capital in the Ming and Ching Eras], Beijing: People's Publishing House.

Fu, Zhengping et al. (2004), *Zhongxiao Qiye Jiqun Shengcheng Jizhi Yanjiu* [A Study on the Formation Mechanism of Small and Medium Enterprises Clusters], Guangzhou: Sun Yat-sen University Press.

Hangzhou University Finance and Trade School Economic Department (HUFTSED) (1996), "Zhuanye Shichang Yu Zhejiang Jingji Congtan" [On the Specialized Market and Zhejiang Economy], *Zhejiang Social Science*, **5**: 16–27.

Ho, Ping-ti (1966), *Zhongguo Huiguan Shilun* [A Historical Survey of Landsmannschaften in China], Taipei: Taiwan Student Press.

Huang, Philip (2000), *Changjiang Sanjiaozhou Xiaonong Jiating Yu Xiangcun Fazhan* [The Peasant Family and Rural Development in the Yangzi Delta], Beijing: Zhonghua Book Company.

Huang, Philip (2008), "Zhongguo De Xiaozichanjieji He Zhongjianjieceng: Beilun De Shehui Xingtai" [China's Petty Bourgeoisie and Middle Class: Paradoxical Social Forms], http://sard.ruc.edu.cn/huang/paper/xiaozichanjiejiweb.pdf, accessed 1 October 2008.

Huang, Philip (2009), "Zhongguo Bei Hushi De Feizhenggui Jingji: Xianshi Yu Lilun" [China's Neglected Informal Economy: Reality and Theory], *Open Times*, **2**: 51–73.

Huzhou Online News Website (6 September 2008), "Zhili Tongzhuang Qiye Yao Zhenghe" [Zhili Children's Wear Companies Need to be Integrated], http://news.hz66.com/main/news/hz/hzsh/2008090608250687.htm, accessed 2 February 2009.

Jiangsu Economic Year Book Editing Committee (JEYBEC) (1987), *Jiangsu Jingji Nianjian 1987* [Jiangsu Economic Yearbook 1987], Nanjing: Nanjing University Press.

Jiangsu SMEs Net (22 January 2007), "Chuangye Jingji Yinling Changshu Hexie Fazhan" [The Economy of Starting New Businesses Led to Harmonized Development in Changshu], http://www.jste.gov.cn/gzdt/100216559.htm, accessed 2 February 2009.

Jin, Xiangrong and Rongzhu Ke (1997), "Dui Zhuanye Shichang De Yizhong Jiaoyifeiyong Jingjixue Jieshi" [An Explanation of the Specialized Market from the Perspective of Transaction Cost Economics], *Economic Research Journal*, **4**: 74–9.

Li & Fung Research Center (ed.) (2003), *Gongyinglian Guanli: Xianggang Lifeng Jituan De Shijian* [Supply Chain Management: The Practice of Hong Kong Li & Fung Group], Beijing: Renmin University Press.

Li, Shi and Ximing Yue (2004), "Zhongguo Chengxiang Shouru Chaju Diaocha" [An Investigation on Rural and Urban Income Gap in China], *Caijing*, **3** and **4**.

Lu, Lijun and Xiaohu Bai (2000), "'Hezuo Jituan Kuozhan Lun': Yiwu Liantuoyun Shichang Zhidu Bianqian Anli Yanjiu" [The Cooperation Group Extension Approach: A Case Study of Institutional Change in Yiwu Logistics Market], *Economic Research Journal*, **8**: 21–7.

Lu, Lijun, Xiaohu Bai and Zuqiang Wang (2003), *Shichang Yiwu – Cong Jimaohuantang Dao Guoji Shangmao* [Market Yiwu: From Jimaohuantang (the exchange of rooster feathers for sugar) to International Business], Hangzhou: Zhejiang People's Publishing House.

Luo, Xiaojun (2005), "Xiaoshangpin Shichang Shangwu Chengben De 'Liangnan Jueze': Yiwu Xiaoshangpin Shichang Shangwu Chengben De Wenjuan Diaocha Yu Fenxi" [The "Dilemma" of Business Costs in a Small Commodity Market: A Questionnaire Survey and Analysis on the Business Costs in Yiwu Small Commodity Market], *Zhejiang Economy*, **5**: 31–3.

Luo, Zhongwei (2001), "'Huanqi Minzhong Qianwan, Tongxingan': Guanyu Yiwushi Xiaoshangpin Shichang Zhong Shehui Zhongjie Zuzhi De Diaoyan Baogao" ["Call Forth Thousands of People, Striving with One Heart": Investigation and Research Report on Social Intermediary Organizations in Yiwu Commodity Market], Unirule Institute of Economics Website, http://www.unirule.org.cn/SecondWeb/Article.asp?ArticleID=2234, accessed 15 October 2008.

Market and Consumption News (2007), "Yiwu: Xinyong Chengjiu Fanrong" [Yiwu: Credibility Brought About Prosperity], 2 November 2007.

Meng, Yang and Yanhong Niu (2006), "Chanye Jiqun Lizai Hangye Lizai Difang Lizai Baixing" [Industrial Cluster Brought About Merits to the Industries, Local Areas, and People], China Textile Economy

Information Net, http://www.ctei.gov.cn/chanyejidi/newshow1. asp?xx=71874, accessed 5 February 2007.

Mocheng Zhenzhi [Mocheng Town Chronicle] (MTC). Preprint.

National Bureau of Statistics in China (NBSC) (1979–2010), *China Statistical Yearbook 1979–2010*, Beijing: China Statistics Press.

National Statistics Trading, Goods and Materials Statistics Secretary (NSTGMSS) (ed.) (1991–2001), *Zhongguo Shichang Tongji Nianjian* [Market Statistical Yearbook of China], Beijing: China Statistics Press.

Ou, Kaipei and Yi Xiao (2007), *Zhongguo Pifashichang De Kunjing Yu Chulu* [Predicament and Solution of China's Wholesale Market], Beijing: Central Compilation & Translation Press.

Peng, Zeyi (1957), *Zhonguo Jindai Shougongyeshi Ziliao (1840–1949)* [China Modern Handicraft Industry Material (1840–1949)], Volume 3, Beijing: SDX Joint Publishing Company.

Ruian Net, http://www.66ruian.com/Html/ramp, accessed 7 February 2007.

Shi, Xianmin (1993), *Tizhi De Tupo: Beijingshi Xichengqu Getihu Yanjiu* [Breakthrough in a Planning System: A Study on Self-employed Enterprises in Xicheng District, Beijing], Beijing: China Social Science Press.

Sipsongpanna Dai Autonomous Prefecture Committee for Economic Affairs (SDAPCEA) Website, "Quanqiu Zuida De Xiaoshangpin Pifashichang: Yiwu Zhonguo Xiaoshangpincheng De Jianshe He Guanli Jingyan" [World's Largest Small Commodity Wholesale Market: The Construction and Management Experience of Yiwu China Commodity City], http://www.xsbnjw.gov.cn/News_03/ReadNews. Asp?BigClassID=4&NewsID=1135, accessed 11 January 2009.

Song, Zhiyong and Yan Han (2 November 2006), "Zhongfei Maoyi Chanpin Jiegou Buduan Youhua" [The Structure of Trade between China and Africa Continues to Optimize], Sina Net, http://chanye. finance.sina.com.cn/sm/2006-11-02/303399.shtml, accessed 15 December 2006.

State Administration for Industry and Commerce Website, http://www. saic.gov.cn, accessed 1 August 2002.

Suzhou Daily (2001), "Nanzhuang Jingpin Yuanhe 'Qinglai' Changshu Zhaoshangcheng" [Why Menswear Boutiques Favored Changshu Zhaoshang City], 26 November 2001.

Wang, Weiping and Jinchun Zhang (ed.) (2000), *Meiyou Weiqiang De Chengshi* [The Unwalled City], Beijing: China Light Industry Press.

Wang, Ziliang and Xueya Qian (2003), *Cong Xiangcun Gongye Dao Chengshihua: Zhejiang Xiandaihua De Guocheng, Tezheng Yu Dongli* [From Rural Industrialization to Urbanization: Process, Characteristics and Dynamics], Hangzhou: Zhejiang University Press.

Workers Daily (2006), "Yiwu Fazhan Jingyan Tanmi" [Seeking the Yiwu Development Experience (I)], 11 July 2006.

Wu, Zhixiong (2004), "Shichang Luodi Qian De Timing" [The Cockcrow that Foretold the Establishment of the Yiwu Market], Yiwu News Net, http://www.ywnews.cn/20040309/ca777.htm, accessed 2 October 2006.

Xia, Zuxing (1988), "Fazhan Nongcun Shangpin Jingji De Youyi Tansuo" [A Good Exploration for the Development of Rural Commodity Economy], Report Provided by Xia Zuxing.

Xia, Zuxing (1992), "Nongmin Shangchang De Xingwang Zhilu: Changshushi Zhaoshangchang De Tansuo Yu Sikao" [Prosperous Road of a Peasant Market: Exploration and Thinking in Changshu Zhaoshang Market], Unpublished Material.

Xie, Jian et al. (2001), *Wenzhou Zhizao: Touguo Minying Qiye Kan Xin Wenzhou Moshi* [Made in Wenzhou: Observing the New Wenzhou Model Through the Perspective of Private Enterprise], Taiyuan: Shanxi Economy Press.

Xinhua Net Jiangsu Channel (2006), "Siwei Gongchen Zonglun Yiwu Shichang De Qianshi Jinsheng (Xia)" [Four Persons of Merit Talk About the History of the Yiwu Market (II)], http://www.zj.xinhuanet. com/tail/2006-06/07/content_7202907.htm, accessed 16 January 2007.

Xinhua Net Zhejiang Channel (9 July 2008), "Kunjing Xia De Yiwu Shichang You Sanda Youshi" [In a Difficult Situation, The Yiwu Market has Three Advantages], http://www.zj.xinhuanet.com/business/2008-07/09/content_13770999.htm, accessed 14 January 2009.

Xu, Xinwu (ed.) (1992), *Jiangnan Tubu Shi* [History of Hand-woven Cloth in Jiangnan], Shanghai: Shanghai Academy of Social Science Press.

Xu, Yuanming (2002), "Changshu Zhaoshangcheng Chenggong De Jingyan Yu Jinyibu Fazhan De Sikao" [The Successful Experience of Changshu Zhaoshang City and the Thinking for Its Further Development], Unpublished Material.

Xu, Yuanming and Zhiming Xu (2005), "Zhonguo Jiangsusheng Nanbu Diqu Chanyejiju Diaochabaogao" [A Research Report on the Industrial Clusters in Southern Jiangsu Province, China], A Report of the Joint Research Project Entitled *East Asian Industrialization and Industrial Clusters*, carried out by Nagoya University Graduate School of Economics and Jiangsu Academy of Social Sciences.

Xue, Ruicheng (2001), *Nongcun Jingji Yu Gaige Fazhan Wenji* [Selected Papers for the Development of the Rural Economy and Reform], Suzhou Rural Economy Academy.

Yang, Xiaokai and Yongsheng Zhang (2003), *Xinxing Gudian Jingjixue Yu Chaobianji Fenxi* [New Classical Economics and Inframarginal Analysis], Beijing: Social Science Literature Press.

Yiwu Administration for Industry and Commerce (Yiwu AIC) (2003), *Yiwushi Gongshang Xingzheng Guanli Zhi (Dier Juan)* [Yiwu Chronicles for Administration for Industry and Commerce (2)].

Yiwu Fair Website, http://www.yiwufair.com/cn/Wizard/Overview, accessed 11 January 2009.

Yiwu Fair Website, http://www.yiwufair.com/cn/about/historyDetails. htm, accessed 11 January 2009.

Yiwu Foreign-Concerning Service Center (YFSC) (2006), *Yiwushi Waiguo Ji Gangaotai Qiye Changzhu Daibiao Jigou Nianjian 2006* [Yiwu Foreign Countries and Hong Kong, Macao, Taiwan Resident Offices Yearbook 2006].

YFSC (2007), *Yiwushi Waiguo Ji Gangaotai Qiye Changzhu Daibiao Jigou Nianjian 2007* [Yiwu Foreign Countries and Hong Kong, Macao, Taiwan Resident Offices Yearbook 2007].

Yiwu Forum Secretariat (ed.) (2005), *Zhuanye Shichang Yu Quyu Fazhan – Guanzhu Yiwu Shichang Fushequan* [Specialized Markets and Regional Development – Focusing on the Range of Economic Impact of the Yiwu Market].

Yiwu News Net (2005), *Guanzhu Yiwu Jingji Fushequan* [Focusing on the Range of Economic Impact of the Yiwu Market], http://www.ywnews. cn/gzywscjj/index.htm, accessed 2 October 2006.

Yiwu Statistics (ed.) (1999–2006), *Yiwu Tongji Nianjian* [Yiwu Statistical Yearbook], Yiwu: Yiwu Statistics.

Yiwu Yearbook Leading Group Editing Office (YYLGEO) (ed.) (1992), *Yiwu Nianjian (1986–1990)* [Yiwu Yearbook (1986–1990)].

Yuan, Enzhen (ed.) (1987), *Wenzhou Moshi Yu Fuyu Zhilu* [The Wenzhou Model and the Road to Prosperity], Shanghai: Shanghai Academy of Social Science Press.

Yushan Town Chronicle Editing Committee (YTCEC) (ed.) (2000), *Yushan Zhenzhi* [Yushan Town Chronicle], Beijing: Zhongyang Wenxian Press.

YTCEC, *Yushan Zhenzhi* [Yushan Town Chronicle], Preprint.

Zhang, Houyi (2003), *Zhongguo Siying Qiye Fazhan Baogao 2002* [China Private Enterprise Development Report 2002], Beijing: Social Science Academic Press.

Zhang, Renshou and Hong Li (1990), *Wenzhou Moshi Yanjiu* [A Study on the Wenzhou Model], Beijing: China Social Science Press.

Zhang, Wenxue et al. (ed.) (1993), *Yiwu Xiaoshangpin Shichang Yanjiu: Shehuizhuyi Shichangjingji Zai Yiwu De Shijian* [A Study on Yiwu Commodity Market: The Practice of the Socialist Market Economy in Yiwu], Beijing: Qunyan Press.

Zhao, Renwei, Shi Li and Carl Riskin (1999), *Zhongguo Jumin Shouru*

Fenpei Zaiyanjiu [Reinvestigation on Distribution of Income in China], Beijing: China Financial and Economic Publishing House.

Zhaoshang City Managing Committee (ZSCMC) (ed.) (1997), *Quanguo Diqijie Gongyepin Pifashichang Lianluohui Lunwen Ziliao Huibian* [Compilation of Papers for The Seventh National Industrial Products Wholesale Markets Association], Internal Material.

Zhaoshang City Self-Employed Enterprises and Private Enterprises Association (2001), "Zhaoshangcheng Geti Siying Jingji Xiehui Diqijie Pianzu Wangluo Zuzhi Mingdan" [The 7th Zone and Group Network Member List of Zhaoshang City Self-Employed Enterprises and Private Enterprises Association].

Zhejiang Daily, 13 January 2005.

Zhejiang Online Jiaxing Channel (11 September 2006), "Huzhou Zhili: 'Zhili Sudu' Zhijiu 'Tongzhuang Zhidu'" [Huzhou Zhili: "The Speed of Zhili" Weaved "the Capital of Children's Wear"], http://www.zjol. com.cn/05jx/system/2006/09/11/007863818.shtml, accessed 2 February 2009.

Zhejiang Province Market Chronicle Editing Committee (ZPMCE) (ed.) (2000), *Zhejiangsheng Shichang Zhi* [Zhejiang Province Market Chronicle], Beijing: Chronicle Press.

Zhejiang Province Zhengxie Historical Data Committee (ZPZHDC) (ed.) (1997), *Xiaoshangpin, Dashichang: Yiwu Zhongguo Xiaoshangpincheng Chuangyezhe Huiyi* [Small Commodities, Big Market: The Memoirs of the Founders of Yiwu China Commodity City], Hangzhou: Zhejiang People's Publishing House.

Zhejiang Statistics (1999), *Zhejiang Tongji Nianjian* [Zhejiang Statistical Yearbook 1999], Beijing: China Statistical Press.

Zhejiang University Economics School Research Group (ZUESRG) (2007), "Zhejiang Sheng De Chanye Jiqun" [The Industrial Clusters in Zhejiang Province], in Ken Imai and Ke Ding (eds), *Dangqian Zhongguo Chanye Shengji Qushi Fenxi: Hangye Anli Yanjiu* [An Analysis on the Trend of Industrial Upgrading in Current China: Case Study of Industries], Chiba: Institute of Developing Economies, Japan External Trade Organization (IDE-JETRO), Joint Research Program Series 143.

Zhejiang University Economics School Research Group (ZUESRG) (2008), "Yiwu Huangyan Diqu De Chanyejiqun: Yingdui Chanyeshengji Tiaozhan De Zhongxiaoqiye" [The Industrial Clusters in Yiwu and Huangyan: Challenge to Industrial Upgrading and Local SMEs], in The Research Group on the Reform and Upgrading of Chinese Enterprises (ed.), *Dangqian Zhongguo Chanye Shengji Qushi Fenxi: Hangye Anli Yanjiu (II)* [An Analysis on the Trend of Industrial Upgrading in Current China: Case Study of Industries (II)], Chiba: Institute of

Developing Economies, Japan External Trade Organization (IDE-JETRO), Joint Research Program Series 144.

Zheng, Yongjun et al. (2003), *Jiedu "Shichang Dasheng": Zhejiang Zhuanyeshichang Xianxiang Yanjiu* [An Interpretation on "The Province of Markets": A Study on the Specialized Market in Zhejiang], Hangzhou: Zhejiang University Press.

Zhu, Huasheng (2003), *Zhejiang Chanyequn: Chanye Wangluo, Chengzhang Guiji Yu Fazhan Dongli* [Zhejiang Industrial Clusters: Industrial Network, Growth Trajectory and Dynamics of Development], Hangzhou: Zhejiang University Press.

JAPANESE PUBLICATIONS

Asanuma, Banri (1997), *Nihon No Kigyo Sosiki Kakushinteki Tekio No Mekanizumu* [The Mechanism of Innovative Adaptation in Japanese Corporate Organizations], Tokyo: Toyo Keizai Inc.

Ding, Ke (2004), "Sonan Chiiki Sengyo Shizyo No Seidoteki Keisei Yoin" [The Institutional Factors for Specialized Market Formation in the Sunan Area], in Johzen Takeuchi (ed.), *Chugoku Kogyoka No Nosonteki Kiso: Choko Karyuiki Wo Chuxin Ni* [The Rural Basis of Chinese Industrialization: With Particular Reference to Downstream Yangtze River Areas], Nagoya: Nagoya University East Asian Study Series I (JSPS Report).

Ding, Ke (2005), "Zyojuku Apareru Sanchi No Sengyoshizyo Ni Kansuru Ichikosatsu" [A Case Study of Changshu Apparel Industrial District with Particular Reference to Its "Specialized Market"], *China Management Studies*, 5: 57–82.

Ding, Ke (2007a), "Chugoku No Tai Afurika Shohizai Boeki" [China's Consumer Goods Trade Towards Africa], in Eiichi Yoshida (ed.), *Afurika Ni Fuku Chugoku No Arashi, Ajia No Senpu* [China's Storm and Asia's Whirlwind Blow Towards Africa], Chiba: IDE-JETRO.

Ding, Ke (2007b), "Chugoku No Zakka Sangyo Niokeru Kodoka – 'Ichiba' Wa Naze Chusyokigyo Katsuyaku No Butai Ni Narerunoka?" [The Industrial Upgrading of Daily Commodity Industry: Did the Marketplace Become a Stage For Supporting Dynamic SMEs?], in Kenichi Imai and Ke Ding (eds), *Chugoku Kodoka No Choryu* [Trends in Industrial Upgrading in China], Chiba: IDE-JETRO.

Ding, Ke (2008a), "Apareru Sangyo No Sangyo Soshiki To Kyosoryoku Keisei: Sangyo Shuseki To Oganaiza No Shiten Kara" [Industrial Organization and Competitiveness Formation in the Apparel Industry: From the Perspective of Industrial Clusters and Organizers], in Kenichi

Imai and Ke Ding (eds), *Chugoku Sangyo Kodoka No Choryu* [Trends in Industrial Upgrading in China], Chiba: IDE-JETRO.

Ding, Ke (2008b), "'Ichiba' Wa Naze Chusyo Kigyo Katsuyaku No Butai Ni Nareru Noka? Zakka Sangyo Ni Miru Shinkou Shizyo Baryuchein No Sosyutu Katei" [Why Did the Marketplace Become a Stage for Supporting Dynamic SMEs? An Observation of the Process of Value Chain Creation in Emerging Markets from the Perspective of the Daily Necessities Industry], in Kenichi Imai and Ke Ding (eds), *Chugoku Sangyo Kodoka No Chouryuu* [Trends in Industrial Upgrading in China], Chiba: IDE-JETRO.

Fujimoto, Takahiro, Toshihiro Nishiguchi and Hideshi Ito (eds) (1998), *Sapuraiya Shisutem: Atarashii Kigyokan Kankei Wo Tsukuru* [Supplier Systems: Creating New Inter-firm Relationships], Tokyo: Yuhikaku Publishing Co.

Goto, Kenta (2005), "Hoh Chi Min Shi No Naizyu Muke Apareru Sangyo No Seisan To Ryutu Kozo" [The Production and Distribution Structure of the Domestic Demand-Oriented Apparel Industry in Ho Chi Minh City], *Asian Economies*, **10**: 2–25.

Hayami, Yujiro (2006), "Keizai Hatten Niokeru Kyodotai To Shizyo No Yakuwari" [The Role of Community and Market in the Economic Development], in Yasuyuki Sawada and Tetsushi Sonobe (eds), *Shizyo To Keizai Hatten* [Market and the Economic Development], Tokyo: Toyo Keizai Inc.

Ikeno, Shun and Shinichi Takeuchi (eds) (1998), *Afurica No Infomarusekuta Saiko* [Reconsidering the Informal Sector in Africa], Tokyo: IDE.

Itami, Noriyuki, Shigeru Matsushima and Takeo Kikkawa (eds) (1998), *Sangyo Syuseki No Honshitsu* [The Nature of the Industrial Cluster], Tokyo: Yuhikaku Publishing Co.

Iwasaki, Yoko (2002), "Teheran No Apareru Oroshiuri Shizyo: Bonakudaru No Serinin Kino" [The Apparel Wholesale Market In Tehran: The Functions of the Bonak-dar as an Auctioneer], *Asian Economies*, **2**: 2–25.

Japan External Trade Organization (JETRO) (2000), *Chugoku Taigai Boeki Tokei* [China Overseas Trade Statistics], Tokyo: JETRO.

JETRO (2005), *Chugoku Taigai Boeki Tokei* [China Overseas Trade Statistics], Tokyo: JETRO.

JETRO (2007), *Chugoku Mihonichi Bijinesu Doko 2007* [Trends in China's Trade Fair Business 2007], Tokyo: JETRO.

Jin, Xiangrong (2004), "Sekkosho Niokeru Sengyoka Sangyoku" [The Industrial Districts of Zhejiang Province], in Johzen Takeuchi (ed.), *Chugoku Kogyoka No Nosonteki Kiso: Choko Karyuiki Wo Chuxin Ni* [The Rural Basis of Chinese Industrialization: with Particular Reference to Downstream Yangtze River Areas], Nagoya University East Asian Study Series I (JSPS Report).

Kim, Yanghee and Makoto Abe (2002), *Kankoku Todaimon Shizyo No Hatten To Aratana Nikkan Apareru Sangyo Nettowaku No Keisei* [The Development of the Dongdaemun Market in South Korea and the Formation of a New Apparel Industrial Network between Japan and South Korea], Chiba: IDE-JETRO, Joint Research Program Series No. 130.

Koike, Yoichi (1999), "Gurobaruka To Sangyo Syuseki: Gifu Apareru Sanchi No Kadai" [Globalization and Industrial Clusters: The Challenge to Gifu Apparel Cluster], in Kayoko Kitamura (ed.), *Higashi Ajia No Chusyo Kigyo No Nettowaku No Genjo To Kadai: Gurobarizeishon eno Sekkyokutekina Taio* [The Current Situation and Challenges to the East Asian Small Business Network: Active Responses to Globalization], Chiba: IDE-JETRO.

Komagata, Tetsuya (2004), "Onshu Moderu Kenkyu No Shikaku: Chugoku Keizai No Taisei Iko Ni Yosete" [The Perspective of Wenzhou Model Studies: On China's Economic Transition], in Keio University 3E Academy (ed.), Small Special Series: *Ikoki – Chugoku Niokeru Shizyokeisei – Seido Kaikaku – Sangyo Hatten: "Onshu Moderu Wo Chushin Ni"* [Transitional Period – Market Formation – Institutional Reform – Industrial Development: With Particular Reference to the Wenzhou Model], *Mita Journal of Economics*, **96**: 467–85.

Li, Ruixue (2003), "Ryutu Shisustemu Niokeru Futatsu No Nami" [Two Waves in the Distribution System], in Tatsuhiko Sakurai and Ruixue Li (eds), *Kawaru Chugoku, Kawaranai Chugoku* [Changing China, Unchanging China], Tokyo: Zen-nichi Publishing Co.

Marukawa, Tomoo (2001), "Chugoku No Sangyo Syuseki: Sono Keisei Katei To Kozo" [Industrial Clusters in China: Their Formation Process and Structure], in Mitsuhiro Seki (ed.), *Ajia No Sangyo Syuseki – Sono Hattenkatei To Tenbo* [Asian Industrial Clusters – Their Development Process and Overlook], Chiba: IDE-JETRO.

Marukawa, Tomoo (2002), "Chugoku Niokeru Jieigyo Eno Shugyo" [Employment in Self-Employed Enterprises in China], *China Management Studies*, **2**: 41–60.

Marukawa, Tomoo (2004b), "Onshu Sangyo Shuseki No Shinka Purosesu" [The Evolutionary Process of Industrial Clusters in Wenzhou], in Keio University 3E Academy (ed.), Small Special Series: *Ikoki – Chugoku Niokeru Shizyokeisei – Seido Kaikaku – Sangyo Hatten: "Onshu Moderu Wo Chushin Ni"* [Transitional Period – Market Formation – Institutional Reform – Industrial Development: With Particular Reference to the Wenzhou Model], *Mita Journal of Economics*, **96**: 521–41.

Marukawa, Tomoo (2007), *Gendai Chugoku No Sangyo – Bokko Suru Chugoku Kigyo No Tsuyosa To Morosa* [Modern China's Industries: The Strong Points and Weak Points of Emerging Chinese Enterprises], Tokyo: Chuokoron-sha Inc.

Matsumoto, Hitokazu (2006), *Afurica No Chugokujin* [The Chinese in Africa], *Asahi Shinbun* series between 8 May and 9 June 2006.

Nakagane, Watsuji (2002), *Keizai Hatten To Taisei Iko* [Economic Development and System Transition], Nagoya: Nagoya University Press.

Ogawa, Hideki (1998), *Itaria No Chusyo Kigyo: Dokuso To Tayosei No Nettowaku* [SMEs in Italy: A Network of Originality and Variety], Tokyo: JETRO.

Sawada, Yasuyuki and Tetsushi Sonobe (eds) (2006), *Shizyo To Keizai Hatten* [Market and the Economic Development], Tokyo: Toyo Keizai Inc.

Seki, Mitsuhiro (2001), "Chiikihatten to Sangyo Syuseki" [Regional Development and Industrial Clusters], in Mitsuhiro Seki (ed.), *Ajia No Sangyo Syuseki – Sono Hattenkatei To Tenbo* [Asian Industrial Clusters – Their Development Process and Overlook], Chiba: IDE-JETRO.

Seoulkankou.Com, http://www,seoulkankou,com/pdt_se,php?cat_id=36& pdt_no=234, accessed 29 January 2009.

Sonobe, Testushi (2006), "Sangyo Syuseki To Shizyo" [Industrial Clusters and Market], in Yasuyuki Sawada and Tetsushi Sonobe (eds), *Shizyo To Keizai Hatten* [Market and the Economic Development], Tokyo: Toyo Keizai Inc.

Sonobe, Tetsushi and Keijiro Otsuka (2004), *Sangyo Hatten No Rutsu To Senryaku: Nicchutai No Keiken Ni Manabu* [Roots and Strategies of Industrial Development: Lessons from the East Asian Experience], Tokyo: Chiizumi Press.

Takaoka, Mika (1998), "Sangyo Syuseki To Maaketto" [Industrial Clusters and Markets], in Noriyuki Itami, Shigeru Matsushima and Takeo Kiikawa (eds), *Sangyo Syuseki No Honshitsu* [The Nature of the Industrial Cluster], Tokyo: Yuhikaku Publishing Co.

Takeuchi, Johzen (1996), "Chusyo Kigyoshi Kenkyu No Kadai To Shikaku" [Subjects and Perspectives of Small Business History Studies], in Johzen Takeuchi, Takeshi Abe and Minoru Sawai (eds), *Kindai Nihon Niokeru Kigyoka No Sho Keifu* [Various Genealogies of Entrepreneurs in Modern Japan], Osaka: Osaka University Press.

Watanabe, Yukio (1979), "Diatoshi Niokeru Kikaikogyo Reisai Keiei No Kino to Sonritsu Kiban: Tokyoto Zyonan Chiiki No Baai" [The Functions and Foundations of SMEs in the Machinery Industry in Conurbations: A Case Study of the Zyonan Area, Tokyo], *Mita Journal of Economics*, **72**: 69–101.

Watanabe, Yukio (2004), "Onshu No Sangyo Hatten Shiron: Jiritsu –
    Kokunai Kanketstugata – Kokunai Shizyo Muke Sangyo Hatten,
    Sono Imi To Tenbo" [An Attempt to Discuss Industrial Development
    in Wenzhou], in Keio University 3E Academy (ed.), Small Special
    Series: *Ikoki – Chugoku Niokeru Shizyokeisei – Seido Kaikaku –
    Sangyo Hatten: "Onshu Moderu Wo Chushin Ni"* [Transitional Period
    – Market Formation – Institutional Reform – Industrial Development:
    With Particular Reference to the Wenzhou Model], *Mita Journal of
    Economics*, **96**: 503–20.
Yoshida, Eiichi (2007), "Afurika No Chiiki Sangyo Wo Meguru Kankyo
    No Henka" [Environmental Changes in African Local Industries], in
    Eiichi Yoshida (ed.), *Afurika Ni Fuku Chugoku No Arashi, Ajia No
    Senpu* [China's Storm and Asia's Whirlwind Blow Towards Africa],
    Chiba: IDE-JETRO.

Index